THE LITURGICAL YEAR

THE
LITURGICAL YEAR

Volume Four

SUNDAYS NINE TO THIRTY-FOUR
IN ORDINARY TIME

by

Adrian Nocent, O.S.B.

translated by

Matthew J. O'Connell

THE LITURGICAL PRESS

COLLEGEVILLE   MINNESOTA

Cover design by Clement Schmidt.

Available in four volumes, THE LITURGICAL YEAR is the authorized English version of *Célébrer Jésus-Christ, L'année Liturgique*, published by Jean-Pierre Delarge, 10, rue Mayet, 75006 Paris, France.

Texts from the Revised Standard Version — Catholic Edition of the Holy Bible contained in this book are used by permission, copyright © 1965 and 1966 by the Division of Christian Education of the National Council of Churches of Christ in the United States of America. All rights reserved.

English translation of excerpts from the Roman Missal, The Roman Calendar, Rite of Marriage, Rite of Baptism for Children, Rite of Blessing of Oils, Rite of Consecrating the Chrism, Rites for Holy Week, original texts of Alternative Opening Prayers, Invitatories and Penitential Rites, the Liturgy of the Hours, Lectionary for Mass, copyright © 1969, 1970, 1972, 1973, 1974, 1975. International Committee on English in the Liturgy, Inc. All rights reserved.

Nihil obstat: William G. Heidt, O.S.B., S.T.D., *Censor deputatus.*
Imprimatur: ✝ George H. Speltz, D.D., Bishop of St. Cloud, October 12, 1977.

Copyright © 1977, The Order of St. Benedict, Inc., Collegeville, Minnesota.

All rights reserved under United States copyright law, and the International and Pan-American Conventions, including the right to reproduce this booklet, or parts thereof, in any form, by mimeograph, or other mechanical or electronic devices.

Printed in the United States of America. ISBN 0-8146-0965-1

CONTENTS

SUNDAYS NINE TO THIRTY-FOUR IN ORDINARY TIME
CYCLE A
Years 1978, 1981, 1984, 1987, 1990

CYCLE B
Years 1979, 1982, 1985, 1988, 1991

CYCLE C
Years 1980, 1983, 1986, 1989, 1992

THE LITURGICAL YEAR

1. THE ORGANIZATION OF ORDINARY TIME

The final volume in this series of commentaries on the liturgical year will be different in format from the first three. This is because the material to be handled is quite different. Each of the special seasons — Advent, Christmas-Epiphany, Lent, and Easter — has its characteristic theology, but the "Sundays after Pentecost" have no special coloring of their own. These Sundays simply celebrate the paschal mystery as it is being fulfilled in the Church and the world. Consequently, except for the theology of Sunday, there is no question of elaborating a special theology for Ordinary Time. Nor is there any point in drawing up tables that would show how the Sundays of Ordinary Time were organized at other periods of history or in other Churches. Since Ordinary Time follows no special line, the choice of readings and prayers has varied without following any pattern.

This volume, then, will be very simple in format and will limit itself almost entirely to commentary. Doubtless such comment could have been organized in various ways. May the one we have chosen serve its purpose to the reader's satisfaction.

1. Work of the Commission for Reform of the Missal

If the reader is to understand what we have attempted to do in this book, he must first be made aware of how the commission for the reform of the Missal understood its role and how it went about achieving the goal it set for itself. The work of the commission is doubtless not beyond criticism, and some of the norms it followed are questionable; but the commission certainly took great pains in its work.

1

Enrichment of the lectionary

The first task of the commission was to greatly expand the lectionary. We need only run our eye over the list of readings in the older lectionary to see that it was quite impoverished. Vatican Council II, therefore, was very insistent in the *Constitution on the Sacred Liturgy* that a richer fare be provided (No. 51). In responding to this strongly worded desire, however, the commission found itself faced with a complicated and ticklish situation. We shall point out some of the complexities so that the reader may understand that no completely satisfactory solution was possible.

A central theme for each Sunday?

The celebrations of the major liturgical seasons have always been so constructed, even in the early Church, as to illustrate a broadly conceived theme. This is evident when we examine, for example, the liturgies for the Sundays of Lent. In the judgment of many, such celebrations organized around a theme are pastorally successful, since the attention of the faithful is not easily dispersed in several different directions. From Advent to Pentecost the congregation is therefore accustomed to hearing readings on a particular mystery, while the chants and prayers likewise call attention to a limited range of ideas. Would there not be an advantage, then, in following a similar pattern for each Sunday of Ordinary Time?

Obviously, the commission asked itself that question. The exegetes, however, did not care for the idea. There is always a danger of telling the texts what they must say and of using them in a subjectivist manner to make them fit into a predefined framework; it cannot be said that the liturgy has always resisted such a temptation. The exegetes' warning was well-grounded, and it would have been imprudent to neglect it. In this day and age, we cannot ignore the scholarly study of Scripture, which has made such great advances. We must indeed respect the special nature of liturgical proclamation, but we must also respect the objective meaning of the texts and not force them into an alien mold.

The members of the commission were in agreement, then, that the Sunday celebrations could have themes only if these were loosely and flexibly conceived. It was possible, for example, during some weeks and on some Sundays, to bring together texts among which there was an objective correspondence; it would be almost impossible, however, to do this for a very large number of celebrations. Experience with "Masses on a theme" had showed that the biblical texts ended up being distorted in the effort to pursue a narrowly conceived theme. The commission therefore rejected outright any effort to implement themes that would have to run through all the texts; they allowed, however, for the possibility of themes conceived more in the Semitic manner and not requiring a material parallelism between the texts.

How organize the readings?

Once this decision had been, the commission faced another complicated problem: What type of readings was to be offered on these Sundays? The question gave rise to endless discussions and a large variety of views. The end sought was to foster contact with Scripture as proclaimed by and in the Church. Was this goal always pursued in a measured way? We shall see. At this point, however, we may say that perhaps the commission was excessively conditioned by its desire to achieve that goal and that the abundance, indeed the superabundance, of the texts proclaimed did not always yield the expected result. We may even say that the goal of proclaiming a great number of texts may have caused distortions in the individual celebrations.

A single cycle

We shall advert briefly to a few of the tendencies at work in the reform commission. Some members wanted a single cycle of readings. They argued that the faithful cannot easily digest a large number of varied passages from the Bible and that the repetition of the same passages year after year was therefore not a bad thing in itself. However, if the commission chose to have a single cycle, it would not be meeting the wishes of Vatican II. The material of Scripture was so vast that a single set of selections for about thirty Sundays would be entirely inadequate, even if further readings were introduced for each weekday. Once this was realized, the only question to be answered was: How many cycles would be needed for a "more abundant" reading of Scripture? The number of cycles did not have to be same for Sundays and for weekdays.

The Gospel

Since the Gospel is the climactic stage in the proclamation of the word, the distribution of the Gospel texts was the necessary starting point for the commission's work. How many cycles would be needed — two, three, or even four — for an adequate distribution with ever new texts?

Some of the experts felt that the Sunday proclamation of the Gospel should be limited solely to the logia or *ipsissima verba* of Christ, that is, to what contemporary critical exegesis regards as the words of Jesus himself; the whole framework added by the evangelists should be dropped. The pericopes would then admittedly be very short, but they would have the striking force of a slogan and would thus prove a valuable pastoral tool. Others, however, were of the opinion that short sentences cannot be thrust upon the faithful without any context and that when thus read in isolation, the sentences do not stick in the mind. Moreover, from the ceremonial viewpoint, how could the solemn ceremonial surrounding the reading of the Gospel be maintained if the text proclaimed were, for example, only a single sentence or even less than that?

There was an even more important objection to the idea, for what the idea represents may at times be only an exegetical hypothesis, not something certain, and it is difficult to involve oneself deeply in a liturgy that rests on such a fluid base. In addition, there is a material stumbling block: the limited number of such pericopes would have made it impossible to proclaim the Old Testament, the text of which is far more extensive than the New, even when the latter is taken in its totality. Other members of the commission, therefore, asked whether, instead of getting involved in exegetical hypotheses, it would not be far better to proclaim almost the entire text of each Gospel. That was the choice the commission finally made.

Three cycles: the Synoptic Gospels

The decision required new choices. Ancient tradition has the Church read the Gospel of John during Lent and the Easter season. It would therefore not be appropriate to begin the reading of John all over again later in the year. Once it was decided to have three cycles, it was also decided to exclude the Gospel of John, inasmuch as it is proclaimed yearly at certain times. However, to fill out the Gospel of Mark, which is shorter than the other two Synoptics, certain passages of John would be introduced into the Sundays of Ordinary Time. Thus, for practical purposes, one of the three Synoptics would be read in each year of the three-year cycle. For weekdays, a two-cycle proclamation of the Gospel was envisaged.

There was no thought of attempting a continuous reading of the Old Testament, for it is simply too long. A number of the experts, however, did want all the other books of the New Testament to be read in the course of the year; the second reading on the Sundays of Ordinary Time was to help in achieving this goal.

The second reading

The decision gave rise to difficulties, however, as we have by now come to experience. The chief difficulty is the following. Since there is no continuous reading of the Old Testament on these Sundays, the reading for each Sunday is chosen with an intelligent eye on the Gospel reading for that day. But the second reading consists of a quasi-continuous reading of the Letters; thus an element that usually has no relation to the other two readings is introduced into each Sunday's liturgy. When such a relation does exist, it does so only by accident.

Here we have a new situation. During the Easter season, for example, the readings may not fit perfectly together, but at least they are all concerned with the mystery of the resurrection, and this gives unity to them. In the case of the Sundays of Ordinary Time, however, the second reading introduces a new factor, being unconnected with the other two readings (unless, of course, you attempt to establish artificial and arbitrary links with them).

The homily

The lack of unity between the second reading, on the one hand, and the first and third, on the other, creates a real and insoluble problem when it comes to the homily. One must either concentrate on the second reading and say nothing about the Old Testament reading and the Gospel, or else say little or nothing about the second reading and concentrate on the Old Testament and the Gospel. Where approved by the conference of bishops, it is permissible indeed to have only two readings; then the first of these, for obvious reasons, must always be from the Old Testament and the second from the Gospel.

Some celebrants have found a solution that makes it possible to retain the three readings and to comment on them all: before the beginning of the penitential act, the second reading is proclaimed, and the penitential act then is structured around the theme of that reading. Then, at the proper time, the liturgy of the word is celebrated, using only the Old Testament reading and the Gospel. In some ways this is a fairly good solution, provided we do not anticipate the liturgy of the word by assigning the same solemnity to the proclamation of the second reading.

The other texts

There is this further difficulty: Except for the responsorial psalm after the Old Testament reading and for the Alleluia that introduces the reading of the Gospel, the chants, like the prayers, are the same in all three years of the cycle. This means further new elements that, like the second reading, often have no connection with the Gospel.

These difficulties are fully real. We had to mention them at the beginning in order to explain why the final volume of this series of commentaries must follow a different format from the first four.

2. Our Commentary

Readings

In light of the problems mentioned, how is this commentary to be arranged? The theme of the second reading, as we said, rarely fits in with the broad theme of the given Sunday. In both the second and the third readings we are admittedly dealing with a continuous reading of the text, but the two cases are nonetheless different. Even though the reading of the Gospel is continuous or quasi-continuous, we cannot be satisfied with a commentary that is exclusively exegetical. This is because the Gospel pericope is related to the first reading, the one from the Old Testament, and this latter reading tells us the point of view from which the Gospel should be read and commented on.

The second reading, on the other hand, is self-contained and unrelated to the other two readings. The solution here is to give a commentary that is pretty much a straight exegesis of it, and to add a spiritual commentary; the fact that the passage is proclaimed in a liturgy will not cause us to read it from some special viewpoint. All this being so, we think it enough to devote a few lines to each of these second readings, offering some reflections that will serve as a guide to the reader and referring him for further developments to some works of exegesis or spiritual commentary on Scripture. As in previous volumes, a heavy line separates the second reading from what precedes in the many instances in which the second reading is not related to the theme of the day's celebration. And in the outline charts preceding the commentary, an asterisk is used to identify such selections.

Prayers

The prayers and chants are the same in all three cycles, except for the responsorial psalm and the chant that introduces the Gospel. There is therefore no advantage to be gained by joining the commentary on them to the commentary on the readings for each Sunday. As a matter of fact, the Entrance and Communion antiphons of Ordinary Time, together with the prayers for these Sundays, form a separate whole that has no necessary relation to the readings. On the one hand, then, the proclamation of the word, the responsorial psalms, and the chants that introduce the Gospel form one whole; on the other, the various prayers and the other chants form a second whole. Each of these wholes is independent of the other.

In view of all this, we judge it better to offer a short general commentary, at least on the prayers, which we shall examine and try to treat synthetically; at the same time, however, we shall be on the watch for the possibility of seeing a given prayer as an integral part of the Sunday to which it is assigned. As for the chants, there would have been little value in attempting a synthesis of them.

There could be no question, of course, of commenting on the liturgy for each weekday of Ordinary Time. To do so would have required several more volumes. Finally, we could, in the course of the commentary, have cited numerous works on the theology of Sunday and especially on the

Scriptures. That would only have made the volume unwieldy and would have added little of value, given the nature of the volume.

2. THE LORD'S DAY:
A Theology of Sunday

We would manifest an odd view of things if we were to maintain that the period between Pentecost and Advent is the time of real spiritual growth, as though the special seasons of Advent, Lent, and Eastertide were not climactic moments in our supernatural odyssey. What we now call "Ordinary Time," because in it we do not celebrate some special mystery of Christ, is not inferior to the other seasons; on the other hand, neither is it superior to them, as though it were the time of fulfillment while the celebrations in the other seasons would be more theological and contemplative. In point of fact, the whole liturgical year is centered on a single mystery: the mystery of Christ's death and resurrection; and we live that mystery, and live by it, at all times. Ordinary Time, like the special seasons of the liturgical Year, is simply a continuation of that basic mystery. The mystery, moreover, is celebrated in a special way on every Sunday of the year. It is rather important, then, that we possess a life-supporting theology of Sunday.

Sunday

For most persons, Sunday means rest and the obligation of attending the Eucharistic celebration. The obligation is too often thought of in disciplinary terms; people do not grasp the real reason for it. Yet, if the Church intended to enrich the Sunday celebration by means of the new lectionary, she did so because she wanted people to understand

once again the true meaning of Sunday. We will not be able
to grasp that meaning unless we recall briefly the situation
in which the newborn Church found itself; the Acts of the
Apostles gives us a picture of that Church and its experiences.

The Jewish week

The Jewish week, as known to the apostles and lived by
Judeo-Christians until their conversion, begins with the
Sabbath and leads back to the Sabbath. The Jewish
theology of the Sabbath is based on the account of creation
in Genesis, in which we are told that God rested after
finishing his work.

It would, however, be simplistic to see in the Jewish
Sabbath nothing but a pious imitation of God's rest. No, the
Sabbath is above all a day of thanksgiving and prayer. The
legalist approach contributed to distorting the real meaning
of the Sabbath, making people forget that it is meant to be a
day of special communion with the Lord of creation. The
Sabbath rest certainly has beneficial social repercussions,
but when it is imposed in an excessively rigid manner, it
can obscure the other possible dimensions of the Sabbath.

The Sabbath was of such central importance for the Jews
that the other days of the week are not even named but only
numbered. Only the eve of the Sabbath has a special name:
parasceve, or "preparation" day, that is, the day when all
that is needed for the Sabbath must be prepared, since on
the Sabbath itself nothing can be bought or prepared. The
Jewish week, then, consists of: the first day (our Sunday),
the second day (Monday), the third day (Tuesday), the
fourth day (Wednesday), the fifth day (Thursday), the sixth
day (Friday), and the Sabbath (our Saturday). The Latin
liturgy has retained this manner of designating the days of
the week: *feria secunda* (Monday), *feria tertia* (Tuesday),
etc.

The planetary week

In antiquity, the Hellenistic contemporaries of the Jews were familiar with a week in which the days were named after the planets. Mars, Mercury, Jupiter, Venus, and Saturn lent their names to the days from Tuesday to Saturday. The sun and moon gave their names to the days that the Germanic world would later call Sunday and Monday, while the Latin world would speak of the "Lord's (day)" for Sunday and of "the day of) *luna*" (Latin for "moon").

The planetary week had no official standing, but it became increasingly popular. People believed that the planet after which a day was named influenced the action of human beings. Christian evangelization did not everywhere succeed in imposing even the new name, "the Lord's day," for the first day of the week (Latin: *dies dominicalis*; Italian: *domenica*; Portuguese: *domingo*; Spanish: *domingo*; French: *dimanche*). The Germanic languages continued to speak of the "sun's day" (German: *Sonntag*; Dutch: *Zondag*). The Hellenistic world accused the Jews of really being followers of Saturn, since they celebrated Saturday, while it accused Christians of being worshippers of the sun, because they celebrated Sunday. Meanwhile, within the Christian community the leaders had to be on guard against the superstitions of the faithful who were at times inclined to overestimate the influence of the stars on their behavior.

Christians chose the name "Lord's day" instead of "Sunday" in order to show that this was a memorial of the Lord's resurrection. Christian symbolism was also to speak of this day as "the eighth day," that is, a day entirely outside of the traditional week, in order to emphasize the fact that a new era had begun with the resurrection of Christ. The name "eighth day" was never officially adopted by the Church, despite the wealth of meaning it conveyed, but the Fathers of the Church did make use of it in their catechetical instructions.

The Lord's day

For Christians, one day of the week had incomparable importance: the first day, immediately after the Sabbath. That is the day on which the evangelists locate the Lord's resurrection (Matthew 28:1; Mark 16:2; Luke 24:1; John 20:1, 19). Christians considered this day to play an unconditionally definitive role in the history of the world, and so they wanted to celebrate it in a special way. As Judeo-Christians, they continued to attend the synagogue on the Sabbath, but they also wanted to celebrate the first day of the week, which the evangelists had said was the day of the resurrection. This day they called "the Lord's day"; the name itself occurs for the first time in the Apocalypse (1:10). There was no possibility of confusing this "day of the Lord" with the "day of the Lord" when he returns at the end of time; the latter was called, in Greek, *hēmera Kyriou*, while Sunday was called *kyriakē hēmera* or simply *kyriakē*. It is the word *kyriakē* that enters the Romance languages by way of Latin (*dominicalis* or *dominica*) and provides the modern Romance word for Sunday: *domenica*, *domingo*, *dimanche*.

Meaning and importance of Sunday

Is Sunday a day just like other days? Is there any point in celebrating the Eucharist on Sunday rather than on some other day of the week? Would it not be possible for each individual to pick any day of the week instead of Sunday and celebrate a weekly liturgy on that day? Isn't the important thing, after all, that the Church should not let too long a time pass without celebrating the Eucharist in memory of Christ's death and resurrection?

We must reflect at least briefly on the answers to these questions. These days we tend to dislike fixed times for doing things; we regard them, perhaps a little too quickly, as artificial. As a matter of fact, in many cases they have been. The question is: Is the choice of Sunday for the

Eucharist something artificial, and can we shift to some other practice without loss?

To get an answer we must first of all look to the past. The ways of those who have gone before us, especially the apostles and the early Church, cannot be a matter of indifference to us, especially if we can determine why they acted as they did. We cannot solve our Christian problems by looking solely to what we call, in a somewhat vague and indefinite way, "modern man" and "contemporary anthropology."

Practice of the early Church

A first and striking fact is that Scripture and the early ecclesiastical writings do not focus attention on a celebration of the annual Pasch; they speak first and foremost of celebrating Sunday as a special day, the day of days for the Christian assembly (1 Cor. 16:2). This is the more remarkable in that, down to the Peace of Constantine, only Saturday was a holiday; Christians had to work on Sunday. That is something we tend to forget. Nowhere do we read that Christians rebelled or suffered martyrdom because they wanted to have Sunday free. This means that the idea of Sunday as a day of rest was not very important and certainly not decisive.

Despite this fact, the Church regarded it as extremely important that the Eucharist should be celebrated on Sunday, the first day of the week. The Acts of the Apostles mentions the Sunday gathering (20:7). At a period when people had to work on Sunday, the idea of Sunday rest was not characteristic of the day. The focus of attention was on celebrating the act of worship that commemorated the resurrection of Christ, an event that occurred on the first day of the week, according to the evangelists.

A creation of the Christian community

The facts show that the early Church was firmly bent on celebrating the first day of the week in a special way, even though in order to do so it had to overcome many obstacles. What we seem to have here is a creation of the early Christian community. Some interpreters have seen in this act a deliberate contrast to Judaism, with the cultic celebration of the first day as a conscious rejection of the Jewish Sabbath. The opposition was intended, in this view, to call attention to the new situation in which Christians found themselves in relation to Judaism.

Other scholars see in the Sunday celebration an extension of a Jewish harvest feast that was celebrated on the first day of the week, although only once a year. Still others have suggested the influence of the planetary cults; the difficulty with this explanation is that nowhere do we find the worship of the sun (to take the most obvious example) being assigned to the first day of the week. The most we can say is that the passages of Scripture relating to Sunday inform us about the customs of Christian communities whose members were converts from paganism (1 Cor. 16:2; Acts 20:7; Apoc. 1:10) and that these communities made the first day, rather than the Sabbath, the most important day of the week.

It seems, however, that we must see in the celebration of Sunday a Christian creation that is neither continuous with, nor set in conscious opposition to, any other celebration, including the Jewish celebration of the Sabbath. For one thing, the content of the Christian celebration of Sunday is completely unrelated to the content of the Jewish Sabbath. In Judeo-Christian communities we find the two observances existing side by side, with Christians observing the Sabbath and even attending the synagogue but also observing Sunday. There is no indication that these Christians saw any continuity between the two observances.

Sabbath and Sunday

The Jewish Sabbath was marked by abstention from all work, whereas Sunday was simply a day of worship in commemoration of the risen Christ. Sunday was not a prolongation, transposition, or revision of the Sabbath. When, finally, Christians no longer observed the Sabbath, Sunday was not taken as a kind of shifting of the Sabbath to another day. Rather, the Sabbath was taken as a "figure," and Sunday as its perfect fulfillment. We pass from the cultic observance and imitation of what had taken place at the first creation to a paschal celebration that renews the creation of man and his world.

Rest and worship

The history of the Christian Sunday thus bids us distinguish carefully between Sunday as a day of worship and Sunday as a day of rest. From the very beginning, Sunday was a day of worship, whereas the idea of rest became the subject of a "precept" only around the sixth century. Even then, we may note, the "rest" meant a more complete focusing of the mind and heart on God rather than a prohibition against all work.

The *Constitution on the Sacred Liturgy* speaks of Sunday in two articles:

> Holy Mother Church believes that it is for her to celebrate the saving work of her divine spouse in a sacred commemoration on certain days throughout the course of the year. Once each week, on the day which she has called the Lord's Day, she keeps the memory of the Lord's resurrection. She also celebrates it once every year, together with his blessed passion, at Easter, that most solemn of all feasts (no. 102; Flannery, pp. 28–29).

> By a tradition handed down from the apostles, which took its origin from the very day of Christ's resurrection, the Church celebrates the paschal mystery every seventh day, which day is appropriately called the Lord's Day or Sunday (no. 106; Flannery, p. 29).

Gospel inspiration for Sunday

The paschal mystery and the resurrection are the events that determined the choice of Sunday or the first day of the week for the Christian assembly and the celebration of the Eucharist. Indeed, the Gospels made the Church's choice of Sunday inevitable. According to the evangelists, the risen Christ first showed himself on the morning of the first day. By so doing, he already made the day a specially holy one; at this point, however, there was nothing to suggest a weekly return of this day of glory. Then, on the following Sunday the risen Lord appeared again to his disciples (John 20:26). Once the apparitions and manifestations of the risen Christ were thus attached to Sunday, there was an evident basis for choosing this day as the day for the Christian assembly; to the Church of the first years the choice must have seemed inevitable.

Chapter 20 of the Acts of the Apostles shows that the celebration of Sunday was already an institution: "On the first day of the week, when we were gathered together to break bread, Paul talked with them" (20:7). When Paul writes to the Corinthians urging them to take up collections, he refers to Sunday as the day for doing this (1 Cor. 16:2). When St. John at a much later date is recounting his visions, he designates "the Lord's day" as the day when he received his revelations (Apoc. 1:10).

Sunday: a permanent institution

We must bear in mind the fact that Christians in the early days still had to work on Sundays; it was on the Sabbath that they rested. This is to say that the choice of the first day of the week was not dictated by convenience and did not fit nicely into the life pattern of the day. The choice of Sunday was thus not an accident or something secondary. Sunday has a quasi-sacramental character about it, so much so that it is hard to imagine the Church leaving open the day on which communities or individuals may celebrate the Lord's resurrection, and not continuing to celebrate it on a fixed day that is in no sense artificial but was chosen by Christ himself for his resurrection and his appearances to his Church. It is important, moreover, that the entire Church should, together and on the same day, celebrate with joyous worship the event of the resurrection, the event that is the ultimate ground of her birth in the Spirit.

Clearly, then, the Church cannot make optional the choice of the day for celebrating the resurrection of Christ. This does not mean that a Christian who is legitimately prevented from joining the celebration on that day may not feel it his duty to celebrate this central event on another day. If he does so, however, that other day does not become the real equivalent of Sunday.

It must be acknowledged that the frequent celebration of the Eucharist during the week has obscured the significance of Sunday as a special day, particularly since every Eucharist commemorates and proclaims the death and resurrection of Christ. Objectively, however, each celebration of the Eucharist has its own proper character; the Sunday Eucharist is not the same as the Easter Eucharist, nor is a weekday Eucharist the same as the Sunday Eucharist or the Easter Eucharist.

Memorial of the resurrection

When the Christian community assembles on Sunday, it does so in order to celebrate the resurrection of Christ, its Lord. His resurrection is the essential object of Christian faith and the basis of the Christian's assurance that he too will pass from death to life. On Sunday the community also celebrates the day when the new and eternal covenant was brought to fulfillment; that covenant is the sign of a new world and a new creation, and thus is the source of the joy that marks the celebration. The Church recalls this world that the Lord created anew by his Cross and his victory over death. The Fathers of the Church compare this new creation, effected in the paschal mystery, with the first creation, and relate them as figure and fulfillment. Every Sunday celebration thus brings joy because of Christ's triumph and present glory, as well as joy because man has been clothed in Christ and transformed into a new creature.

Presence of Christ

Every celebration of the Church means the presence of the past. Sunday brings Christians together around the victorious Christ, for if the Church is the Body of Christ, that Christ must be the risen Christ. In his defense of the Christians to Emperor Antoninus Pius, St. Justin Martyr describes a Christian assembly of about the year 150 and tells how the Christians of Rome came together joyously to praise their Lord, hear his word, and celebrate his Eucharist. Justin thus shows us how the local Church of Rome considered it extremely important to celebrate the Eucharist, the sacrifice of praise, as the crown of the Sunday liturgy of the word.

The risen Christ is present in his word; he is also present in his Eucharist. When the Church celebrates the resurrection of the Christ who is present in her midst, she also celebrates her own resurrection. She knows that her Lord communicates himself to her; that the risen Lord who is present in his word and present, body and blood, in the Eucharistic bread and wine, gives her an ever new life that will make her perpetually youthful through the centuries. It is on Sunday above all that the Church approaches the Father through Jesus in the Spirit, and thanks him for the creation of the world, for redemption, and for the whole plan of salvation that has been carried out and is now bearing its fruit.

Sign of the world that is coming

If every celebration in the Church makes the past present, it also actualizes the future, that is, gives it a presence here and now. The Church now awaits the risen Lord whom she celebrates each Sunday; she proclaims him until he comes. Sunday is thus linked to the future, the end of time. On Sunday we utter our *Marana tha*, "Our Lord, come!" It is thus a day on which we have a foretaste of the kingdom that will not pass away and of our future rest in the Lord.

This explains why Christian symbolism has thought of Sunday as the "eighth day." The First Letter of St. Peter speaks of it, while the Second Letter presents Noah as the eighth man saved (2 Peter 2:5). In the fourth century, the ogdoad (the number eight) symbolized the resurrection itself, because the resurrection occurred on a Sunday and Sunday is the eighth day. If the risen Christ lives in the unending eighth day, the baptized person too lives in the same eighth day because he is already risen with Christ.

The concept of obligation can evidently not do justice to the Christian reality of Sunday and its celebration. We can understand, then, the attitude of some of the Fathers of Vatican II who wished to remove Sunday from the realm of juridical obligation. They were doubtless being very idealistic, and yet we can certainly deplore the lack of enthusiasm Christians have for Sunday and the fact that they attach so little importance to its celebration. Perhaps the fault is to be found in an excessively juridical training and the lack of an authentic catechesis in regard to Sunday.

3. LET US GIVE THANKS TO THE FATHER ON THE LORD'S DAY

Sunday is marked chiefly by the celebration of the Eucharist. We think it very important, therefore, to dwell on the theology contained in the Eucharistic Prayers that are now used in the Western Church and to see how they are to affect our lives. Every Catholic who realizes what he has become through his baptism should study these prayers so that he may make more profitable use of them, draw sustenance from them, and make them the basis of his habitual personal prayer.

1. The Prefaces

The first part of the Eucharistic Prayer is chiefly exclamatory in tone; it reminds us of our duty to praise the Lord for what he has done. In the Eastern liturgy this first part of the Eucharistic Prayer has always been unvarying and closely connected with the body of the anaphora.[1] The Roman liturgy, on the other hand, has shown great creativity in this first part of the Eucharistic Prayer, and the old liturgical books, such as the Gelasian Sacramentary (the manuscript dates from about 750, but the texts are often at least a century older), provide quite a large number of prefaces. For several reasons, however — the variety itself; the singing of the *Sanctus*, which at times became quite ornate; the solemn singing of the preface as contrasted with the silence of the Canon — the participants in the liturgy could be led to think that the preface, with its more exclamatory style, was not part of the Eucharistic Prayer, whereas in fact it is the opening part of that prayer.

The illuminated manuscripts, later imitated by the printed books, contributed to foster the same misunderstanding. The Roman Canon begins with the Latin words *Te igitur*; the letter *T* was embellished by artists to from a cross, and the painting became so important that it was blown up to full-page size, thus separating the preface from the body of the Eucharistic Prayer or Canon (this last word then being written at the top of the next page in large capitals).

In the reformed liturgy we have recovered a sense of the unity of the Eucharistic Prayer — this, despite an increased number of prefaces, since these, though quite varied, are always in evident continuity with the Eucharistic Prayer, of which they are a part.

Our reason for these initial remarks about the preface will

become clearer as we go through the texts of the Eucharistic Prayers.

Theology of the prefaces

It is our intention here to give a short synthesis of the content of the prefaces, in order to show the wealth they contain. Eight prefaces are provided for Ordinary Time. They remind us of the story of creation (Preface V) and the history of salvation (Preface IV). We are urged to meditate on the mystery of salvation within which we live our lives (Preface II). Moving more deeply into the theology of this mystery of salvation, we see how mankind was saved through the manhood of Christ (Preface III) or, more accurately, through the obedience of the Son who had become man (Preface VII) and who by accomplishing his paschal mystery gives birth to the new people of God (Preface I). We live now as members of the one Church, the Body of Christ, and as sharers in the life of the Blessed Trinity (Preface VIII). Every celebration of the Eucharist, which is the Pasch of Christ and his Church, gives us a more secure possession of the first fruits produced by the new Passover (Preface VI).

Creation (Preface V)

We noted earlier that Sunday represents to some degree a break with the Sabbath. The reason for this is that the central factor in the Christian Sunday is the celebration of Christ's resurrection, whereby he creates a new people and brings a new creation into existence. At the same time, however, the biblical components of the Jewish Sabbath are to be retained, although within a Christian perspective. In fact, it is especially necessary that the Christian of our time learn to contemplate the God of whom the preface says: "All things are of your making, all times and seasons obey your laws." Otherwise he may well succumb to the pervasive pride that marks the mind of the day. Our age is very much under the impression that it has replaced the Creator, that it is lord of time and history, and that it is at the root of reality. There is danger that this outlook may find its way even into the liturgy, as though man is to be the norm, whereas in fact everything originates in God and leads back to him.

Our forgetfulness of God

The mentality to which we refer is doubtless to some extent a reaction against a contempt for the real and even sacred values of the world, against the tendency to curse the world and forget that it too had come from the creative hand of God. These attitudes, however, have in large measure changed; Vatican II's *Pastoral Constitution on the Church in the Modern World* faced up to that kind of pessimism and general distrust of earthly values.

But this justifiable reaction has gotten out of hand. As a result, we who work for the advancement of the world, whether in the technological or in the social spheres, are forgetful of him who created all things, the world and all that is in it; we forget that all we can do is transform the elements God himself has prepared for us. In our anxious concern for the ongoing evolution of the world, we forget that in the last analysis God alone is Lord of time and history, and that we indulge in naive and dangerous presumption when we imagine that we can infallibly influence the course of history.

The Christian attitude

Preface V defines the Christian attitude by telling us that the Lord has entrusted his creation to us. But he has not done so in order that we might simply restore it to him exactly as it was, thus imitating the steward whose master gave him a sum of money to invest and who returned the exact amount he had originally received. On the other hand, the created world has not been entrusted to us so that we might pursue our selfish goals and seek a well-being that puts paradise to shame. No, if God entrusted the created world to us, it was in order that we might "praise you day by day for the marvels of your wisdom and power." To forget this aspect of things is to betray the trust God has placed in us; it is to use his blessings for limited purposes, while forgetting the will and intentions of him who created what he entrusted to us. The Christian attitude toward creation, then, should be one of wonder and thanksgiving; such is the Christian meaning of all work, and the Christian way of using created things.

This preface shows us where every work for the advancement of man and his world should start. It tells the Christian what his basic attitude should be to the real values God has created and incorporated in his world.

The history of salvation (Preface IV)

If the creation of the world and its component elements should constantly inspire us to thanksgiving, the Church should also ceaselessly proclaim the history of salvation.

The history of the world has been, and continues to be, conditioned by the Passion and resurrection of Christ, by his ascension, and by his sending of the Spirit. In the Christian view, the whole history of the world, and not merely the history recorded in the Old Testament, must be read in the light of those decisive events, as well as of the events we experience in our own time and those yet to come. We are really not sufficiently aware of the revolutionary force that Christ introduced into the world through his paschal mystery. He brought a new people into existence: the baptized, who are in the world without being of it and who already belong to the world of God even while being constantly filled with concern for the fears and anxieties of our age. The paschal mystery created not only a new people but a new world, one that is slowly being renewed until it attains the better state that it had at its first creation.

The history of salvation is our personal history; it is the

history we should be living and helping others to live. That means that our value judgments should constantly be undergoing revision, until what is foolishness in men's eyes becomes for us the way to God.

The mystery of salvation (Preface II)

As we continue to contemplate and live the history of salvation, we see this mystery reaching its climax in Christ, who "out of love for sinful man. . . . humbled himself to be born of the Virgin." That is the root and foundation of everything. (The birth of Christ raised problems for the Church from the very beginning, and especially from the fourth century on. The reality of the human nature likewise raised serious problems, as did the unity of this complete human nature [which is composed of a soul as well as of a body] with the divine nature; these problems the Councils tackled and solved. This is not the place for discussing these various issues.)

We should ask ourselves whether we keep the incarnation of the Word of God constantly in mind and whether we see in it an event that has reshaped the whole course of history. St. Leo the Great, with his usual clarity, points out to the Christians of Rome the conclusions to be drawn from the great event of Christ's birth:

> Thus, by being born a real man while never ceasing to be true God as well, our Lord Jesus Christ became the beginning of the new creature. By the manner of his birth he established a spiritual origin for the human race so that the contamination attached to carnal generation might be eliminated and that those to be reborn might have an origin unconnected with the seed that transmits original sin. Of the men and women thus reborn Scripture says: "They are born not of blood nor the desire of the flesh nor the desire of man, but of God." What human mind can grasp this mystery, what tongue tell of this gift? Guilt reverts to innocence, the old becomes new; strangers become

adopted children, and outsiders enter into the inheritance. The wicked become just, the avaricious generous, the lecherous chaste, and the earthbound
heavenly.[2]

The Saint is not exaggerating. We have all frequently observed how the history of the world and of man can take a
new direction. We have been made aware (too rarely, indeed) of how men's lives are transformed; I refer not only
to the transformations recorded for our edification in the
lives of the saints, but the transformations that sometimes
occur without publicity, in silence and hiddenness. The
sight of the evils that afflict the present world should not
make us forget that things can always change, and indeed
that all is already changed in principle once a man adverts
to the incarnation of God.

Mankind saved by the manhood of Christ (Preface III)

"You came to our rescue by your power as God, but you
wanted us to be saved by one like us."
Everyone says that mankind is sick and in need of healing; and, beyond a doubt, mankind is indeed sick — physi-
cally, psychologically, spiritually, and politically. Well, in
principle we are already freed in all these areas, even
though, as we are well aware, there is so much still to be
done to make freedom reign.
We are freed because one of our number had the power
to free us, and he had the power because he came from God
and was God. By his own dying he overcame death and
thus freed us. Do we believe that? Our liberation will not,
of course, take place without our own efforts — not in the
sense that we are able to save ourselves, but in the sense
that our liberation cannot be effectively implemented unless we cooperate with the man Jesus and with the God
who Jesus is. The liberation of mankind is the joint work of
God and men, although God always has the initiative in it
and can alone make our cooperation effective.
The Spirit who dwells in the Church continues the work

of redemption and calls us to collaborate with him. It is accurate to say that mankind has been saved by the manhood of Christ, but we must add that, on the basis of what Jesus did and under the powerful influence of the Spirit, mankind saves itself and works for its own liberation until Christ comes again. The astounding, magnificent fact that we can thus collaborate with Christ, the God-man, no longer moves us to wonder, and that is too bad. We really need to recover a sense of wonder in the face of this absolutely fundamental divine work that is our liberation.

We have forgotten, for example, how sublime is the attitude of the sick person who is apparently useless but offers his life and suffering to God, thereby helping to liberate the world, in union with Christ, his fellow in the flesh. We no longer understand the life of a man who withdraws into solitude and by his very existence gives striking proof that Christ can enable a human being to live in utter independence, with God alone for company. We take a purely political view of those who seek to better the lot of their fellows; and yet there are men who work with Christ to save mankind. We judge the specialist only in terms of the success of his inventions, and we forget that he too is working, with the Word-made-flesh, for the liberation of mankind.

We could easily go on listing the people all around us who can, if they wish, transform their own lives by helping in the liberation of mankind. Because Christ has become incarnate, there is not a single human being that cannot play a useful role in the vast workshop where the world is being rebuilt. Perhaps if men realized this, they would find life a time of joy: the joy of being liberated themselves and of joining Christ in the liberation of their fellow-men.

We are, then, not freed from outside ourselves; rather, we free ourselves, and mankind in its entirety is called to achieve this kind of self-liberation. Christ came among us as a man in order to teach us to free ourselves, and he gives us all the tools we need for effecting this liberation. Moreover, in thinking of this liberation, we must not limit our sights to only one aspect, namely, the restoration of man's state before the original sin. There are two other aspects of it that we must bear in mind: the continuation of the work of creation, and divinization.

The discoveries made by science have perhaps made us more aware than our forebears were that the process of creation is continuing and that the created world is constantly being made more perfect. People used to think of creation as having been perfect at the beginning and as having then gradually been spoiled. We, however, are in a position to observe that the created world is becoming better. This aspect of liberation fits in with what St. John writes: "My Father is working still, and I am working" (5:17). The created world is still the work of God and Christ. The Word Incarnate, acting in our midst and with us, continues the work of creation, and one of the ways he does so is to send his Spirit and make us more conscious of God's plan for the world and each of us, and of our duty to cooperate with him.

The obedience of the Son (Preface VII)

All that we have been saying would be inexplicable if we were not living under the new covenant that was sealed by the blood of Christ. "Your gifts of grace, lost by disobedience, are now restored by the obedience of your Son." To accept humiliation and be "one like ourselves, though free from sin" was the attitude of the obedient Christ, and his obedience in turn is the basis for our liberation and our ability to cooperate in our own redemption. If we are saved and can work for our own liberation, it is because God chose to "see and love in us what you see and love in Christ." In the Son, the Father found a world that subjected itself to him through the sacrifice of the Son's life.

The paschal mystery and the people of God (Preface I)

"Through his cross and resurrection he freed us from sin and death and called us to the glory that has made us a chosen race, a royal priesthood, a holy nation, a people set apart."

Jesus willed to unite into a single people those whom he had liberated. Yet the Church is not a world within the world; it continues to be part of mankind and is to be thought of rather as the leaven in the mass. The Church does not always clearly act as such, and we for our part are more sensitive to the scandals that can be attributed to her than we are to the power given her by the continued presence of Christ her Head and by the action in her of the Holy Spirit. Yet this presence and activity are fully real and cause the Church to be not isolated but constantly growing. The Church, then, is truly human, and as such is a community of sinners who are only more or less faithful and who share the weakness and corruption of the rest of mankind. At the same time, however, the Spirit of God is constantly at work in the Church and proceeding with his constructive work. The Church is scandalous at times because she is human, but she is also divine and clad with majesty and power.

We are a new people and must make ourselves conscious of that fact. But then it should not surprise us that we cannot always go along with the principles the world accepts. We sometimes feel inferior because we are afraid of appearing reactionary; we are not always at ease in the new world of those who have been redeemed by the mystery of Christ. The Sundays of Ordinary Time will provide material for meditating on our state as Christians. It is a glorious thing, but also a burden and a duty, to be "a chosen race, a royal priesthood, a holy nation, a people set apart."

The one Church and the Blessed Trinity (Preface VIII)

The Church is a holy people because the Blessed Trinity wills her to be such and is constantly making her such.

> When your children sinned
> and wandered far from your friendship,

you reunited them with yourself
through the blood of your Son
and the power of the Holy Spirit.

You gather them into your Church
to be one as you, Father, are one
with your Son and the Holy Spirit.
You call them to be your people,
to praise your wisdom in all your works.
You make them the body of Christ
and the dwelling-place of the Holy Spirit.

If we form a united body, it is because the Blessed Trinity dwells in each of us; it is because we are the object of the Trinity's activity and enter into the very sphere of that activity. The Father has eternally loved us to the point of sending his Son. The Son has given his life for us, has risen from the dead, and has sent us his Holy Spirit, who creates in us the image of the Son. As a result, every time the Father gazes upon us, he now sees in us the image of his own Son. By the power of the Spirit, then, we have become a single being in Christ, to the glory of the Father. The liturgical assembly, and especially the liturgical assembly on Sunday, is the image of this Body of Christ that the Spirit has brought together under the benevolent eye of the Father of all things.

Pledge of eternal life (Preface VI)

The life of the Church, the people of God, seems to pass as all lives do: in an everyday greyness and dullness. Even the series of Sundays may strike the Christian as simply another set of joyless, or even sad and gloomy, days. And yet, "each day you show us a Father's love; your Holy Spirit, dwelling within us, gives us on earth the hope of unending joy." We need faith, however, if we are to be convinced of what the words are saying; if we look only at the earthly dimension of things, there is nothing to show us what lies deeper. There is no proof that eternal life is there and that we already lay hold of it. Only faith can make that a vital conviction for us.

Such a conviction is, however, essential for the life of God's people, the holy nation, because on it depend the Church's energy and her criteria for judging and acting.

Eternal life has already begun. The "proof": we have "your gift of the Spirit who raised Jesus from the dead." It is a proof, however, only for those who believe in the testimony of Scripture as proclaimed in the Church and by the Church. The gift of the Spirit and his charisms makes us live in hope that the paschal mystery will be fulfilled in us. The definitive and irreversible passage to eternal life still lies before us; at that moment all mere signs will be done away with because we will be in direct contact with the divine realities and will contemplate and touch them through love. There will be no more reason for faith and hope.

Such is the teaching contained in the prefaces for the Sundays of Ordinary Time. They are short poems that seek to capture the reality of our daily lives, a reality we seek to make new again for us each Sunday as we exercise our faith and strive to recognize the signs of God's infinite wisdom at work in our history. The prefaces thus sum up the whole meaning of our Christian life. They make us mindful again of true reality and introduce us to the great Eucharist in which we sing the Father's glory through Christ in the Spirit.

2. The Eucharistic Prayers

The Structure of the Eucharistic Prayer

When commenting on Holy Thursday, we recalled the Jewish framework within which the Last Supper must be set if it is to be entirely comprehensible. We refer the reader to the description there given.[3]

By way of further background, we must turn here to the structure of the Eucharistic Prayer in the early Church. The structure was in fact very simple. The prayer began with an exclamation of wonder at what the Lord had done: "It is truly right and fitting that we should praise you. . . ." In this, Christians were making their own the manner in which Jewish prayer had begun.

The second component is closely linked to the first and consists of an enumeration of the reasons for the praise and thanksgiving. This part will later on be given the technical name of "anamnesis," or "remembrance": "We give you thanks because you have. . . ." As we noted elsewhere, many of the Old Testament prayers follow this pattern, as do the New Testament canticles in the infancy narrative: "Blessed be the Lord God of Israel, for he has visited and redeemed his people . . ." (Luke 1:68); "My soul magnifies the Lord . . . for he has regarded the low estate of his handmaiden" (Luke 1:46-47). This second part may be quite lengthy; some of the psalms, for example, recall the whole history of salvation in outline.

The recall or anamnesis leads psychologically to a further development, which is the third component in the structure. The remembrance of what God has done contains an implicit praise of his power, and the person praying instinctively turns to this new aspect: "You have done thus and so in the past; grant us now this new favor." In other words, the grateful remembrance of God's past favors leads to petitions, or intercessions as they are technically called. The realization of the power that God exercises in all he does rouses confidence that he will meet man's further needs. We can see from this that the distinction between prayer of praise and prayer of petition is rather artificial, since in asking we acknowledge the Lord's power and, at least implicitly, give him praise.

The fourth and final section of the prayer is a return to the element of praise. He has done the wonderful things we have recalled, and we confidently await new deeds from him: "To him be glory forever!"

These four parts, which are closely linked and correspond so well to man's instinctive way of praying, are to be found in all the Eucharistic prayers. They may be differently arranged or there may be repetitions, but the four parts are always evidently present. It was a prayer of this kind that Christ himself used when celebrating the Last Supper with his disciples. Christians should be encouraged to make this simple prayer formula their own in personal prayer; it will familiarize them with liturgical prayer and make it easier to pass from personal (private) prayer to liturgical prayer.

The plurality of Eucharistic Prayers

The Jewish elements present in Christ's prayer at the Last Supper have remained through the centuries. The first disciples, after all, continued to attend the temple, as the Acts of the Apostles remind us (2:46). We are told, by way of summary, that the first Christians "devoted themselves to the apostles' teaching and fellowship, to the breaking of bread and the prayers" (Acts 2:42). As a result, the early Christians probably accepted as obligatory and even inevitable the prayer structure we have just analyzed.

The first known text of a Eucharistic Prayer comes to us from Rome and is contained in the book *Apostolic Tradition*, which St. Hippolytus wrote around 217. In context, the prayer is suggested for the use of a bishop who has just been consecrated and is presiding for the first time, as bishop, at the Eucharist of his community. The prayer follows the pattern we have indicated; we shall give the text of it a little further on because the Second Eucharistic Prayer in use today is based on it.

Beginning in the fourth century, a variety of Eucharistic Prayers came into existence, and the Eastern liturgies would end up with a large number of them. They can be reduced to two main types, according to their structure. Liturgies of the Antiochene type have Eucharistic Prayers organized as follows: exclamation; account of the history of salvation (anamnesis); consecration; continuation of the anamnesis and act of offering; prayers of petition (intercessions), among them a petition for the sending of the Spirit (epiclesis); final doxology. This is the more simple structure, and closer to the Jewish prayer of blessing. The Byzantine Liturgy, which is the Eastern liturgy most familiar to us, usually uses a Eucharistic Prayer of this type.

Liturgies of the Alexandrian type have Eucharistic Prayers that follow a somewhat different structure: exclamation; intercessions and first epiclesis; consecration; anamnesis; second epiclesis and second group of intercessions; final doxology. The distinguishing mark of this group is that they introduce intercessions and an epiclesis before the consecration, and then have a second epiclesis and a second group of intercessions after the consecration. The first of our present-day Eucharistic Prayers, i.e., the old Roman Canon, is of this type.

The Eucharistic Prayers in use today

The single Eucharistic Prayer that was used for centuries down to our own time and is still used as the First Eucharistic Prayer was already known, in a primitive form, to St. Ambrose, who records it in his little book *De sacramentis*. We cannot, of course, claim that such a prayer was used at Rome around 378 (the date of composition for the *De sacramentis*).

Why has the Church not continued to use only this single Eucharistic Prayer, which is after all quite beautiful? The answer is somewhat complex. From a catechetical viewpoint, the Roman Canon is not a whole whose internal structure can be readily grasped. It stands, as we indicated, in the Alexandrian line of Eucharistic Prayers, which have two epicleses and two groups of intercessions. The Antiochene pattern, on the contrary, is very simple and corresponds to an almost instinctive way of praying. Moreover, it is closer to the Jewish prayer of blessing and thus closer to the prayer Christ himself would have used. Thus the adoption of other Eucharistic Prayers would be useful from both the historical and the catechetical points of view.

Furthermore, though the Roman Canon is a very beautiful composition, it does not bring out the action of the Holy Spirit in the Eucharistic celebration. The Canon could have been "corrected," of course, but that would have been to mar an ancient composition that has its own values.

The choice was made, therefore, to introduce three new Eucharistic Prayers. What is now our Second Eucharistic Prayer is largely inspired by the prayer St. Hippolytus suggests for a newly consecrated bishop; we shall give the two texts side by side below. The Third Eucharistic Prayer is a new composition, inspired by the Eastern anaphoras, as is the Fourth, which contains a lengthy anamnesis.

The pattern of the new Eucharistic Prayers

What scheme was adopted for the new Eucharistic prayers? Well, to begin with, the theologians and liturgists faced a problem: the epiclesis. We must say a few words about this.

The epiclesis (Greek: *epikalein*, "to appeal to for help; invoke upon") is a prayer asking the Father to send the Holy Spirit. In itself, the term might be applied to any such prayer; in practice, the name is usually reserved for the prayer asking the Father to send the Holy Spirit upon the gifts that the Church is offering.

Our Roman Canon seems never to have known an epiclesis. St. Ambrose, in his *De sacramentis*, lays a great deal of emphasis on the dynamic power of the word, and the "words of institution," of course, form the center of the Eucharistic prayer. According to the traditional faith of the Church, it is these words that effect the change of the bread and wine into the body and blood of Christ.[4]

On the other hand, the Eucharistic Prayer of St. Hippolytus and the various Eastern Eucharistic prayers all contain one or two epicleses. This epiclesis, however, raises a problem, though this is less true of St. Hippolytus's prayer than of the others. The epiclesis is a prayer that the Holy Spirit transform the bread and wine into the body and blood of Christ. But is that not accomplished by the words of institution? When the epiclesis comes before the consecration, it can be taken as a petition that the Spirit would come and act through the words the priest utters and thereby change the bread and wine into Christ's body and blood. But when the epiclesis comes after the consecration, as it does in some liturgies, does it not implicitly deny the power of the words of institution? Such seemed to be the problem.

As a matter of fact, this statement of the problem reflects a typically Western outlook. Once the schism occurred between the Eastern and Western Churches, the problem thus posed became increasingly important, and we find both sides marshalling even the most recondite and least probative arguments in order to brand the other side heretical. And yet Eastern Catholics use the Eastern Eucharistic Prayers, for example those of St. John Chrysostom and St. Basil, in which there is only one epiclesis, and it comes after the consecration — but they have never felt the slightest theological scruple!

If we look at the problem a little more carefully, we find that it is not as important as the theologians like to think. The theologians are the ones who have gotten themselves into difficulty by the way they carve up reality; the Christian people see no problem, because they hardly raise questions of this kind. Nonetheless, the Church has thought it wise not to cause possible disturbance to Western Christians and has therefore introduced two epicleses into each of the new Eucharistic Prayers: the first comes before the consecration and relates to it (a consecratory epiclesis); the second comes after the consecration and relates chiefly to the union to be effected among those who will participate in the sacrifice by receiving Communion (a Communion epiclesis).

The new Eucharistic Prayers are thus of the Alexandrian type as far as the epiclesis is concerned, because there are two epicleses. They are, however, of the Antiochene type as far as the other intercessions are concerned, because they appear only at the end of the Eucharistic Prayer. The Eucharistic Prayers of the Alexandrian type, as we saw, have intercessions both before and after the consecration.

Before proceeding to a short analysis of the texts of the new Eucharistic Prayers, we should recall that the word *anaphora*, which Eastern Christians use, designates the Eucharistic Prayer as an "offering" of the sacrifice of Christ, whereas the Latin word *canon* designates the manner (*canon* = norm) in which the sacrifice of Christ is to be offered. "Anaphora" refers to the content of the prayer, while "canon" refers to the rule the prayer must follow in its construction.

A. The Second Eucharistic Prayer

The anaphora of Hippolytus of Rome, the source of Eucharistic Prayer II

The best and simplest way to approach our Second Eucharistic Prayer is to compare it with its source, the anaphora of St. Hippolytus, which we mentioned above. Here, then, is a literal tranalation of Hippolytus's text set side by side with the official English translation of the new Eucharistic Prayer II:[5]

Anaphora of St. Hippolytus

We thank you, God, through your beloved Child Jesus Christ, whom you have sent to us in the last age as Savior and Redeemer and messenger of your will. He is your Word, inseparable from you, through whom you made all things and whom in accordance with your good pleasure you sent from heaven into the Vir-

Eucharistic Prayer II

Father, it is our duty and our salvation, always and everywhere to give you thanks through your beloved Son, Jesus Christ. He is the Word through whom you made the universe, the Savior you sent to redeem us. By the power of the Holy Spirit he took flesh and was born of the Virgin Mary.

gin's womb. Having been conceived, he took flesh and was manifested as your Son, born of the Holy Spirit and the Virgin.

Carrying out your will and acquiring for you a holy people, he stretched out his hands when he suffered in order to free from suffering those who believed in you. When he was about to be handed over to voluntary suffering so that he might destroy death and break the devil's chains, tread hell underfoot and enlighten the just, establish the rule (of faith) and manifest the resurrection, he took bread, gave you thanks, and said: "Take, eat, this is my body which will be broken for you." Likewise the cup, saying: "This is my blood which is poured out for you. When you do this, you make commemoration of me."

Mindful, therefore, of his death and resurrection, we offer you the bread and the cup, thanking you for judging us worthy to stand before you and serve you.

And we ask you to send your Holy Spirit upon the offering of the holy Church.

For our sake he opened his arms on the cross; he put an end to death and revealed the resurrection. In this he fulfilled your will and won for you a holy people. And so we join the angels and the saints in proclaiming your glory as we say: Holy, holy, holy Lord, God of power and might, heaven and earth are full of your glory. Hosanna in the highest. Blessed is he who comes in the name of the Lord. Hosanna in the highest.

Lord, you are holy indeed, the fountain of all holiness. Let your Spirit come upon these gifts to make them holy, so that they may become for us the body and blood of our Lord, Jesus Christ. Before he was given up to death, a death he freely accepted, he took bread and gave you thanks. [Text of consecration follows, as in the other Eucharistic Prayers.]

In memory of his death and resurrection, we offer you, Father, this life-giving bread, this saving cup. We thank you for counting us worthy to stand in your presence and serve you.

Bring into unity all who partake of the holy things, and grant that they may partake so as to be filled with the Holy Spirit and be strengthened in their faith in the truth, so that we praise and glorify you through your Child Jesus Christ, through whom be glory and honor to you, Father, and to the Son with the Holy Spirit in your holy Church, now and for ever. Amen.

May all of us who share in the body and blood of Christ be brought together in unity by the Holy Spirit.

Lord, remember your Church . . . [intercessions for Church, pope, clergy, the dead, and the living].

Through him, with him, in him, in the unity of the Holy Spirit, all honor and glory is yours, almighty Father, for ever and ever. Amen.

Even a cursory reading of the two texts shows that there are likenesses, but also rather profound differences, between them. We shall first offer some general reflections on them and then go on to particular points.

Why revise Hippolytus's text?

Just as we would have found it regrettable had the ancient Roman Canon been revised, so we find it regrettable that Hippolytus's text has been altered in the process of turning it into our present Eucharistic Prayer II. Why did this happen? We can see two motives operating: one was the desire to have its language resemble that of the other new Eucharistic Prayers; the other was the fear lest certain expressions or prayers undermine the orthodox faith.

The desire for *likeness* or parallelism is what led to the modification of the words of institution as found in Hippolytus, as well as to the modification of the very beautiful, original, and theologically rich final doxology. *Fears* with regard to orthodoxy, on the other hand, led to the alteration of some expressions, to the introduction of an epiclesis before the consecration, and to the almost complete revision of the epiclesis after the consecration.

Likeness

In dealing with the first point, that is, the likeness between the Eucharistic Prayers, we shall enlarge the scope of the problem a bit by looking more closely at several expressions.

The anaphora of Hippolytus is addressed simply to "God," and not explicitly to the Father: "We thank you, God. . . ." Yet clearly enough the Father is meant, since we thank God "through your beloved Child Jesus Christ." Hippolytus's words "your beloved Child" have, however, a fullness of meaning that is not quite captured by the English "your beloved Son." The Greek word for "child" also means "servant," and thus is linked up with the terminology of Isaiah and with his poem about the servant who gives his life for the multitude. When the first part of the anaphora was turned into a "preface," the experts preferred to make the text resemble other prefaces in style and language.

Hippolytus's Eucharistic Prayer contains no *Sanctus*. It was decided to introduce one; this in turn made it necessary to introduce the words that traditionally lead into the *Sanctus*.

In addition, it was quite to be expected that some expressions that are vague and difficult to understand should be eliminated; for example, "establish the rule (of faith)." On the other hand, there was perhaps an excessive fear of such expressions as "break the devil's chains" and "tread hell underfoot." After all, it would have been easy for anyone who understood the text to read it with the eyes of those who lived at the time of its composition and to draw profit from these vivid, visual expressions.

The modification of the doxology was probably due to the desire to be able to sing it according to the familiar melody. Yet it would not have been difficult to compose another doxology for use in singing, while preserving Hippolytus's doxology for use when the prayer was to be spoken rather than sung. The reason for thus preserving it is that it contains a theology that is of some interest. It expresses very well the meaning of the Eucharistic offering: the praise and glory of the Father, which, however, we cannot give without faith and the interior action of the Holy Spirit. Then, too, the expression "with the Holy Spirit in your holy Church" (a favorite of Hippolytus and found elsewhere in his *Apostolic Tradition*), offers a perspective with which Western Christians are unfamiliar. It emphasizes the importance of the Holy Spirit's action in everything the Church does.

Fears

Some corrections were motivated by fear of doctrinal confusion. Thus, early in the anaphora Hippolytus speaks in a way that might have caused the modern Christian to raise an eyebrow: "Having been conceived, he took flesh and was manifested as your Son." On first hearing this, we might suppose Hippolytus to be saying that the Son became the Son through the incarnation, whereas in fact the Son, like the Father, is from all eternity.

That is not what Hippolytus means. His theology is in fact very close to that of St. John. In St. John's view, that which characterizes the Son and gives the very name "Son" its full depth of meaning is Christ's will to be obedient and to serve. He came on earth to do the Father's will, and that meant becoming incarnate; it was this act of obedience that elicited the Father's words at the transfiguration: "This is my beloved Son" (Matthew 17:5). Thus the incarnation earned the name of "Son" for Jesus even more than before; that is to say, he shows himself to be truly the Son by becoming incarnate out of obedience. He is certainly the Son from all eternity, but the incarnation, like the paschal mystery, reveals him more than ever to be the Son who makes his own the Father's eternal plan and carries out the Father's redemptive will. Hippolytus expresses the same idea in the next sentence when he speaks of Christ as "carrying out your will and acquiring for you a holy people."

The most important changes introduced into Hippolytus's

text relate to the epicleses. We mentioned the problem of the epiclesis earlier; let us dwell on it here again for a moment.

It is not exceptional to find a single anaphora containing two prayers asking the Father to send the Spirit; the various anaphoras of the Alexandrian type have two epicleses. Hippolytus's prayer, however, has only one and thus resembles anaphoras of the Antiochene type.

The old Roman Canon has no epiclesis before the consecration, but it does have a prayer asking for the consecration. In order to make the new Eucharistic Prayer II resemble the Roman Canon more closely, it was decided to introduce into it a pre-consecration epiclesis. (The prayer in the Roman Canon reads: "Bless and approve our offering; make it acceptable to you in spirit and in truth. Let it become for us the body and blood of Jesus Christ, your only Son, our Lord.")

The chief purpose in thus making the two Eucharistic Prayers parallel was to highlight the full consecratory power of the words of institution. It is a matter of faith that the words of Christ are what effects the consecration of the bread and wine. The power of the word is much stressed by the Fathers, and especially by St. Ambrose, whose treatise *De sacramentis* quotes the central section of the Roman Canon, as we shall see. In this treatise the Saint coins a phrase that expresses the power of the words used in the sacraments: *operatorius sermo*, "effective words."[6] In the context, he is speaking of baptism and of Christ's words at the end of St. Matthew's Gospel, but he makes the same claim with regard to the Eucharist:

> By what words is the consecration effected, and whose words are they? The words of the Lord Jesus. . . . It is the words of Christ that produce the sacrament.
> What is the nature of this word of Christ? It is the word by which all things were made. . . . He spoke and it [the body of Christ] was made; he issued the order and it was created. . . . Understand, then, that

the word of Christ is accustomed to transforming every creature and that it changes the very laws of nature when he so wills.[7]

In another little work, the *De mysteriis*, we find the same emphasis on the power of Christ's words:

If a blessing bestowed by a man [Eliseus] was powerful enough to change nature, what are we to say of a consecration that God himself effects, that is, a consecration in which the words of the Lord and Savior himself are the active force at work? For the sacrament you receive is produced by the words of Christ. ... If the word of Christ could make out of nothing that which previously did not exist, can it not change what exists into what previously did not exist?[8]

It was this power of the word that the liturgical experts and theologians wished to emphasize, and they were afraid that if the Eucharistic Prayer had only an epiclesis after the consecration, this epiclesis would lessen the importance of the consecration itself in the minds of those listening to the prayer. A pre-consecration epiclesis, on the other hand, directs attention ahead to the consecration that will take place through the intervention of the Spirit, as the Spirit gives power once again to the words that Christ once spoke and that he now speaks again.

As for the post-consecration epiclesis common to all the Eastern anaphoras, it was decided not to eliminate it. The text has, however, been much altered.

Hippolytus asks simply that God would send his Holy Spirit upon the Church's offering. He is not explicitly asking for the Spirit to effect the change of the elements, though many have so interpreted him. In what, then, does the activity of the Spirit consist? Hippolytus seems to tell us in his next sentence: The Spirit's activity consists in uniting the faithful who participate in the mysteries. The Spirit is to act within them and strengthen their faith in the truth.

We should note the connection Hippolytus establishes

between participation in the Eucharist (the point at which the Spirit intervenes), the unification of the faithful, and the strengthening of their faith. In Eucharistic Prayer II the connection is weakened because the components of Hippolytus's epiclesis are separated and distributed in two epicleses: the pre-consecration epiclesis asks that the Spirit be sent for the consecration, while the post-consecration epiclesis asks that, having shared in the body and blood of Christ, we may be gathered by the Spirit into a single body. It is not quite clear that the reason why we are gathered into a single body is because we share in the body and blood of Christ in which the Spirit works upon us.

A final point to be made is that the intercessions of Eucharistic Prayers II are not to be found in Hippolytus's anaphora.

In summary, the Eucharistic Prayer of Hippolytus is of the Antiochene type, while the new Eucharistic Prayer II is of a mixed type: it is Alexandrian in that it contains two epicleses, and Antiochene in that it contains intercessions only after the consecration.

One last note: The anaphora of Hippolytus contains a number of expressions that match typical expressions of St. Irenaeus that are found nowhere else. As such, this venerable prayer is a real jewel. We should learn to love it, use it, and meditate on it. We shall have an even better understanding of it after we have studied the other Eucharistic Prayers now in use.

B. Eucharistic Prayer III

This Eucharistic Prayer, like the Fourth, is a recent composition inspired by the Eastern anaphoras.

Its structure

The preface of this Eucharistic Prayer can vary; the body of the prayer is linked to what precedes the *Sanctus*, by means of the words: "Father, you are holy indeed . . ."

The structure of the prayer is quite simple. It begins with

an exclamation of praise: "Father, you are holy indeed, and all creation rightly gives you praise." This is followed by the motives for the exclamation: the gift of life, the sanctification of all things, the gathering of a people that is capable of offering the Father a pure sacrifice. These motives form the anamnesis, or "remembering," which actualizes the mysteries now past.

The intervention of the Spirit is required if the Church is to be able to offer this pure sacrifice. Therefore there is a first epiclesis, which asks for the consecration that will immediately follow. We bring the gifts, but it is God who must consecrate them by sending his Spirit upon them.

After the consecration there is a continuation of the anamnesis, with reference now to the mysteries of Christ: his Passion, resurrection, and ascension. This is followed by the climactic act of offering: Together with Christ and his Church, we offer the holy and living sacrifice that is now present on the altar, thanks to the intervention of the Holy Spirit. We make this offering as a people that awaits Christ's return at his second coming. Each Eucharist advances us on the road toward the last day.

There is now a second epiclesis, which asks that the Holy Spirit would fill us at our reception of the body and blood of Christ and unite us all into a single body.

The second epiclesis is followed by intercessions. We should note the emphasis on reconciliation with God, on salvation that is meant to reach the entire world, and on the strengthening of faith and love. As for the commendations of human beings to God, there could have been a different order in the listing. As it stands, the list begins with the Pope and ends with "the entire people your Son has gained for you." Vatican II's *Dogmatic Constitution on the Church* gives first place to the people of God; perhaps the list should have been modified slightly to begin with the people of God and then move on to its head, the Pope, and the local bishop, priests, and deacons.

At the end of the intercession for the living, there is a

happy repetition of the prayer for unity: "In mercy and love unite all your children wherever they may be." The phrasing of the intercession for the dead is excellent: "Welcome into your kingdom our departed brothers and sisters, and all who have left this world in your friendship." The Eucharistic Prayer ends with the doxology.

The structure, then, is the same as in Eucharistic Prayer II, but it is filled out somewhat more. This is a prayer all of us should love and use in our personal prayer.

C. Eucharistic Prayer IV

Its structure

Although broken up to a certain extent by the *Sanctus*, this prayer is nicely unified. It is the prayer closest to the Jewish blessing that we mentioned earlier. Unfortunately, it is used too infrequently, and this for a paltry reason: "It's too long!" Its structure, again, is simple, but its content is rich.

Following the normal structure of an anaphora, the prayer begins with an exclamation of praise — in this instance, praise of God for creation. The Father is the source of life and has created the world so that he might heap his blessings upon his creatures. This first part of the anamnesis leads us into the *Sanctus*, after which the anamnesis resumes. The focus shifts now to the creation of man in God's image and to the history of salvation: sin, repeated covenants, and finally the sending of the Son and the mystery of our redemption.

The Holy Spirit brings Christ's work in the world to completion; it is appropriate at this point, therefore, to ask the Father to let the Spirit sanctify the gifts so that they may become the body and blood of the Son (first epiclesis). After the words of institution, the anamnesis resumes once again and terminates in the offering of the Son's body and blood to the Father. It is followed in turn by the second epiclesis, which asks that the Holy Spirit make one body of all who participate in Christ's body and blood so that the participants may themselves become, in Christ, a living sacrifice to the praise of God's glory.

At this point the intercessions begin. Here again (as in Eucharistic Prayer III), the list of those commended to God could have begun with the holy people of God and then gone on to the visible head (the Pope), the local bishop, all the bishops, etc. Note the fine prayer for all who seek God with a sincere heart. The prayer ends with the classical doxology.

Value of the new Eucharistic Prayers

It must be acknowledged that the new Eucharistic Prayers form an attractive initiation to prayer. If trouble were taken to teach people the very simple scheme followed in these prayers, the scheme that is almost instinctive when man enters into conversation with God, the results would be most advantageous for the prayer life of the Church. The divorce too often found between personal prayer and liturgical prayer would be ended, since the style of prayer would be the same in both cases. If we ignore the technical aspect of the Eucharistic Prayers and focus our attention on their basic form, must we not judge them capable of leading many to a kind of prayer that they have hitherto thought beyond them? How readily the Christian might learn to respond almost instinctively to any event of the week with a prayer along the lines of these anaphoras! The habit of quick and spontaneous dialogue with God would soon develop.

D. Eucharistic Prayer I and the Roman Canon

Why do we consider last the Roman Canon, which is the first of our present-day Eucharistic prayers? We do so because we think the Roman Canon becomes more accessible once we have examined the other three prayers, which in their structure are more like the original source, namely, the Jewish blessing. The problem with the Roman Canon, which is an anaphora of the Alexandrian type in that it has intercessions both before and after the consecration, is that it does not strike us as a unified whole; it gives the false impression of being a composite of elements juxtaposed and artificially united. This impression used to be intensified by the fact that "Amens" had been introduced into the body of the text, as acclamations that rendered possible a certain amount of active participation by the faithful.

We will gain a better understanding of the Roman Canon if we look at its sources and evolution. It is clearly impossible, of course, to do a complete study that would begin with St. Ambrose's *De sacramentis* and follow the development of the text through the intermediate forms to the time of St. Gregory the Great, when the text achieved a form almost identical with the one we now have. We must be satisfied to give the text as found in St. Ambrose, then the text used in the Old Spanish Liturgy, and finally the Canon as we have known it in modern times.

Here is what St. Ambrose says about the part of the Canon that precedes the consecration:

> By what words is the consecration effected, and whose words are they? The words of the Lord Jesus. *Everything that is said up to this point is said by the priest: praise is given to God, prayer is offered to him, intercessions are made for the people, the rulers, and everyone else.* But when the moment comes to produce the august Sacrament, the priest no longer uses his own words but the words of Christ.[9]

That is a description of how the Eucharistic prayer began in the time of St. Ambrose. As we can see, there was an exclamation of praise, along with intercessions whose objects are named.

We can turn now to the heart of the Canon. We shall place in parallel columns the text given by St. Ambrose, the text found in the Old Spanish Liturgy, and the text of the Roman Canon of St. Gregory the Great (which we shall here translate in a literal manner, for the sake of the parallelism):

St. Ambrose

Grant that this offering may be approved, spiritual, acceptable, for it is the figure of the body and blood of our Lord Jesus Christ. On the day before he suffered, he took bread in his holy hands, looked up to heaven to you, holy Father, almighty everlasting God, and giving thanks, he blessed it, broke it, and gave it to his apostles and disciples, saying: "Take and eat of this, all of you, for this is my body which will be broken for many."[10]

Spanish Liturgy

Grant that this offering be blessed and ratified: it is the image and likeness of the body and blood of Jesus Christ.[11]

Roman Canon

Grant, O God, that in every respect this offering be blessed, approved, ratified, spiritual, and acceptable, so that it may become for us the body and blood of your beloved Son, our Lord Jesus Christ. On the day before he suffered, he took bread into his holy and venerable hands, and raising his eyes to heaven to you, God, his almighty Father, and thanking you, he blessed it, broke it, and gave it to his disciples, saying: "Take and eat of this, all of you, for this is my body which will be delivered up for you."

Mindful, therefore, of his most glorious Passion and resurrection from the dead and ascension into heaven, we offer you this spotless victim, this spiritual victim, this unbloody victim, this holy bread and cup of eternal life,

Mindful, eternal and almighty God, of the most glorious Passion of your Son, our Lord Jesus Christ, and of his resurrection and his ascension. . . .

B

As it pleased you to accept the gifts of your just servant Abel, the sacrifice of our father Abraham, and that which the high priest Melchisedech offered you.

Let your blessing descend here invisibly, we pray you, as once it descended visibly on the sacrifices of our fathers.

Mindful, therefore, Lord, of the blessed Passion of Christ, your Son, our Lord, and of his resurrection from the dead and his glorious ascension into heaven, we your servants and your holy people offer to your glorious Majesty, from among the gifts you yourself have given us, this pure victim, this holy victim, this spotless victim: the holy bread of eternal life and the cup of everlasting salvation.

A

and we ask and pray that you would accept this offering on your heavenly altar through the hands of your angels,

B

as you deigned to accept the gifts of your just servant Abel and the sacrifice of our father Abraham, and that which the high priest Melchisedech offered you.[12]

A

Let the offering rise up with a sweet odor, from this sublime altar which belongs to you, into your glorious presence through the hands of your angel.[13]

B

Look with mercy and gladness on them, and accept them as you deigned to accept the gifts of your just servant Abel, the sacrifice of our father Abraham, and that which your high priest Melchisedech offered you, a holy sacrifice, a spotless victim.

A

We humbly beg you, almighty God, command that they be carried by the hands of your holy angel to the heavenly altar, into the presence of your divine Majesty, so that all of us who in communion with that altar receive the most holy body and blood of your Son may be filled with every heavenly grace and blessing.

Likeness of the three prayers

Let us stop here after this first half of the Canon. The likeness of each of the three prayers to the others is striking. The most important thing to be noted, however, is the Eucharistic theology that finds expression in the three prayers.

The Roman Canon has omitted the words "figure," "image," and "likeness." On the other hand, it connects the acceptance of the offering by God with the fact that the offering becomes the body and blood of Christ.

For St. Ambrose, the Father accepts the sacrifice because it is "the figure" of the body and blood of our Lord Jesus Christ. In the Spanish prayer, he accepts it because it is "the image and likeness" of the body and blood of Jesus Christ. The Roman Canon does not contain this idea, though it is an important one, for it expresses a sacramental theology we cannot afford to neglect.

The *Euchologion* (prayer book) of Bishop Serapion of Thmuis contains an anaphora of the Alexandrian type in which the term "likeness" occurs with relation to the body and blood of Christ:

> We offer you this bread, the likeness of the body of the Only-Begotten. This bread is the likeness of the holy body. For the Lord Jesus Christ, on the night he was handed over, took bread and broke it and gave it to his disciples, saying: "Take and eat, this is my body which is broken for you for the forgiveness of sins." Therefore, celebrating the likeness of his death, we have offered the bread, and we pray: Through this sacrifice be reconciled with all of us and have mercy, God of truth.[14]

The same expressions are then repeated in regard to the cup.

There is thus only one sacrifice, that of the Cross, but it is actualized, that is, made present and operative here and now. This element of actualization is proper to Catholic worship. We do not celebrate just any sacrifice; we offer *the* sacrifice, namely, the sacrifice of Christ himself. "Likeness" does not mean something that resembles that sacrifice, just as "image" does not mean a simple analogue, or "figure" an object that is somehow like another. Each of these terms, on the contrary, signifies the reality itself as present in a different mode. They all mean, concretely, what we in the West speak of as "the unbloody manner" in which the historical sacrifice of Christ is present.

The key idea, then, is that our offering is accepted precisely because it contains the very reality of the one sacrifice of Christ. St. Ambrose and the Roman Canon emphasize this when they speak of the offering as "spiritual." It is accepted because it is spiritual; the Lord has no need of material offerings.

Differences

The Spanish Liturgy and the Roman Canon contain some important modifications in comparison with the text of St. Ambrose. In St. Ambrose the sections we have marked *A* and *B* form a single whole. The prayer begins by asking that God would have his angel bring the offering to the heavenly altar and that he would accept it. It then goes on to give examples of such acceptance by God in the pre-Christian period: Let God accept the offering as he accepted those of Abel, Abraham, and Melchisedech.

In the Spanish Liturgy and the Roman Canon, *A* and *B* are reversed. That is to say, the prayer begins with the plea for acceptance and the giving of the motivating parallels from the Old Testament. In the Roman Canon, this first part, or *B*, is an independent entity. In the Spanish Liturgy, the examples are given in the very first place and are followed by the prayer that God would accept the present sacrifice in the same way; this prayer is expanded, however, and runs over into *A*, that is, the prayer that God would let the sacrifice ascend into his glorious presence.

In the Roman Canon, *B*, as we said, is an independent

entity, clearly distinct and separate from what follows. *A* is introduced, in fact, by a formula frequently used at the beginning of presidential prayers: "We humbly beg you, almighty God." It would seem that the introduction of this formula took place at a relatively late date and had the effect of separating *A* from *B*. The Canon asks not only that an angel carry the sacrifice into God's presence but also that God would bestow his heavenly blessings on all who receive the body and blood of Christ; thus the latter becomes an epiclesis in the broad sense (the Spirit is not explicitly mentioned), comparable to the post-consecration epiclesis in Hippolytus.

We may note also that the Spanish prayer does not ask that the offering be taken to the heavenly altar, as the Roman Canon does, but rather that it be taken from the earthly altar of the Lord into his heavenly presence. Ambrose's prayer asks that the offering be taken in the hands of *angels*, while the Spanish prayer and the Roman Canon speak of it being carried by *an angel*. Consequently, there is no reason to see in the angel of the Roman Canon a reference to Christ or the Holy Spirit or some other non-angelic personage.

It is easy, in the light of our analysis, to discern the Alexandrian structure of the Roman Canon: exclamation, beginning of an anamnesis, intercessions, prayer for the consecration, consecration, anamnesis, offering and petition for acceptance of the sacrifice, intercessions, and doxology.

This Eucharistic Prayer has certain deficiencies, such as the lack of an explicit prayer for the intervention of the Holy Spirit. It has the great merit, however, of strongly emphasizing the sacrificial aspect of the Mass. It also makes it clear that the one sacrifice of Christ, which is actualized in the Mass, is present and manifested through an unbloody rite. This is a theology we find in both Serapion and Ambrose, and later in the teaching of the Council of Trent.

4. LITURGICAL THEOLOGY OF THE PRESIDENTIAL PRAYERS: God's Love for Men, Men's Love for God

The various presidential prayers of the Sundays of Ordinary Time were not chosen with the readings or chants in mind, they are, in fact, used in all three years of the cycle. Consequently, it is neither necessary nor useful to comment on them when dealing with the readings for each Sunday.

On the other hand, these prayers should not simply be overlooked, and we have therefore decided to offer a synthetic presentation of them. They contain a theology we should not neglect; in fact, when we bring together those that follow the same general line of thought, we find a theology that is quite rich. We shall, of course, make no effort to exhaust the content of these prayers; this essay should rather be thought of as a first approach to the prayers. Since our interest here is pastoral, we shall not indicate the ancient sources of the prayers or, alternatively, the fact that they are modern compositions; that kind of information can easily be found elsewhere. The reader can consult the articles published by the experts who worked on the revision of the Roman Missal.[15] (In the following pages, the bracketed numbers indicate the Sunday of Ordinary Time to which the prayer in question belongs.)

1. The Opening Prayers

These prayers used to be called "collects," that is, prayers in which the celebrant gathered together and summarized in a general statement the intentions of all.

A simple survey of these prayers will bring to light the broad range of themes that find expression in them. The prayers have to do with the history of creation, with the guidance of providence, and above all with the love of God, with his grace that anticipates and accompanies our actions, and with the response we should make to God's concern for us. We must eliminate evil from our lives and keep ever before our minds the blessings to come. Such are the main thoughts to be found in these prayers.

Creation, providence, today's world

The Lord is Creator and Master of all reality [24]; he is the God of the universe who rules heaven and earth [2]; he is also the King of the universe (feast of Christ the King) and guides the world with a providence that is unerring in the carrying out of its plans [9].

When we contemplate the whole work of creation and the whole divine plan of salvation, we are proud that God is our Creator and all-providing Lord [18]. The proof of God's power is given to us not only by his creative action and his providential guidance of all things, but also by his unwearying patience and mercy [26].

Creation was ruined by sin, and the sins of men continue to deface it. We ask the Lord to restore his creation [18] and to free it from its enslavement (feast of Christ the King). He alone can establish in the world the peace that we need [8] and that our age seeks [2]. Amid a world that is constantly changing, we ask him to establish us in true and lasting joy [21].

God's love for us

God's love is limitless [27]. He loves us like a father [23], and his kindness to us, like his love, is inexhaustible [18].

This love is manifested in the blessings that God constantly bestows so lavishly upon us. The first and greatest blessing is his very own Son, whom he sent so that we might become adoptive sons [23]. His grace has made us children of light and will keep us ever within the radiance of his truth [13]. We are capable of manifesting the light because God himself shows us that light and points out the true way to us [15]. It is from him that every perfect gift comes [22]; he is the source of every blessing [10].

God's basic action in the world's behalf is his will to raise it up through the humiliation of his own Son [14]. God's love for men is so great that he desires to dwell in upright and sincere hearts and to make of us his dwelling place [6].

His love is constantly being manifested by the way he protects and watches over his family, the Church [5].

The response to love

The aim of every Christian must be to ground his heart solidly in the love of God, a respectful love [12] that allows us to call God our Father [19].

The proper response to love consists in observing the commandments and in devoting ourselves, in will and action, to what the love of God requires of us [11]. Our weakness, however, does not allow us to live in so perfect a way, and God himself therefore must give us the power to love what he commands [30]. He must instill a filial spirit in us and make it grow [19]; he must pour into our hearts a fervent love for him [20]; he must make love for his name take root in us [22] and direct our actions as love requires [3]. In this way we shall gradually come to love God above all things [20], for it will be God himself who makes us love what he commands [30] and will what he wills [29].

The love of God and the unconditional worship he requires necessarily imply a love for men that springs from genuine charity [4]. The law requires that we love not only God but our neighbor too [25].

If the faithful who have been rescued from slavery thus conform themselves to God's will in all they say and do [7], they will live in a holy joy [14] and will feel the effects of the love the Lord has for them [24]. Their joy will be the joy of a people that serves the Lord in peace [8] because it serves him wholeheartedly [24]. This people will know the deep and lasting happiness that springs from service [33] rendered to the glory of the Lord [29]; their happiness will be all the greater because they know that the Lord himself must give his grace if men are to be able to serve him worthily [31].

God, the Servant of man

God is truly at the service of man when it comes to inspiring man and remaining at his side in all he does [28]. God constantly guides men [12], inspires them to do what is right, and helps them in the doing [10]. He fills them with his blessing far beyond their deserts and even their desires [27]; he will even bestow upon them what they do not dare to ask for [27]. He multiplies his gifts of grace [16], which alone gives man hope [5], and without which he can do nothing [11] and nothing is holy or worthwhile [17].

We look to the gracious God to intensify our faith, hope, and love [30]. Only if he grants us true freedom [23] and enables us to focus our hearts upon a single goal [21] will we be able to live always in accordance with the grace [6] that God, ever at our service, constantly wishes to give us.

Called in Christ's name

Because of God's gifts to us, we can live in Christ's name, rejecting what is unworthy of that name and pursuing what does it honor [15]. Such a rejection and pursuit presuppose that we are free enough to do God's will [32] with a joyous fidelity [33] and a peaceful conscience [27]. No one is perfect, however; each in the course of his life experiences the unwearying patience and mercy of God [26].

We cannot successfully make good use of temporal goods and set our hearts on those that abide [17] unless the Lord gives us power to do what is right [28] and fosters what is good in us, by watching over us and protecting the fruits of grace he produces in us [22]. Consequently, if we bear fruit in Christ's name, that too is already God's gift to us [3].

The vision of the world to come

In accord with our baptismal promises we are to live a life of love by observing the commandments and keeping our eyes turned toward eternal life [25]. But we must even look to God for the power to set his will upon what

God promises [21]. God must enable the faithful to advance [31], indeed to hasten [26], toward the promised blessings. It is the Lord himself who must give them knowledge of inexhaustible happiness [14] and the invisible blessings prepared for them [20]. The Christian therefore has but one desire: to obtain what God promises [30], to enter into the promised inheritance, which surpasses all human desire [19; 20], and to reach the happiness of heaven [26]. Such a concentration on the world to come, while we are still residents of this world, would be impossible if God himself were not the strength of those who hope in him [11].

The opening prayers thus contain a rich teaching about the encounter between God and man, between God's generous, indeed limitless, initiative and man's need. These prayers were certainly not selected in order to present a carefully elaborated systematic theology, but nonetheless, Sunday after Sunday, they do help deepen our appreciation of the divine realities that are the basis of our life, though only too often we not reflect upon them.

2. The Prayers over the Gifts

The opening prayers were fairly general in their statements. The prayers over the gifts will now offer us an experiential theology of the life of worship. In these prayers the worshippers are seen offering with Christ and the Church the sacrifice that establishes the world in unity and leads it toward its final salvation. The prayers contain a profound theology of the Eucharist and of the meaning of the sacrifice; they also bring to light the various effects of the spiritual sacrifice that is offered in the celebration, especially the effects of pardon and purification, which are an aspect of the Eucharistic celebration that is too often neglected.

We offer what the Lord has given to us

Four of the prayers over the gifts emphasize the fact that it is God himself who has given us what we are now offering to him. (This idea found expression long ago in the Roman Canon, which is now our First Eucharistic Prayer.) The Lord gives us what we are then to offer to the glory of his name [8]; the gifts we give we have because of his generosity to us [17]. It is in an act of mercy that he has given them to us so that we may offer them back to him [19]. One of the four prayers gives a more theological expression to the deeper meaning of our offering: The offering of the Eucharistic gifts is part of a marvelous exchange in which we offer God what he has first given us, and then he in turn gives us his very self [20]. This last happens because when we offer the gifts we have received, they are transformed into the body and blood of the Word.

A spiritual sacrifice

Our offering is first and foremost an act of love, the love being signified by what we offer [8]. We must be careful to understand what is meant by our placing our offerings on the altar [4] and the Lord's receiving them from the hands of the faithful [16]. There is in fact a single sacrificial offering; it was made by the one Priest, Christ, as a spiritual sacrifice [18]. We, however, participate in the offering of that sacrifice [2] and thereby enter into the mystery of Christ's Passion [32].

The gifts we bring signify our interior disposition; they will be consecrated [3] and become for us the sacrament of a new life and a food to sustain that same life [11].

The Lord can make of our offering the sacrament of our salvation [19]; the bread and wine God originally gave us for our earthly nourishment become here the sacrament of an eternal life [5]. The Eucharistic celebration actualizes the paschal mystery (i.e., makes it present and effective here and now), for every time this memorial sacrifice is celebrated, the work of our redemption is accomplished [2]. The power of the Lord himself accomplishes what we celebrate in the liturgy [22], that is, in the commemoration of the sacrifice of the Cross, which itself brought to fulfillment the sacrifices of the old law [16].

The Eucharistic celebration thereby gives glory to the Father for what he has done; we pray that the celebration may contribute to his glorification [23; 30]. In fact, since the offerings represent us, we can ask the Lord to turn us, and not only our gifts, into an everlasting sacrifice to his glory [18].

A people of sons and daughters who are united by love

The sacrifice of the Cross was a covenant sacrifice that re-established the world in unity. Through the one sacrifice of the Cross, the Lord acquired a people of adopted children [21]. Participation in the Eucharist is meant to strengthen the bonds of unity among us [23]; our offering will obtain an intensification of love [10]. In the Eucharistic celebration the Lord bestows upon his Church the graces of unity and peace [21], so that the gifts offered by each one contribute to the salvation of all [16].

We are purified and renewed

The effect of purification and forgiveness, which in the past was frequently mentioned in the postcommunion prayers as a reminder to those who had shared in the body and blood of Christ, is now more frequently to be found in the prayers over the gifts.

The Eucharist purifies and renews us [6]; we are purified by the sacrifice we offer [9]. The sacrifice we offer is one of praise and expiation [12], and the Lord responds to it with foregiveness and peace [32]. The Eucharist is a generous gift of the merciful God to us [31], and we are purified by the very mystery we celebrate [14; 29].

Our bodies and our souls both profit by the sacramental sustenance given us for our new life [11]; the Eucharist sanctifies those whom the Father has saved through his Son [27]. The faithful who receive these gifts advance toward greater holiness [15], for in these mysteries divine grace is powerfully at work [17] to sanctify us in our everyday lives [17].

Salvation and the blessings to come

One of the most common themes is the effectiveness of the Eucharist in leading us to salvation; we pray that the offerings may become the sacrament of our salvation [3; 4; 7; 22]. The Eucharistic celebration wins for the faithful those blessings on which they set their hopes [25]. Faith and hope, though, are not enough; the Christian must also do the Father's will, for it is to those who do God's will that the Eucharist gives the promised happiness [6]. If we have faith and hope and if we do God's will, the mysteries will lead us to the everlasting joys of a blessed eternity [17; 33]. The gifts we offer will then bear the fruit of eternal happiness [8]. The Eucharistic sacrifice leads us day by day to the kingdom [14], and the liturgy, when celebrated with love, guides us to the glory of heaven [28].

3. The Prayers after Communion

As we would expect, these prayers likewise provide a rich experiential theology of the Eucharistic celebration. Our effort here, once again, will simply be to outline the content of the prayers, with a minimum of interpretive commentary.

Become what we have received

Our deeply intimate union with the Christ we have received is one of the favorite themes of these prayers after Communion. The idea that we will become what we have received [27] best sums up the hope of the believer who participates in the body and blood of Christ. Communion with the holy mysteries prefigures the union of the faithful with Christ [11] and deepens it [20]. Participation in the Eucharist makes us like Christ while we are on earth [20] and also makes us participants in the divine nature [28].

The prayers are thus emphasizing the profound renewal and transformation that takes place. The Eucharist is meant to heal and transform us [21]. It frees us from our evil inclinations and directs us toward the good [10], giving us new strength for the purpose [29]. Participation in the Eucharist affects spirit and body [24], renewing them both [26]. This idea of the renewal of man is a frequent theme: we are renewed by the bread of heaven [18], by the body and blood of Christ [12]; we receive the grace of a new life [3], into which our Communion makes us enter [16].

The sacraments thus produce in us what they signify [30]. The Eucharistic celebration is a commemoration and actualization of the Passion of Christ [17], and from it we are to derive fruit for our salvation [14]. Bound now to Christ by a love that will never pass away, we are to produce fruit that will likewise remain forever [13], while the activities of our lives strengthen us to do so [25].

The Eucharist is in all truth the sacrament of our redemption [4]; it keeps us faithful [19] and intensifies the effects of salvation [15]. It makes us advance in true faith [19] and grounds us more deeply in the truth [19]. The influence of Eucharistic grace prevails over our selfishness [24], to the point that our thoughts and actions become a witness to the Lord [9].

The action of the Holy Spirit is perhaps too infrequently mentioned in these prayers, but it is extremely important. Now that God has fed us with his Son's body and blood, may he also guide us through his Spirit [9]; now that we have received power from on high, may the Spirit keep us on the right path [32].

The sacrament of unity

We have been fed with the one bread; may we now be one in love [2]. Such unity demands that we serve one another; the Eucharist intensifies our love and rouses us to serve the brethren [22]. Being the actualization of the paschal mystery, the Eucharist unites the Church, and our Communion contributes to this unity [11].

The Eucharist has effects beyond the Church, however, for it transforms the world as a whole, inasmuch as we who eat the one bread and drink the one cup must be so one with Christ in our lives that we will be able to bear fruit for the salvation of the world [5].

The sacrament of the kingdom

What do we do in the Eucharist if not praise the Father for all he has accomplished through the paschal mystery of his Son? We therefore ask that we may be fully redeemed and share in what we celebrate in each Eucharist [12]. We are destined one day to enter into the full, unveiled possession of the realities we celebrate now in sacramental form [30]. Communion penetrates us with the heavenly mysteries [16] and enables us to enter the kingdom of heaven [9]. It gives us knowledge of the eternal blessings of the kingdom [29] by giving us a taste of heavenly delights and a thirst for the sources of true life [6].

The Eucharist is wholly focused on eternity. We pray, in the prayers after Communion, that the sacrament that feeds us while on earth may also make us live forever with God [8] and may make us sharers forever in the life of the Son [23] and in his heavenly glory [20]. The Eucharist is the pledge and promise of the fruits of salvation [7]; it makes us worthy of salvation [18] and thus helps us attain it [17]. It bestows a share in the glorious inheritance [26] and prepares us to enter into the joy that the sacrament promises [31].

SUNDAYS NINE TO THIRTY-FOUR
IN ORDINARY TIME

CYCLE A
Years 1978, 1981, 1984, 1987, 1990

TABLE OF SUNDAY READINGS

In the following table, the general theme of each celebration and the particular theme of each reading are indicated. If the second reading is connected with the general theme of the day, it will be commented on together with the first reading and the Gospel (these second readings are marked by an asterisk in the following list). If the second reading does not fit in with the theme of the day, a heavy line separates the commentary given from the preceding.

Comment on Sundays one to nine in ordinary time may be found in volume one, pages 308-311; 332-432.

CYCLE A

Years 1978, 1981, 1984, 1987, 1990

Sunday 9   The obedience of the heart
            Matthew 7:21-27   Do the Father's will
            Deut. 11:18, 26-28   Lay up the commandments in your heart
            *Rom. 3:21-25a, 28   Justified by faith

Sunday 10   Love, not ritualism
            Matthew 9:9-13   Yes to mercy, not to ritualism
            Hos. 6:3-6   Yes to love, not to holocausts
            Rom. 4:18-25   Faith made Abraham strong

Sunday 11   Men chosen by God
            Matthew 9:36–10:8   Chosen and sent to the lost sheep
            Exod. 19:2-6a   A kingdom of priests
            Rom. 5:6-11   Saved by the death of Christ

Sunday 12   Proclaim the will of God
            Matthew 10:26-33   Do not fear men
            Jer. 20:10-13   The persecutors will fail
            Rom. 5:12-15   Where sin was, grace now abounds

Sunday 13	Receive the Lord Matthew 10:37-42 2 Kings 4:8-11, 14-16a Rom. 6:3-4, 8-11	He who receives you receives me Receive the holy man of God We died with Christ and now live with him
Sunday 14	The Lord is humble Matthew 11:25-30 Zech. 9:9-10 Rom. 8:9, 11-13	Gentle and lowly in heart A humble king To live, put to death the disorders of sinful man
Sunday 15	The efficacious word Matthew 13:1-23 Is. 55:10-11 Rom. 8:18-23	Receive the word The word of God Creation longs to see God's sons revealed
Sunday 16	The patient justice of God Matthew 13:24-43 Wis. 12:13, 16-19 Rom. 8:26-27	The justice that saves You judge with mildness The Holy Spirit prays in us
Sunday 17	Choose the real treasure Matthew 13:44-52 1 Kings 3:5, 7-12 Rom. 8:28-30	Sell all for the real treasure Ask for the real treasure Become the image of God's Son

Sunday 18   A God who feeds men
             Matthew 14:13-21   They ate their fill
             Is. 55:1-3   Be filled
             Rom. 8:35, 37-39   Who can separate us from the love of Christ?

Sunday 19   Face the obstacles and advance toward the Lord
             Matthew 14:22-33   Bid me come to you
             1 Kings 19:9a, 11-13a   Stand before the Lord as he passes
             Rom. 9:1-5   I could wish even to be accursed for the
                                                    sake of my brothers, the Jews

Sunday 20   A house for all peoples
             Matthew 15:21-28   Israel, but all believers as well
             Is. 56:1, 6-7   A house of prayer for all peoples
             *Rom. 11:13-15, 29-32   All peoples can obtain mercy

Sunday 21   Firm ground
             Matthew 16:13-20   On this rock I will build my church
             Is. 22:19-23   A peg in a sure place
             Rom. 11:33-36   From him and through him and to him are
                                                    all things

Sunday 22   The suffering required of the disciple
             Matthew 16:21-27   Renounce self and follow the Lord
             Jer. 20:7-9   I am insulted and mocked
             *Rom. 12:1-2   Offer one's person and life in sacrifice

Sunday 23   Fraternal correction
             Matthew 18:15-20   Win your brother over
             Ezek. 33:7-9   Warn the wicked man
             *Rom. 13:8-10   Love fulfills the law

Sunday 24   Forgiveness
             Matthew 18:21-35   Forgive seventy times seven times
             Sir. 27:30—28:7   Forgiveness of neighbor and forgiveness of sins
             *Rom. 14:7-9   We live and die for the Lord. Why judge?

Sunday 25   God's thoughts and value judgments
             Matthew 20:1-16   Do you begrudge my generosity?
             Is. 55:6-9   My thoughts are not your thoughts
             Phil. 1:20c-24, 27a   For me to live is Christ

Sunday 26   Repent and live
             Matthew 21:28-32   Sinners are saved by faith and repentance
             Ezek. 18:25-28   Turn from your sins and be saved
             Phil. 2:1-11   Have the mind of Christ

Sunday 27   The fruitless vineyard
Matthew 21:33-43
Is. 5:1-7
Phil. 4:6-9

He will lease his vineyard to others
The Lord's vineyard is the house of Israel
The God of peace will be with you

Sunday 28   The banquet of the Lord
Matthew 22:1-14
Is. 25:6-10a
Phil. 4:12-14, 19-20

Those invited to the wedding feast
The banquet of the saved
Bear with everything by the power of Christ

Sunday 29   The primacy of God's service
Matthew 22:15-21
Is. 45:1, 4-6
1 Thess. 1:1-5b

Give to Caesar what is Caesar's
I am the Lord, and there is no other
A life of faith, love, and hope

Sunday 30   Love of neighbor
Matthew 22:34-40
Exod. 22:21-27

1 Thess. 1:5c-10

Love your neighbor as yourself
Love the orphan, the widow, the foreigner, and
the poor
Turn from idols and serve God

Sunday 31   The law and obedience to it
            Matthew 23:1-12
            Mal. 1:14b–2:2b, 8-10
            *1 Thess. 2:7-9, 13

            They speak but do not act
            Watering down the law
            Give the Good News and your very selves

Sunday 32   Watch and wait
            Matthew 25:1-13
            Wis. 6:12-16
            1 Thess. 4:13-18

            Watch, for we know not the day or the hour
            Watch, and find wisdom
            God will bring forth those who have fallen
                asleep in Jesus

Sunday 33   Fidelity to duty and work
            Matthew 25:14-30

            Prov. 31:10-13, 19-20, 30-31
            1 Thess. 5:1-6

            You have been faithful in small things: enter
                into the joy of your Lord
            A worthy wife is a precious jewel
            If we are watchful and sober, we will not
                be taken by surprise

Sunday 34   Christ, King of the universe
            Matthew 25:31-46

            Ezek. 34:11-12, 15-17
            *1 Cor. 15:20-26, 28

            The Son of Man, the shepherd who will separate the sheep from the goats
            The Lord will judge between sheep and sheep
            The final reign of the glorious Christ

NINTH SUNDAY

The Obedience of the Heart

Do the Father's will (Matthew 7:21-27)

Neither petitions to the Lord nor outward marks of honor given to him are enough — such is the clear point made in today's text. Nor does the text mean only that liturgical prayer is not enough; the same must be said even of activities that themselves depend on God and seem at first sight to be surely inspired by a desire to serve him, such as prophesying, expelling demons, and performing miracles. The mere cry of faith, the mere calling on God's name — these are not enough. What more is required? The doing of the will of the heavenly Father. The person who does not do it will find God treating him as a stranger and an evildoer.

Jesus' words are important and always relevant. The man who does as Christ teaches here, that is, who seeks to do the Father's will, builds his house on solid rock, so that nothing can shake it. The person who does not do as Christ instructs him here builds on sand, and his house will collapse.

The example is simple and illuminating, and should make us stop and reflect. Faith alone or devotion or even confidence in the Lord is not enough. In fact, we must go even further: pious practices, attendance at the liturgy, and the reception of the sacraments can delude us about the real quality of our Christian lives. And yet there is a way of preventing self-deception and judging our situation accurately by asking ourselves, "Do we do the Father's will?" We may act in the name of Jesus, we may even act as his ministers and representatives, but none of that is relevant on the last day if we have not done the Father's will.

The Gospel pericope thus urges the Christian to test his conduct. No practice, even sacramental, and no devotion to the "cause" of God is of any value if there has not been the practical will to do what God wants us to do.

These words of Jesus exclude any possible hypocrisy and tell us clearly what awaits us at the end. God will not acknowledge us because of our prayer or Christian practices if these are simply formalities or actions that spring simply from our own liking. No, we must submit to God's will and seek to know what he wants of us. There is no secret about what he wants; it is expressed in the commandments and especially in the commandment of love for God and neighbor. Faith, prayer, and devotion acquire value only if they are built upon the doing of God's will.

Does this mean that the Gospel is here preaching a more external conformity? Not at all, since in doing the Father's will we are not simply being automatons but are forming our very selves according to revelation and right reason. The parable of the house built on rock or on sand shows that this is the case. To do God's will is to form ourselves in harmony with divine wisdom for life on earth and for eternal life. The solidly built man, who will enter the kingdom as "justified" and "built" in God, is the man who does the Father's will.

Lay up the commandments in your hearts (Deut. 11:18, 26-28)

Had St. Matthew wished to give scriptural backing to Jesus' words about the disciple who does God's will, he could have simply cited the Book of Deuteronomy. The passage used in today's liturgy helps us grasp the constructive aspect of obedience to God's will.

In the first part of the Book of Deuteronomy, Moses explains at length the meaning and importance of the law. It was first and foremost a love-inspired gift of God, who wanted to form his people. The law was a seal upon the covenant, guaranteeing its permanence and solidity, while at the same time constantly reminding the people of the duty of fidelity. By obeying the law, the people of God would gradually form themselves and build themselves up; they were responsible, therefore, for what they were and would be. That is why the passage we read in today's liturgy uses so many images in its exhortation: "You shall lay up these words of mine in your heart and in your soul; and you shall bind them as a sign upon your hand, and they shall be as frontlets between your eyes" (v. 18).

This people whom God loved was thus obliged constantly to choose, and it would be blessed or cursed by God, depending on the choice it made. The central choice demanded was, of course, fidelity to the one God and rejection of every other god. In a second stage, the choice was to follow the way of the Lord (an expression used with great frequency in the Old Testament, especially in the psalms).

To do as the Lord commanded was to keep the covenant and to walk in his ways. Doing God's will was thus something very positive, not merely a passive acceptance of obligation. In the same way, when the Christian of today does the Father's will, he is cooperating with the Lord in the formation and building up of God's people.

People are not entirely wrong in seeing Catholicism at times as a religion of cultus and sacramental practice; they are simply judging Catholicism by Catholics. And yet the Lord spoke clearly enough; we need only read his words to realize that neither faith nor sacraments are enough to guarantee true Christianity and to build the kingdom. The true builder is God himself. He is the Lord of the covenant, and the covenant will be fruitful and turn into a genuine dialogue between God and man only when man is willing to choose and do God's will.

Justified by faith (Rom. 3:21-25a, 28)

This short passage from St. Paul's Letter to the Romans gives us an opportunity to state in a more nuanced way the teaching given in the passages from the Book of Deuteronomy and the Gospel of St. Matthew.

On the surface, St. Paul is contradicting the teaching of Christ. A superficial reading of the passage might suggest that far from realizing the importance of practical obedience, the Apostle is making faith the essential thing: "We hold that a man is justified by faith apart from the works of the law" (v. 28). We seem to be faced with a dilemma, for Jesus says in St. Matthew that neither faith nor prayers nor devotions are enough to save man, while St. Paul says that faith justifies independently of actions or works. Which of the two are we to choose?

The Church, as we know, does not accept the Protestant position that faith "alone" saves. Is the Church departing from the teaching of St. Paul, or has Protestantism somehow exaggerated what St. Paul is saying? We cannot enter here into all the theological discussions, and yet at the same time we cannot simply pass the problem by, especially since the principle of continuous reading has accidentally led to this passage of St. Paul being set side by side with the passages from St. Matthew and the Book of Deuteronomy. Paul either contradicts the other two, or he sheds a further indispensable light on the subject.

A first point to be made is one that Paul himself makes in this passage: All men are under the domination of sin. Men must therefore inevitably despair if God does not intervene with his mercy. That is precisely what God has done: he has shown mercy and of his own accord justified men. But there is a condition that must be met if God's mercy is to be effective in us, and that condition is faith in Jesus Christ. The one who decided on this new order of things is God himself, and his decision was that salvation through Jesus Christ should be independent of the old law. Yet the decision does not come suddenly, for Scripture had predicted this new way of salvation, and the law and the prophets have their fulfillment in Christ.

Since we are all sinners and since we cannot by our own efforts free ourselves from this situation, God freely saves us by giving us his grace in virtue of the redemption wrought by Jesus. Our part is to accept the gift by believing in him who wins it for us through his death. "God put

[Christ Jesus] forward as an expiation by his blood, to be received by faith" (Rom. 3:25). Jesus has become for us wisdom, righteousness, sanctification, and redemption (1 Cor. 1:30). In his blood the new covenant has been sealed (1 Cor. 11:25). Though Jesus was without sin, God made him to be sin for our sake, so that we might become the righteousness of God (2 Cor. 5:21). To be saved, therefore, we must through faith accept God's love for us and the gift of salvation he offers us in Jesus Christ. In this passage, then, what St. Paul is emphasizing is the gift-character of salvation and, on our part, the fact that faith is an indispensable condition for our receiving the gift.

At this point, however, we must be careful in interpreting St. Paul's thought. If we put the thought of the present passage into the context formed by his other letters, we see that he is much concerned with those who imagine that they can find salvation by their own efforts. Consequently, he lays a great deal of stress on the fact that salvation is God's gift to us. At the same time, however, the man who is to receive the gift must believe. Faith, in turn, does not relieve men of any further efforts. In the Letter to the Galatians, Paul reminds his readers that a Christian must be active and that good deeds are needed if a man is to be saved. He tells his readers that they must produce in themselves the fruits of the Spirit who dwells and acts in them, and he lists the vices that exclude a person from the kingdom; he bids his readers crucify their flesh with its passions and lusts (Gal. 5:16-25).

What does all this mean? It means that while the Christian is no longer subject to the old law, he is certainly subject to the law of Christ, which he fulfills by "bearing one another's burdens" (Gal. 6:2). Paul writes: "He who sows to the Spirit will from the Spirit reap eternal life. . . . Let us do good to all men" (Gal. 6:8-10). He bids his Roman readers renounce sin (Rom. 6:2, 6, 12-14); he tells the Philippians that they must work out their salvation with fear and trembling (Phil. 2:12). Elsewhere he depicts the preacher as one who exhorts his hearers to an obedient faith (Rom.

1:5), and later on in the same letter, in a fine passage on the righteousness of God foretold by Moses, he speaks of obedience to the Good News (Rom. 10:16). At the end of the letter he refers again to obedient faith, this time with regard to the Gentiles (Rom. 16:26).

Evidently, then, while faith in Christ is the only way to attain to salvation, this faith supposes and indeed consists in obedience to the gospel. Faith requires the involvement of the person's entire existence, for while faith alone can save (since Christ alone can give us salvation), it presupposes a response to Christ, an adherence to his person and his Good News. The Christian thus sees himself obliged to a choice that frees him and makes him responsible for his own formation and the building of the kingdom.

TENTH SUNDAY

Love, Not Ritualism

Yes to mercy, not to ritualism (Matthew 9:9-13)

St. Matthew records his own calling in a simple, straightforward way. The story is marked, in fact, by the moving simplicity of all the vocation narratives in the New Testament: Christ chooses and calls; the person chosen and called immediately leaves everything and follows Jesus. In its very simplicity, the calling is so wonderful that it defies commentary. In this instance, however, the choice is quite unusual, and St. Matthew deliberately emphasizes this aspect of it by describing the sequel. Jesus comes to dine with Matthew and the other disciples in Matthew's house at Capharnaum; they are joined at table by many tax collectors and sinners, to whose ranks Matthew has belonged until now.

It is easy to see the point Matthew wants to make, namely, that Jesus has come into the world to save not only Jews but others as well, including sinners. When Jesus is challenged for eating with sinners, we observe that he does not justify himself but simply speaks of himself as "a physician." A physician does not have to justify his presence among the sick; neither does Jesus. Matthew is thus once again offering us a theology of the Christ. Jesus is characterized by mercy, because his Father is mercy itself and he, Jesus, has been sent in order to communicate God's mercy.

Those who listened to Jesus must have had at least a rudimentary understanding of what "mercy" meant when applied to God. The Old Testament was filled with passages on divine mercy. The Old Testament expression "God of mercy" or "merciful God" was the concise statement of a whole theology. For the Book of Deuteronomy, God is the "meriful God" (Deut. 4:31), as he is for the Book of Wisdom (Wis. 9:1) and the Book of Psalms (Ps. 86:15).

It would be impossible, of course, to list here all the Old Testament passages that speak of God's mercy, since mercy is one of his constant attributes. Here are a few texts. "The Lord is merciful and gracious, slow to anger and abounding in steadfast love" (Ps. 103:8). "The Lord is gracious and merciful" (Ps. 111:4). How often had not the people of Israel experienced that mercy! "I the Lord your God am a jealous God . . . but showing steadfast love to thousands . . ." (Exod. 20:6); ". . . showing steadfast love to thousands" (Deut. 5:10); "Righteous art thou, O Lord; all thy deeds and all thy ways are mercy and truth" (Tob. 3:2).

The psalms especially are full of references to God's mercy: "I have trusted in thy steadfast love" (Ps. 13:5); "Be mindful of thy mercy, O Lord, and of thy steadfast love" (Ps. 25:6); "All the paths of the Lord are steadfast love and faithfulness" (Ps. 25:10); "We have thought on thy steadfast love, O Lord, in the midst of thy temple" (Ps. 48:9); ". . . to declare thy steadfast love in the morning" (Ps. 92:2). This mercy is immense and limitless: "Thy steadfast love is great to the heavens" (Ps. 57:9); "Great is his steadfast love toward us" (Ps. 117:2). This mercy is also eternal (Pss. 100:5; 103:17; 107:1; 118:1, 29; 136:1). The psalms are often an appeal for God's mercy: "Wondrously show thy steadfast love" (Ps. 17:7); "Hear, O Lord, and be gracious to me!" (Ps. 30:10); "Let thy steadfast love, O Lord, be upon us" (Ps. 33:22). God's mercy is identical with his loving concern for mankind which he wants to save.

Jesus' hearers, then, must have understood quite well what he meant. Being God's Son, Jesus must himself be merciful as God is merciful. He came on a mission of mercy, and to him mercy shown to our fellow-men was far more important than ritual observances. Christianity is a religion of love, not of ritual.

At the same time, however, the catechist must be careful in explaining this passage. Elsewhere, in explaining the Gospel in which Jesus pardons the adulterous woman because she loved much, an undemanding catechesis might justify a facile forgiveness of all the sins of the flesh. So here a simplistic and opportunistic catechesis might be built on the fact that Jesus ate with tax collectors and sinners, that he chose an apostle from among them, and that he says his chief desire is for mercy. But the fact that Jesus ate with sinners and tax collectors is not a legitimate basis for propaganda in favor of a party and of overturning the existing social structure. Jesus is not talking politics in this passage. His teaching does not aim at creating new human and social situations but at establishing justice and bestowing on all mankind a salvation that is to be enjoyed in the world to come.

The emphasis here must be on the fact that Jesus, in working for the conversion and salvation of the world, brings together in the group of disciples who will form the Church all sorts of people, without regard to their race or social class or previous moral status. He does the choosing, and he makes it possible for individuals so different in cultural background, social status, and moral quality to live together and cooperate in spreading the kingdom. He came

to call sinners, not to confuse sinners with a particular social class, as though sinners were not to be found in every
social class. It may be necessary to overhaul certain attitudes cultivated in the past and to overcome a certain fear
of sinners that sometimes affects present-day apostles. This
is a far cry from saying that the Church of today must side
with every claim against society or be concerned only with
sinners and rebels. Every age must examine its conscience,
but it must do so honestly and within an understanding of
the kingdom for which the Church toils.

It is true enough, however, that the Church and the faithful cannot withdraw into the celebration of the liturgy,
prayer, and the sacraments, while paying no heed to the
needs of contemporary man and forming a kind of elitist
Church that is concerned only for the pious. If the Church
or Christians were to take such an attitude, they would soon
learn from today's Gospel that they were traveling a different road than Christ.

Yes to love, not to holocausts (Osee 6:3-6)

Love, not burnt sacrifices: God makes this statement in
connection with a penitential liturgy being celebrated by
the people. We cannot assert, however, that the liturgy was
hypocritical and an example of the kind of thing often at-
tacked by the prophets when they saw men seeking pardon
out of simple fear and without any desire for real conversion. This passage from Osee does not support such an interpretation. What God complains of is something different,
though quite serious: The love of his people for him is as
fleeting as the morning dew. The people are inconstant in
their fidelity, and the text hints at a kind of infinite sadness
in the heart of God.

Jesus cites this passage in the Gospel pericope we have
just been reading: "I desire mercy, and not sacrifice" (Osee
6:6; Matthew 9:13). The prophet adds: "the knowledge of
God, rather than burnt offerings." What the Lord wants is
that men should be united to him in intimate, faithful love.

Here again a crucial problem is raised for our meditation. Is not today's Christian, like the believer of the Old Testament, tempted to opt for an easy sacramental ritualism that would dispense him from the hard task of loving? Does he look for sacramental forgiveness rather than to be truly converted and become more loving? Does he not tend to take refuge in ritual and forget about forgiveness and love of others? Each of us must face the question and try to answer it without self-indulgence.

Faith made Abraham strong (Rom. 4:18-25)

Paul has launched into his dissertation on "justification." He tells us that it is through faith in Christ that God "justifies," i.e., saves man. In simplest terms: Faith in Christ saves.

The present pericope has two themes: the faith of Abraham as a model of saving faith, and the Christian's saving faith. Abraham's faith justified him. He believed against all hope; he believed in the promise God had made; because of that faith, God declared him just. Paul had explained, a bit further back (see last Sunday), that Abraham was justified, not by any merit attaching to his works, but by God's free gift, given on account of Abraham's faith in God's promise and without any dependence on the observance of the law. Neither the law nor works justified Abraham; he was justified on account of his faith and by a free gift.

Because of his faith, Abraham became the father of many peoples. Paul tells us that Abraham's faith never wavered. In all simplicity he believed God's promise, despite all the human circumstances that seemed to say the promise would not be kept. Faith made Abraham strong; he glorified God and remained convinced that God would do as he had promised.

It was this faith that justified Abraham. His faith was, in

fact, a certainty that God is Lord of everything; it was based on God's power, whereby he can do what he chooses to do. This attitude of Abraham pleased God, who justified him for his abandonment to the divine will and his utter reliance on the divine power. Abraham did not merit justification as a reward but received it as a gift from God. God made justification dependent on man's loving him and accepting whatever he sent.

St. Paul, who bases his teaching on Scripture, notes that the latter speaks not only of Abraham but of all Christians as well; it speaks of us all. If we have faith, we are the heirs of Abraham; we inherit justification if we believe as he did. We receive this justification, not because of our merits, but as a free gift given to us by God at the moment we abandon ourselves into his hands. We Christians, however, believe in a God who raised Jesus from the dead, for our justification, after he had handed himself over on account of our sins. What was still lacking in Abraham's faith was belief in the merciful power of God as manifested in the sending of the Son and raising him from the dead.

ELEVENTH SUNDAY

Men Chosen by God

Chosen and sent to the lost sheep (Matthew 9:36–10:8)

This passage is basic for an understanding of what the Church is meant to be through the centuries that will pass before Christ's return. It sketches for us, in broad strokes, the missions of the apostles and the Church.

The pericope begins with the mention of Jesus' compassion for the crowds. This is not the only time an important passage begins with this mention; we find a similar remark in the second Gospel in the account of the multiplication of the loaves (Mark 6:34). The Lord sees the needs of the crowd, and he is moved by them. In our present passage, the crowd is in need of someone to lead it. It is like fruitful seed that could produce a great yield, but there are few laborers to work in these fields. Christ urges prayer to the owner of the harvest that he would send workers out to gather it.

This is the moment Jesus chooses for selecting a group of men who will be the first workers to go into the field. Thus it is the boundless compassion of Jesus for the crowd that leads to the selection of the apostles, their mission, and the mission of the future Church.

Jesus sees the crowd prostrate, exhausted, shepherdless. The shepherd who leads his flock is an image that frequently recurs in the Old Testament, which so often records the experience of a people in distress. The Book of Numbers, for example, shows Moses fearful for a prostrate and leaderless people; he begs God to send a guide who will go before them (Num. 27:17). The prophet Zechariah describes the people as wandering like sheep, afflicted for want of a shepherd (10:2). Jesus, the great Shepherd, is likewise deeply moved and longs for the coming of leaders for the flock and workers for the harvest. The workers are few, and this should move the apostles to pray that God might send workers to offer their services.

The image of the harvest, too, is not rare in the Old Testament, although there it signifies chiefly the judgment on the last day (see Jer. 51:33; Joel 4:13). In the New Testament, the image is associated with the work that makes the grain grow, and the dividing of the good grain from the bad, with the Lord who himself sows the good seed and hopes that it will fall on good soil, and finally with the last day and the final judgment (Matthew 13:30, 39). Yet men must pray that the harvest be gathered; they must pray because it is the Lord, not man, who is lord of the harvest.

Christ chooses the first harvesters; he calls the Twelve

and bestows powers on them. These powers, which are
carefully spelled out in the text, may surprise us: the power
to expel evil spirits, the power to heal every illness and
infirmity. Such powers seem strange to us at first sight, and
yet if we look back, we see that they were the powers that
Christ exercised in his own missionary activity: "He went
about all Galilee, teaching in their synagogues and preaching the gospel of the kingdom and healing every disease
and infirmity among the people" (Matthew 4:23); "Jesus
went about all the cities and villages, teaching their synagogues and preaching the gospel of the kingdom, and
healing every disease and every infirmity" (Matthew 9:35).
Thus, if the Twelve are given these powers, it is because
their mission is the same as Christ's.

We are also invited, however, to look beyond purely physical sufferings. According to St. Matthew, the disciples are
called to do what Christ did. The latter, however, fulfilled
the Isaian prophecy that St. Matthew himself quotes (8:17):
he bore our griefs and carried our sorrows (Is. 53:4). As
servant of God, the missionary must carry the burdens of
others. As proclaimer of the coming kingdom, he expels
demons and heals the sick.

St. Matthew then gives the list of the apostles chosen by
Jesus. Finally, he reports the careful instructions that Jesus
gives the Twelve: They are not to approach the Gentiles or
the Samaritans, but are to concentrate on the lost sheep of
the house of Israel. We must bear in mind that we are seeing here the very beginning of the apostles' mission, at a
time before Jesus has carried out his own mission fully
through his paschal mystery. That is why he limits the field
of their work to Israel; after Easter, missionaries will be
sent to "make disciples of all nations" (Matthew 28:19).

The activity of the apostles is chiefly to proclaim the
kingdom. That is why, as we have seen, they heal the sick,
raise the dead, cleanse lepers, and expel demons, for all
these are signs of the kingdom. They have been called by
Christ without any merit on their own part, and therefore
they must give freely and without requiring recompense.

A kingdom of priests (Exod. 19:2-6a)

What the Lord Jesus here does for his apostles, the God of Israel had done, in a measure, for his whole people. His entire people was to be a missionary people, proclaiming to the nations that their God was one and that he had entered into a covenant with them. The people of Israel were not allowed to be a people closed in on themselves. If they were privileged and were bound to make their privileged status manifest, this was for the sake of the Gentiles who would come to see the witness to the covenant.

It is along these lines that we must understand the phrase "a kingdom of priests." The words do not mean that all of Israel formed a priestly class but that the entire people had a ministry, and that this ministry was, on the one hand, a participation in the kingship of their God and, on the other, was priestly inasmuch as this people was set apart and bidden to pray, to intercede for the other peoples, to offer sacrifice, and to make their Lord known to all mankind. The people was thus a holy people, that is, a people living in close ties with its Lord; its chief mission was to tell other nations of this intimate relationship. Thus, just as Moses was sent to tell a discouraged people that they were a kingdom of priests and a holy nation that had the special mission to tell others of God's closeness to Israel, so Christ chose his apostles and sent them out to the lost sheep of Israel.

These two readings, from the Gospel of Matthew and the Book of Exodus, are richly instructive for us, and this at two levels.

First of all, they are instructive with regard to universalism. A certain universalism is already implicit in the texts when the Book of Exodus shows us a people chosen for a mission, and when St. Matthew tells us of the first stage in the apostles' mission, a stage that will soon be replaced by the proclamation of the kingdom to all the peoples of the world. The role of Israel was to bear witness that it was a holy nation, and it was to do this for all the nations of the world. In like manner, the Church can never become a self-enclosed entity, for her missionary vocation and her apostolate to all mankind are part of her very being.

The second area in which the texts are instructive is that of "priesthood." The Second Vatican Council, in its *Dogmatic Constitution on the Church* (nos. 10–11), has emphasized the priestly character of the entire new people of God. After stating that Christ is the one true Priest, the Council shows that others participate in his priesthood in two essentially distinct ways. In other words, the entire people of God is priestly, but the priestliness is of two kinds. There is a priesthood of the faithful, which is a true priesthood and not merely so called by analogy. But this priesthood is essentially different from the ministerial priesthood, or priesthood received through ordination.

The entire people of God is called to be missionary, to intercede, to offer sacrifice, and yet their activity is not the same as that of the ministerial or ordained priesthood. The latter is a special participation in Christ's priesthood; it is higher in degree and possesses essentially different powers. The ordained priest is commissioned to make the mysteries of salvation present and operative here and now; the faithful, as priests, can share intimately in the mysteries thus rendered present and operative.

This careful explanation by the Council and this renewed understanding of the priestly character of the entire people of God are very important. The Church is not only an institution, a hierarchic body. It is also a single unified reality, although unity does not eliminate distinction and organization. Each member has his place and his missionary function; each member prays, teaches, and offers the one sacrifice according to the place and position that has been given to him.

Each believer is thus invited to reflect on how he thinks of the Church and his role in it. He must face the fact that he cannot be truly a Christian unless he carries out his mission as someone chosen and sent in accordance with God's plan.

Psalm 100, used as the responsorial psalm after the first reading, sings our gratitude to the Lord for all that he has made of us: "Know that the Lord is God! It is he that made us, and we are his; we are his people, and the sheep of his pasture."

────

Saved by the death of Christ (Rom. 5:6-11)

Paul is filled with amazement at the mystery of our salvation, for he sees God accomplishing it, not when we were already justified, but when we were still sinners. The sending of the Son into the world was thus the work of the freely bestowed love of the God who loved us before we loved him or could love him.

It is against this background that Paul views our present justification. For if God did all that for men who were still sinners, much more, now that Christ has washed us in his blood and reconciled us to God, will we be saved by the life of the risen Christ.

This is the reason for our boasting. God is the source of our pride and joy, because now we are reconciled with him and we are sure that he is saving us.

Paul's basic thesis that our salvation is utterly unmerited clearly lies behind the theology of this passage. As far as daily living is concerned, however, only one point in the passage is absolutely basic and essential: we must really live out the paschal mystery of death and resurrection. It is precisely in this that the greatness of our Catholic religion consists, and not in a multiplicity of observances; the latter, after all, are but means to help us achieve our real goal, which is to live in close union with Christ and his mysteries.

Even though we are sinners, we do not lose hope. The past is the guarantee of the future, for if God concerned himself with us when we were sinners, then surely, now that

Christ has died for us and despite the weaknesses that persist in us after our rebirth, God continues to love us. We can regard ourselves as saved in hope, in the hope of something that is certain.

TWELFTH SUNDAY

Proclaim the Will of God

Do not fear men (Matthew 10:26-33)

Today's Gospel is a lesson on what the disciple should be. Jesus has chosen his apostles; they are his messengers. How should they act when they meet with opposition? Today's reading is an answer to this question.

A basic principle is: Do not be afraid. We speak here of the Christian rather than of the apostles Christ chose, because it was for the Christians of his day that Matthew was writing. What he is saying to them he says to all of us.

There is nothing to fear, because when we proclaim the teaching of Christ, we are making an act of confidence in the effectiveness of his work that is being revealed to others. We must therefore not fear those who can kill the body, but only him who can cast both body and soul into hell. Christ is uncompromising here. The Christian must choose; he must also realize that Christ cannot save the person who does not have the courage to profess his faith. Besides, what is there really to fear? God takes care of us; nothing happens that he does not will. He watches over his creatures, even the least of them, even the very birds of the air.

This first attitude, which is not in any proper sense negative, since it is already an act of faith in divine Providence, must be accompanied by another: the readiness to, confess to the Lord, to acknowledge before men the demands made by the Father. If we do this, Christ himself will defend us when we come before the Father for judgment. In all his actions the Christian must keep the last day in mind; his value judgments must be related to the judgment he knows God will pass on his actions.

The persecutors will fail (Jer. 20:10-13)

This reading tells us of the prophet's response to persecution. Faced with a plot against him, he trusts unwaveringly in the Lord's help; he asks the Lord to avenge him against his enemies; finally, he bids us praise the Lord who saves the poor.

Jeremias is telling us of his own experience, and it is very much like what Jesus anticipates for his apostles and for all of us. When Jeremias answered the call to be a prophet, he did not do so blindly, for the Lord told him in advance of the kind of conflicts he would have to face. The Church does the same thing today when she accepts an adult into the catechumenate after telling him of the difficulties he must meet with; later, at the candidate's baptism, the triple renunciation and the triple profession of faith will again remind him of what the future holds.

Jeremias will be especially tested, for he will have to meet opposition without the support of a family (he must be a celibate: 16:1-4) or of friends (15:17; 16:8). He provides us with a detailed description of the sufferings that his persecutors inflict on him (15:11; 17:16; 18:20; 20:7-9), and we should not imagine him facing all these trials unshaken. On the contrary, he is almost overcome with discouragement (15:18; 20:14-18). And yet, amid it all, he goes on preaching the word of the Lord.

He has very great confidence in the Lord (15:16) and voices it in his prayers (15:15; 17:14, 18). He is sure that he is being heard, and therefore urges us to praise the Lord: "Sing to the Lord; praise the Lord! For he has delivered the life of the needy from the hand of evildoers" (20:13).

The teaching given in these readings is one that we

need today. Not all of us live in countries where not only our faith but our very lives are seriously threatened, but in every life there are moments when we must stand up to men in behalf of our faith. This may happen within the family; it may even happen between husband and wife. Then we must have the strength and courage to keep the promise we made when we professed the faith and to renounce for ever what we then renounced. If we refuse, for example, to be dishonest in business, our professional life may be rendered more difficult, we may lose friends, we may be less well off. The Catholic who is a businessman, the Catholic who has many friends, will often find himself persecuted and forced to confess to the Lord.

Let us therefore meditate on today's readings, stir up our courage, deepen our trust in divine Providence, and learn to pray to God and praise him for the strength he gives us so that we may persevere in his ways and confess him before men. Every one must face his own special kind of martyrdom; it may be a hidden martyrdom, but it has nonetheless its value and greatness.

Where sin was, grace now abounds (Rom. 5:12-15)

The force of this passage may be very much weakened by our contemporary outlook and by various theological inquiries whose dubious findings have gotten out to some of the faithful and made them skeptical about original sin. The parallelism that St. Paul sets up between Adam ("one man") and Christ now seems to us rather weak, because the word "Adam" signifies not an individual but man generally. Though our translations do not register the fact, there are many passages in which Scripture uses the word "Adam" to mean man generally.

Without entering here into theological discussions that have thus far not reached any satisfactory conclusions, and though I believe it is difficult not to think here of the sin of an individual (despite the theories currently being circulated about the sin of the world), I think that in any case the Apostle's comparison remains fully valid. In other words, even if its historical basis is removed, it keeps its full force if we look less at what would then be a simple image and more at the reality being expressed.

The whole passage can be summed up in this very simple comparison between the free gift of grace and sin. The sin of one man brought death to mankind, and the grace given in a single man, Jesus Christ, is given to all mankind, but the grace is given in far greater abundance. God's gift and sin follow different measures.

THIRTEENTH SUNDAY

Receive the Lord

He who receives you receives me (Matthew 10:37-42)

Today's Gospel contains some important themes. One such is the necessity of taking up our cross if we are to follow Christ (see twelfth Sunday, Cycle C). The central point of the reading, however, is indicated by the context afforded by the Old Testament reading, namely, that we must receive the Lord. It is on this point that we shall dwell briefly.

In the commandment to be receptive we must not see simply a moral precept; there is more to it than that. Christ strongly emphasizes the "him who sent me." There is an identification of the one we receive and the one who sent him; to accept the person, moreover, is to accept his teaching and his word. Consequently, there is an identification of

Jesus with the one who sent him, and there is an identification of the apostles with Jesus who sends them. The Lord is
thus laying a heavy burden on his disciples: they must take
his place and let others see that they are indeed one with
him who sent them.

At the same time we must respect the differences that do
exist. Evidently the kind of identity that exists between
Jesus and the Father who sent him cannot be simply transferred to the relation between the apostles and Jesus who
sends them. In the former case the Persons are distinct but
have a single nature. The apostles, on the other hand, are
identical with Jesus neither in nature nor in person; they
are simply invested with his powers. When we receive an
apostle, we receive him insofar as he is sent by Christ; we
acknowledge his authority even while we register and recognize his personal defects. Here we have the basis of
Christian teaching on the apostolic and priestly ministry:
those whom Christ sends are to be received because they
are his messengers, whatever be their personal moral eleva-
tion or lack of it.

In the Church there are prophets as well as apostles.
Jesus tells us that if we receive a prophet, we will be rewarded. The same holds if we receive a righteous man,
and even if we receive the lowliest of the disciples of
Jesus. Observe that Jesus is not speaking here of the chari-
table welcome we are to give to every human being. What
he is focusing on here is the acceptance of a messenger as a
messenger, a prophet as a prophet, a righteous man as a
righteous man, and a disciple as a disciple. We are thus
being bidden to be discerning and to make objective value
judgments on the persons we receive.

Receive the holy man of God (2 Kings 4:8-11, 14-16a)

The first reading offers an example of the kind of reception being urged upon us. The story is simple and might
have been written in our own day. A woman intuitively
realizes that the prophet who is visiting them is truly a man

of God, a person who is very close to the Lord. She therefore receives him with special marks of kindness, and Eliseus promises her a reward.

These texts — the Old Testament reading and the Gospel — tell us how individuals should be received in the Christian community: how God's ministers should be received, but also how each and every one of our brothers and sisters should be received. Recent study of the Scriptures has given us a better understanding of what it is to receive someone "in the name of the Lord."

Every baptized person has received some special mission; in any event, he or she is clothed in Christ. We must therefore receive each person in a Christian manner, not simply out of human courtesy, but as a joyous duty, knowing by faith that we touch Christ himself.

The duty of receiving others is not limited, however, to hospitality. Receptiveness is, more importantly and more profoundly, an openness to the other. It means that when we offer our hospitality we do not also impose on him our way of looking at things, but instead open ourselves to him and try to enter into his person, especially if there is something about him or her that we do not find congenial. We must try to understand, even if we cannot always approve. When we thus open ourselves to everyone, though without necessarily making our own all that they say and do, when we try to understand without passing a negative judgment, we are not only acting in a moral way but are also building the Church and the kingdom.

●●●

We died with Christ and now live with him (Rom. 6:3-4, 8-11)

St. Paul has exalted the new life and the new world that Christ has brought into existence. In the present reading he develops the theme further.

The passage we hear proclaimed today develops on the basis of a brief theology of baptism. In baptism we were immersed in the death of Christ and buried in the tomb with him, but we were also raised up with him so that we might live a new life. It is through baptism that we share fully in the paschal mystery of the Lord, for the sacramental sign is a likeness to Christ's death and resurrection but also contains the full reality and operative power of that death and resurrection.

From the moment of baptism on, our life is a new one, and its whole direction is new. Since we have become Christ and have been clothed in him, and since he died to sin and now lives for God, so we must die to sin and live for God. That is what Christian life is: a dying to sin and living for God in Christ.

The doctrine is simple and logical; its application proves difficult, a task that must constantly be begun anew. Every individual baptized in Christ is called upon to engage in certain basic activities: changing his outlook, making his value judgments accord with his new being. But the difficulty of this kind of life is only one side of the coin. Those who make the effort at constant adaptation so that they may live up to what they have become, know that it brings hope and enthusiasm, peace and joy. We must all want to taste this peace and joy, and not let ourselves believe that it is reserved for some kind of "specialist" in the Christian life. It is, on the contrary, the ideal toward which all who have chosen Christ must strive.

FOURTEENTH SUNDAY

The Lord is Humble

Gentle and lowly in heart (Matthew 11:25-30)

This passage was used earlier for the feast of the Sacred Heart (Cycle A), but here, with the help of the first reading, we approach it from a different angle. We see Jesus as the humble Messiah. In considering him thus, we shall try to forget such instances in which the humility and gentleness of Jesus is treated in an insipidly sentimental way. What we want to do is to put ourselves to school with Jesus because he is humble and because humility is, in God's plan, the condition for access to the secrets of revelation. Those who are not humble and lowly do not receive the revelation.

The words of Jesus are a classical prayer of blessing. First there is the exclamation of praise: "I thank thee, Father, Lord of heaven and earth." Then the reason for the exclamation is given: "that thou hast hidden these things from the wise and understanding and revealed them to babes."

The Father expressly wishes to hide the plan of salvation from the learned and clever and to reveal it to mere children. We find this same will taking concrete form at many points in the Gospel. Only the Son, and those to whom the Son chooses to reveal him, can know the Father. To receive this revelation from the Son, a person must set aside all human wisdom and become a "child." We must also set aside human wisdom if we are to recognize the Son present in our midst through his miracles and words.

All this means that if we want to know the Father and the Son, we must become pupils in the school of Christ. We must become his disciples, that is, become gentle and lowly in heart like him. If we do, we will find rest and peace, even while we carry the Lord's yoke.

A humble king (Zech. 9:9-10)

The Messiah who comes among us is humble, as Jesus himself tells us in the Gospel. In this passage the prophet Zechariah bids us rejoice at the coming of the king. The prophet's language is poetic and may possibly reflect a community liturgy in which the people of God proclaimed their joy. In any event, the prophet is trying to prepare the people to be receptive.

The king is portrayed as "triumphant and victorious," or, in a better interpretation, "just and victorious." These two adjectives doubtless expressed a traditional ideal for a king, but we may ask whether they do not have a special connotation here. As we just indicated, there was nothing new about the idea that a king should be just and victorious. But the adjective "just" certainly acquired a new wealth of meaning in, for example, Isaiah's fourth song of the Suffering Servant, where the latter is said to be "just" because he is the object of divine concern, so much so indeed that the Lord makes him victorious (see Is. 53:11-12). The prophet Zechariah seems to be using "just and victorious" with the same messianic meaning. The adjective "humble" (or "meek" or "lowly") likewise reminds us of Isaiah, who has the Lord say that "this is the man to whom I will look, he that is humble and contrite in spirit" (Is. 66:2).

This Messiah who comes in poverty and humility refuses the kind of mount that the great men of the world would use and prefers to ride on an ass. The prophets were critical of the use of horses in processions, for they saw them as the embodiment of the warrior's pride and aggressiveness (see, e.g., Is. 2:7). Even back in the Book of Genesis, the liberator is described as one who will "bind his foal to the vine and his ass's colt to the choice vine" (49:11). The Messiah who comes in humility will establish peace, breaking the bow of war.

Today's readings encourage us to become pupils of Christ and to learn two lessons from him. First of all, Jesus portrays himself as gentle and lowly in heart, a humble king. We too should banish from our lives all doctrinal pride and every authoritarian, domineering, and triumphalistic approach to the Church. There are in the Church doctrinal and institutional structures that may not be tampered with or bent to suit our liking, but this does not mean we must present them to others with the proud and boastful inflexibility that men often show with regard to human doctrines and power structures. The Church, her teachings, and her institutions should be presented to men firmly indeed, but also gently and in a spirit of humility.

A further lesson is that all theological reflection should be marked by the humility proper to doctrinal study. This does not mean that we are to give up on penetrating more deeply into the mysteries of God. It means simply that prayer and humility are the basic conditions needed in the study of doctrine. Similarly, the proclamation of the truth should be characterized by humility. We who proclaim the truth are weak and we proclaim only the little that our defective humility has allowed us to grasp of the mysteries of God, Christ, and the Church.

To live, put to death the disorders of sinful man (Rom. 8:9, 11-13)

When we first hear this passage, we may find ourselves somewhat at a loss. The writing is clear, but the sentences are compact, and it is not easy to follow the development of the thought. On the other hand, once we do grasp the line of thought, we hardly need to go into the details of the passage.

The Spirit of God and Christ is within us, and consequently we live in the Spirit. Because we live with the Christ who dwells in us, we are dead to sin and have our life from the Spirit of him who raised Jesus from the dead. We are therefore in debt now, not to the flesh, but to the Spirit, and therefore ought to live according to the Spirit.

It is important that we correctly understand the opposition St. Paul is setting up between flesh and Spirit. In Paul's mind, "flesh" is a theological and religious term, not a biological or metaphysical one. As he elsewhere express- es it in this same Letter to the Romans, the "flesh" is "the sinful flesh" (6:6). These last words might suggest sexual sin to us, but we must put that out of our minds, for the "sinful flesh" is meant to sum up the historical situation of man. "Sinful flesh" designates the creature as one who has rebelled against God and succumbed to sin, and who is now doomed to death. Christ is distinguished from the rest of us precisely in that he took flesh that was like the sinful flesh but was in fact without sin (Rom. 8:3). The Spirit, on the other hand, is the divine Spirit; the Spirit of God is power itself.

This opposition between "flesh" and Spirit enables us to grasp the full lesson St. Paul is teaching us in today's liturgy. The Christian lives in union with God and the Spirit. His baptism has, in principle, removed him from the sphere of the sinful flesh; he now lives a life that is the Spirit's gift. This new situation entails radical conse- quences in daily living. He must be wholly dedicated to the struggle against the ascendancy of the sinful flesh, from which he has indeed been liberated but to which the rem- nants of weakness in him still incline him; he must put to death the disordered actions of the sinful self so that he may be able to live. In other words, the Christian must ac- tualize in himself the paschal mystery of crucifixion, joining Christ in the destruction of all evil in himself so that he may rise from the dead and live with Christ.

FIFTEENTH SUNDAY

The Efficacious Word

Receive the word (Matthew 13:1-23)

Two points are made in this Sunday's Gospel, but the more important of them, as indicated by the Old Testament reading chosen to accompany the Gospel, is the reception and effectiveness of the word. This is also the point with which the passage begins.

Jesus here uses the parable of the sower. We are quite familiar with it, and there is no point in reviewing it in detail. The exegetes maintain that we must distinguish, as far as Jesus himself is concerned, between the parable and its explanation. The celebrant is free to omit the latter and to read only verses 1-9, but the explanation is important, even if it represents the reaction of the evangelist rather than the words of Jesus. It is important because it shows us how the early Church thought about the word of God, about its effectiveness depending on the soil into which it fell, and about what we might call the catechetical technique of Jesus himself.

The focus of the parable is on the seed and the soils into which it falls. The sower plays a necessary but secondary role; Jesus is concerned, not with the sower, but with the seed that yields various results and with the different kinds of soil that receive it. We see seed being sown on four different kinds of ground, and we are familiar with the value set on the various crops produced. There are failures and successes. The successes must be judged in relation to the failures, and vice versa.

As we said, there is no need for a detailed commentary on each part of the text. In any case, the Gospel really provides its own commentary, doubtless one that Matthew himself is elaborating for the sake of the Church he is addressing in his Gospel. We shall come back to this point. The important thing is for us to get a grasp of the parable as a whole, since it sums up the results of Jesus' own ministry and (in Matthew's eyes) the results of the apostolic missions of his own day. The summary is an honest one and begins with the deficit side of the ledger. The first three results are poor or at least mediocre. This was true in Jesus' time, it was true in Matthew's day, it is true in our own day.

The parable is precisely a parable, and to insist on every least detail would be to go astray. To see in the "sower" only Christ would be to give the figure too much importance in the story. St. Matthew is concerned to present the situation of the Church in his own day; his account, however, also reflects the situation in our day as well. Matthew is a realist but not a pessimist. The last of the four soils is good soil; the word is heard and bears abundant fruit. The emphasis at the end is not on the precise value to be assigned to the fruit; the purpose is rather to stir the Church to wonder and thanksgiving.

The word of God (Is. 55:10-11)

This short passage from Isaiah is a hymn of praise to God for the effectiveness of his word. The word is, in Semitic fashion, treated as a material thing. Second Isaiah intends to express himself as forcefully as he can because he wants to stay up the courage of his demoralized countrymen. The Exile had been a heavy blow for them, not only in material and patriotic terms but in religious terms as well. It seemed to them that the Lord had ceased being faithful to them and that his promises had gone unfulfilled. Given this situation, we can better understand the way in which Isaiah speaks, putting the effectiveness of the word in the strongest possible terms. The Lord sends his word as an act of good will, and because he is the Lord, his word is and must be efficacious. The power of the Lord is everlasting, even if at times it is a power that seems to fail.

This Old Testament reading sheds further light on the

Gospel pericope. The parable of the sower, as a summary of the situation of the Church and her missionary effectiveness, should not render us pessimistic but, on the contrary, rouse our confidence in the word of God. The problem implicit in the Gospel parable is still a problem for the reflective Christian of today; in fact, the problem seems more acute than in St. Matthew's time. After so many centuries of evangelizing activity by the Church, has the kingdom of God really spread? How many Christians in the various countries of the world really believe in the kingdom and its presence? The number of unbelievers remains vast; men's vices are permanent and even seem to have become more refined. The Christian reading the parable with these thoughts in the back of his mind might well feel a deep anxiety.

But such a reading does not come to grips with the power of God and of his word. The Lord continues to be the Lord, and his power and the power of the word remain fully effective, despite appearances. We must go on, in blind faith, preparing the soil and preaching the word of God. We must also develop catechetical methods and use the most up-to-date means of communication, but the faith that we must intensify in order to encourage ourselves is not faith in these means and methods, but faith in the efficacy of the word that we receive and proclaim in an attitude of adoration and prayer.

It is perhaps precisely here that we can perceive our age going astray. The efficacy of the word does not depend on our activism, but it does depend, to a certain extent, on the quality of our faith and our prayer. It is amazing, is it not, that after so many centuries and despite all the means we have at our disposal, we seem to have advanced no further than the point the Church reached in apostolic times! This relative failure is undoubtedly to be attributed to a lack of faith and of profound prayer. A "relative failure," because we must read any such summary with minds receptive to the Spirit of God. If we do so, our reading can be stern and demanding, but it will also be optimistic, because we know

that God's word does not return to him fruitless. To deny
this would be to deny God.

The response to the responsorial psalm gives voice to this
optimism in words derived from the Gospel. So does the
psalm itself: "So thou hast prepared it [the earth]. Thou
waterest its furrows abundantly, settling its ridges, soften-
ing it with showers, and blessing its growth" (Ps. 65:9-10).

—————

Creation longs to see God's sons revealed (Rom. 8:18-23)

This reading bids us change our habits of judging and our
way of seeing the world. The world is not what we think it
is, that is, simply a world subject to cosmological laws that
make it an agreeable place, but also a place difficult to live
in because of the struggle going on between the opposing
elements and causing catastrophes from time to time. For
living things, too, the world is an unbalanced environment.
In his poem on the golden age, the prophet Isaiah foresees
the world being made over in unity so that the lion and the
lamb may live together in it. Man himself is often plagued
by inner contradictions; his body is no longer simply the
outward manifestation of his soul, but a law of opposition
now holds sway and must be eliminated.

We must, however, look at this present situation in the
light of the future. There is simply no proportion between
the disorders of the present time and the glory that God
will soon reveal in us. Moreover, the whole of creation
yearns with every fiber of its being to see this revelation of
God's sons. And by "creation" here we mean not just Christians and not just human beings; we mean the universe in
its entirety. The whole universe, now affected by sin,
awaits its liberation. Meanwhile, we and all creation with
us must pass through time and the pains of birth; we must
be willing to groan in travail, but with a hope in our hearts

that does not disappoint. For while we have already received the Spirit, we still await the completion of our redemption.

What Paul gives us here is in fact a description of our state as Christians and of the state of the world as a whole. This is why the progress of the world cannot be a matter of indifference to Christians, since this progress is a sign that the world is being rebuilt and gradually restored to unity. The disorders we experience should not be allowed to destroy our hope. Instead, we must accept the dissatisfaction every creature feels as a sign of the future toward which we are moving and of which the Spirit has already given us a pledge and foretaste.

SIXTEENTH SUNDAY

The Patient Justice of God

The justice that saves (Matthew 13:24-43)

Today's passage from St. Matthew's Gospel is full of substance and leads us in different directions. We must first reflect on the passage in its entirety; then, oriented by the main theme in the first reading, we can focus our commentary on the intention that should guide us in our meditation on this day.

It is easy to see that, as so often, St. Matthew takes St. Mark as his source but then freely rearranges the material. He brings together various parables with the same theme, namely, the final judgment that shall be given when the kingdom reaches its full form. In the latter part of the passage, we find something we have already met elsewhere: a short statement about Jesus' use of parables in speaking to the multitudes and a commentary on one of the parables to the disciples. The wealth of material in these verses should not be allowed to distract our attention in different directions. The liturgy does not ask us to meditate on why Jesus uses parables or to reflect on the parable as a literary genre. The Old Testament reading makes it quite clear what we should focus our attention on: the long-suffering patience of God, his merciful judgment, and his gift of conversion to those who have sinned.

The parable of the weeds is the most important one in the series. Jesus himself explains it in a commentary. In addition, this parable is complemented by the other two parables, one of which tells us of the kingdom's growth by comparing it to a mustard seed, which is the smallest of all seeds but becomes a great tree, and the other of which brings out the same process of growth by comparing the kingdom to yeast, which eventually causes the whole mass of dough to rise.

If Jesus speaks in parables, he does so in order to fulfill the prediction of the prophet: "I will open my mouth in parables, I will utter what has been hidden since the foundation of the world." It is not possible to determine who the prophet was to whom St. Matthew is referring, but we do find the words themselves in Psalm 78, "I will open my mouth in a parable; I will utter dark sayings from of old" (v. 2). That which "has been hidden since the foundation of the world" doubtless means the mystery of the kingdom, which is now revealed, but only to the disciples.

The other two parables emphasize chiefly the slow growth of the kingdom. We might even say the inexorable growth, in which man plays no part. Only the power of God, who creates all things, explains this growth that nothing can prevent. Men live just lives or lives dominated by evil, but meanwhile the kingdom continues to grow, and the power of God brings it to maturity. In these two parables of growth we catch a glimpse of the long-suffering, creative patience of God as he brings to perfection a work — the plan of salvation — that he had conceived from all eternity for man's sake.

This same patient expectation is brought out in the parable of the weeds, which is the center of today's Gospel.

The field is properly sown, and with good grain: the Son of Man has sown the children of the kingdom in the field of the world. During the night Satan comes and sows weeds; the result is confusion in the world as the good and the wicked grow together. The superficial mind even finds it hard at times not to judge God: How can he let evil thus grow great? Why, the evil seem at times to be more prosperous materially than the good! These are everyday problems, and not just for simple people. Why does God let things go on unchecked?

The "accusation" is true. God does allow what he has sown to grow: his adopted children, those to whom he has given baptismal grace, those whom the Spirit has transformed into the image of his Son. But at the same time he allows the weeds to continue their growth; the weeds he did not sow and could not possibly have sown. But God is simply waiting patiently. The world must go its way, and God allows it to do so. He is waiting for the harvest; meanwhile good and evil are so intermingled in this world that it is better not to intervene too soon, lest the good be uprooted along with the evil. The kingdom, however, is constantly growing, like the mustard seed, like the yeast spreading through the dough. The Lord is waiting for the kingdom to reach maturity.

In recording these parables, St. Matthew was certainly well aware of the state of the community for which he was responsible. He could see the community growing like the mustard seed — starting as a tiny seed, then becoming a large tree. He was aware that the yeast was at work in the mass of dough, but he could also see the weeds mingling with the good grain. The situation was undoubtedly a problem for his faithful, as it is for us today, and it was no simple matter to allay their doubts and to rekindle their faith in divine Providence. His purpose in the Gospel, therefore, had to be to show the dynamics of the kingdom and how the kingdom was growing despite the enemies and failures;

he had to rouse the community to reflect on its own responsibility as it waited for the great Day of God's coming.

You judge with mildness (Wis. 12:13, 16-19)

God's love for the human beings he created is a constant theme throughout the Old Testament. The history of salvation that we can now read and that we know is continuing and will be continued by us makes manifest to us the love God has for us.

Today's first reading is a meditation on the justice or righteousness of God throughout history. History is a long succession of merciful acts on the part of the Lord who is Israel's leader. God's righteousness as manifested in history proves to be quite different from the righteousness of men or the righteousness of the law. God is concerned about everything, and he thus makes it clear that when he judges, he judges with full knowledge of every case. His righteousness has its origins in his power, and his sovereignty over all things makes him patient with all. He has plenty of time at his disposal. Man, because his power is limited, represses those who oppose him; God alone, because he created everything and holds sway over all, can be patient and can judge mercifully. One sentence in this reading casts a brilliant light on today's text from the Gospel: "Thou hast filled thy sons with good hope, because thou givest repentance for sins."

The responsorial psalm sings of God's mercy: "But thou, O Lord, art a God merciful and gracious, slow to anger and abounding in steadfast love and faithfulness. Turn to me and take pity on me" (Ps. 86:15-16).

The Holy Spirit prays in us (Rom. 8:26-27)

The most marvelous fruit of the Spirit's presence in us is the possibility we now have of reaching God. The end of the reading for the fifteenth Sunday (Cycle A: Rom. 8:18-23) reminded us that we possess the Spirit as the fruit fruits of salvation. Our salvation in its entirety, however, continues to be an object of hope. To hope for what we do not yet see is to await it perseveringly.

This last statement brings out the difficulty of our present situation, for we are pulled, as it were, between what we already possess and what we hope for; since the latter is full and definitive salvation, we must sigh and pray and ask for it. Of ourselves, however, we are incapable of praying rightly. At this point the Spirit intervenes and helps us in our weakness, which is not necessarily a moral weakness but arises rather from our deficient sense of the spiritual and our lack of hope.

The strongly felt tension between what we now have in our grasp as a beginning of the definitive reality and the definitive reality itself, which is not fully guaranteed us, is not such as to leave man in peace, for we are too weak to be patient amid such a tension. We even feel incapable of the energetic reaction that is prayer. Our finiteness prevents us from penetrating the plans of God, while the prison formed by our bodies threatens to keep us from reaching the goal of our deepest desires.

The Spirit therefore prays in us, and his intercession for us is in perfect accord with God's plans. What God wants is that the plan of salvation be carried out and that he be glorified. Just as the Spirit unites Christians with one another in a single community and makes one being of them, so his oneness with the Father allows him to know the Father's plans and to ask him for what is best for us as we live through the complex process that is the re-creation of the world in unity.

SEVENTEENTH SUNDAY

Choose the Real Treasure

Sell all for the real treasure (Matthew 13:44-52)

The real or true treasure is the kingdom of God, of which Jesus speaks, as usual, in parables. The Lord here uses three such parables in an effort to help his hearers understand what the kingdom is. The three are: the treasure hidden in a field that a man sells all he has in order to buy; the merchant who comes upon a fine pearl and sells all he owns in order to buy it; the net that is cast into the sea and emerges containing all kinds of fish, of which only the good fish are kept, the rest being thrown away. To these three we may add a fourth, which is to be found in verse 52: the scribe who has become a disciple of the kingdom and is compared to a householder who brings forth from his treasure things new and old. In fact, however, verse 52 is rather a conclusion to the preceding series of parables, although this conclusion is presented in the guise of an opening for a parable.

The first two of today's three parables are fully parallel. Both concern a precious object, for the sake of which a person sells everything else he owns. However, the two individuals in question represent two different situations. In the first, a man who is not wealthy sells what little he has in order to acquire the treasure; in the second, the subject is a merchant, presumably a man of means. In this second parable we think spontaneously of the rich young man whom Jesus called to follow him: "Go, sell what you have, and give to the poor, and you will have treasure in heaven" (Mark 10:21).

The two parables offer perfectly clear models for all who wish to be Christians in more than name. The danger is that we may think of them simply as parables and fail to see the radical demand they proclaim. They are telling us that no one can be part of God's kingdom without the kind of definitive renunciation that allows for no compromise: one must either sell all or not belong to the kingdom. The kingdom requires a positive acceptance; it cannot be acquired by neutrality. The tepid, whom God vomits from his mouth, are not admitted into the kingdom.

The third parable gives a brief but stern description of those who during their lives do not do all they can to win the kingdom and are therefore not among the "good fish." As fishermen open their nets and choose the good fish and reject the bad, so it is with the kingdom; those who are rejected "will weep and gnash their teeth." This is not the first time Jesus threatens punishment to those who do not accept and live by the word. He uses the same language in the first Gospel when explaining the parable of the weeds in the field (Matthew 13:42).

This group of parables on the kingdom — the sower, the weeds, the mustard seed, the yeast, the treasure, and the pearl — ends with the parable of the net and the good and bad fishes. A general conclusion follows: "Have you understood all this?" When the disciples answer that they have indeed understood, Jesus states the lesson in a form that might be taken, as we indicated, as the beginning of a further parable. He speaks once again of a treasure, but a treasure of a different kind than in the earlier parable of the field. Here the treasure is contained in a householder's box in which the well-off proprietor keeps certain objects. A person who has become a disciple of the kingdom now resembles such a householder. Concretely, the scribe, the disciple of the kingdom, is the disciples of Jesus who have heard and understood the parables of the kingdom, for they now possess new things and old. The new is the gospel teaching, the Good News. This new is, however, closely connected with the old, that is, with what the Old Testament had taught through the law and the prophets; Jesus has come not to eliminate but to fulfill that teaching. The person who understands the parables of the kingdom and sells all he has in order to become a disciple possesses the wealth of the gospel that is grounded in Old Testament teaching and that he is now called on to proclaim in his turn.

Ask for the real treasure (1 Kings 3:5, 7-12)

The requirements of the kingdom suppose that the person who seeks to possess it has the true wisdom for which Solomon asked when God appeared to him in a dream and said: "Ask what I shall give you." Solomon asked for "an understanding mind . . . that I may discern between good and evil."

In reading this passage from the Old Testament, we are dealing once again with a liturgical reading of a text. If we make a purely exegetical reading of this passage, we must see as its intention the desire to legitimate Solomon's succession to David's throne. Because this successor prays humbly to God, the latter gives him the qualities that make a good king. When, however, the Church reads the passage in today's liturgy, she is not concerned with the political purpose behind the text. Her concern in the liturgy is rather with the desire a person must cultivate who wishes to be in the kingdom: the desire for a heart that is docile to God's word.

The responsorial psalm (some verses from Psalm 119) makes this liturgical interpretation clear: "The Lord is my portion; I promise to keep thy words. . . . The unfolding of thy words gives light; it imparts understanding to the simple." As the Gospel makes clear, if a man is to belong to the kingdom, there is a gift he must have, namely, a wisdom that comes only through listening to God's word.

Become the image of God's Son (Rom. 8:28-30)

God's love for us wants but one thing for us: that we be like the image of the Son. That has been the goal of the whole divine, centuries-long strategy.

That God should mean such a goal for us is a grace. He calls us to it, it is he who must destine us for it. This same chapter of Romans has already emphasized the presence of the Spirit in us (sixteenth Sunday). The Spirit makes it possible for us to pray; he even prays in us. Thanks to the operation of the Spirit, the Son is constantly and dynamically present in us. St. Paul likes to express this interior presence of Christ in forceful ways; for example, "it is no longer I who live, but Christ lives in me" (Gal. 2:20), and "to me to live is Christ" (Phil. 1:21).

The language of today's passage from the Letter to the Romans causes us a certain difficulty, however: God "predestined" us to be in his Son's image; "and those whom he predestined" to this, "he also called."

We must not look in the Scriptures for a treatise on predestination nor read into St. Paul the theological problems that arose later on, especially from the time of St. Augustine. Neither is this the place to show both the clarity and the confusion that theology has brought to the question.

For purposes of our meditation on the text, we must first of all change our habitual way of looking at it. Paul is speaking not of individuals but of a people, and this realization immediately changes the whole perspective. A second misunderstanding has to do with the language Paul uses. It disturbs us because of our ideas of freedom; we tend to question God's justice in this matter of predestination. In fact, however, "predestination" and "predestining" are words that convey an idea of anteriority, but this anteriority in no way eliminates freedom. The "pre" (= "before") in the word "predestination" says that the initiative comes from God. In other words, we are not chosen because we wanted to be but because God freely took the initiative and chose us. But while the initiative comes from God and not from man, this does not mean that man remains inactive. "Pre-destination" accents the divine initiative, but it also implies a free, active response. St. John sums up the whole meaning admirably when he writes: "We love, because he first loved us" (1 John 4:19).

The passage reminds us also of the process whereby we are divinized and glorified. God foreknew us, that is, he loved us; he "predestined us to be conformed to the image of his Son," that is, he took the initiative in bringing about such a transformation. Our response of active faith gained for us the gift of being "justified," that is, of sharing in God's life and therefore in his glory.

EIGHTEENTH SUNDAY

A God Who Feeds Men

For a better understanding of today's passage from St. Matthew, we must consult chapter 6 of the Fourth Gospel, the discourse on the bread of life.

We shall reverse our usual procedure and start with the first reading, from the Old Testament. This will help us in grasping the meaning of the Gospel text and St. Matthew's intention.

Be filled (Is. 55:1-3)

In approaching the Gospel text, we must always bear in mind that the evangelist is writing for Christians. He and his readers share the experience of the signs given by Christ, and his purpose is help them understand and enter into that experience more fully. Now, St. Matthew is writing chiefly for Jewish Christians, and he is here offering them an account that must bring to mind what they know of God's plan from the Old Testament.

If we look through the Old Testament, the passage most like our present passage from St. Matthew is to be found in the Second Book of Kings, when the prophet Eliseus multiplies loaves of bread (2 Kings 4:42-44). There is a point-for-point parallelism between the two texts.

Matthew 14:16-21	2 Kings 4:42-44
You give them something to eat.	Give to the men, that they may eat.
We have only five loaves here and two fish.	
Those who ate were about five thousand men, besides women and children.	How am I set this [twenty loaves of barley, and fresh ears of grain] before a hundred men?
He . . . gave the loaves to the disciples, and the disciples gave them to the crowds. And they all ate and were satisfied. And they took up twelve baskets full of the broken pieces left over.	Give them to the men, that they may eat, for thus says the Lord, "They shall eat and have some left."

Being filled is an idea that is entirely human but is at the same time linked to the goodness of God in his covenant. The idea recurs often in the Old Testament. In the psalms, for example, we read: "My soul is feasted as with marrow and fat" (Ps. 63:5); "I would feed you with the finest of the wheat, and with honey from the rock I would satisfy you" (Ps. 81:16); "I will abundantly bless her provisions; I will satisfy her poor with bread" (Ps. 132:15). On the other hand, man experiences situations in which to eat is not to be filled and satisfied: "They shall eat, but not be satisfied" (Osee 4:10); "You shall eat, but not be satisfied" (Micheas 6:14); "You drink, but you never have your fill" (Aggeus 1:6).

In today's celebration Isaiah speaks of a food and drink given by God in fulfillment of the covenant in which his goodness is so manifested. The passage gives us a glimpse of how superior the food is that the Lord wants to give: "Why do you spend your money for that which is not bread, and your labor for that which does not satisfy? Hearken diligently to me, and eat what is good, and delight yourselves in fatness. Incline your ear, and come to me; hear, that your soul may live; and I will make with you an everlasting covenant."

Psalm 145, which serves today as the responsorial psalm, has been used from very early times as a prayer before meals: "The eyes of all look to thee, and thou givest them their food in due season. Thou openest thy hand, thou satisfiest the desire of every living thing."

They ate their fill (Matthew 14:13-21)

It is easy to see that St. Matthew, like St. John, here draws inspiration from the texts of the Old Testament. He models his own account on those texts, because Old Testament events are "types" — not "examples," but rather points of departure and events that anticipate in a lesser way, and are fulfilled by, what Christ does.

The evangelist offers his community an account that they read against the Old Testament background but also in the light of their experience of the Eucharist. It is not accidental that Matthew here describes Jesus' actions in the same terms he will use in describing the Lord's actions at the Last Supper (Matthew 26:26-29).

For the Christian community, the account of the multiplication of the loaves is situated on a line between the Old Testament anticipation and foreshadowing, and the later definitive fulfillment by Christ, that is, the multiplication of Christ's nourishing presence in the Eucharistic bread and wine, a multiplication that still occurs and is experienced by the community. At the multiplication of the loaves, Jesus is present with his disciples, as at the Supper, and the disciples serve as his instruments in the distribution of the bread, as they will later when they celebrate the Eucharist themselves. Evidently, then, the whole atmosphere of this account is inevitably Eucharistic for the Christian reader, whether of the early Church or of today. At the same time, the meal of the crowds for which the bread was multiplied also signifies, in the eyes of the believing community, the presence of the kingdom and the banquet at the end of time.

The account of the multiplication of the loaves also clarifies the definitive covenant that is soon to be established. It shows that this covenant will be a gift of God, a gift symbolized and expressed by a munificence exceeding anything man can expect or imagine. The situation at the end of Jesus' life will be tragic and beyond any human resolution. The Lord alone can bring that resolution, but he will use his apostles in providing the world with the food of the eternal covenant.

Today's passage from St. Matthew's Gospel is very helpful for our understanding of a truly liturgical proclamation. For the event narrated has a basis in the Old Testament for its telling; it will reveal its full meaning when Jesus later institutes the Eucharist; it continues to be proclaimed in the Christian community at the moment when the sign given at the Supper is repeated and makes the bread of life a present, efficacious gift.

Who can separate us from the love of Christ (Rom. 8:35, 37-39)

On the preceding Sunday we saw how St. Paul regards us as justified, glorified, and transformed into the image of the Son. Under such conditions the judgment we must someday face should not worry us. Nothing can separate us from Christ! Using expressions habitual with him, Paul enumerates the things that might be thought able to separate us from Christ but that in fact are powerless to do so. The last one he mentions, the sword, occurs only here. Perhaps he was thinking of the executioner. The Apostle also quotes Psalm 44:22, "For thy sake we are being killed all the day long; we are regarded as sheep to be slaughtered." Yet we conquer all these things. Nothing can keep Christ from loving us and God from showing his love for us through Christ.

NINETEENTH SUNDAY

Face the Obstacles and Advance Toward the Lord

Bid me come to you (Matthew 14:22-33)

Before coming to the main story, this passage first mentions two points that are not without their own importance. The first is this: Now that the miracle of the multiplication of the loaves is over, Jesus bids his disciples enter their boat and set sail. Why does he thus force them to leave the scene? St. Matthew gives no reason, but perhaps an explanation is to be found in St. John. At any rate, the latter tells us that after witnessing the miracle, the crowd wants to take Jesus and make him their king (John 6:15). It may be, then, that Jesus did not want his disciples to be aware of this desire on the part of the crowd and be tempted to join them.

The second point is that, as in St. John's account, Jesus withdraws into the hills by himself to pray. It has been observed that the area is not in fact a hilly one. It seems, then, that the words "into the hills" is a notation with a spiritual meaning rather than a physical one. In other words, St. Matthew uses "hills" to designate a place where an important event is to take place. Both in the Old Testament and in St. Matthew's Gospel, the hill or mountain is the preferred place for encounters with God and for theophanies. St. Luke, too, shows us Jesus praying in the hills (Luke 6:12; 9:28-29).

Now to the main part of the story. Jesus had stayed on the shore, and the boat was now a good distance from the land and was being beaten about by the waves, since the wind was against it. Suddenly Jesus is there, walking on the water toward the disciples. The disciples are fear-stricken; their faith is not yet such as to make them instinctively realize that Jesus is master of the elements.

There are really two central points to the story. One is that Jesus manifests himself as God and Lord of the elements. The other is to show the level of faith of the disciples and especially of Peter, and then their common profession of faith: "Truly you are the Son of God."

St. Matthew alone tells us of Peter walking on the water. The other two evangelists who tell the story (Mark and John) mention only Jesus as walking over the waves. Peter's request to Jesus reveals his faith but at the same time his inadequate trust: he wants to go to Christ, but at the same time he wants Christ to call him as a proof that it is truly he and not a phantom: "Lord, if it is you, bid me come to you on the water."

Stand before the Lord as he passes (1 Kings 19:9a, 11-13a)

The Old Testament reading reports an event somewhat like that of the Gospel, one that brings the elements into play on the occasion of a theophany. Like Moses, Elias must meet the Lord on Sinai and experience the fury of the elements. But the Lord is not to be found in these furious elements — not in the strong wind or earthquake or fire. Only in the soft breeze is Elias able to perceive the presence of God. He then covers his head and stands at the entrance of the cave, for no man can see Yahweh and live (cf. Exod. 33:20-33).

Psalm 85 provides us with a commentary on this text and its meaning for us today. The refrain suggested for our use expresses our desire: "Lord, let us see your kindness, and grant us your salvation." If our desire is to be satisfied, we must bear in mind that an encounter with God, even in the depths of the heart, cannot be self-centered, though it is indeed highly personal; it must bear fruit for the world. That is precisely the deeper meaning of the "contemplative" life: "Let me hear what the Lord will speak, for he will speak peace. . . . Surely his salvation is at hand for those who fear him, that glory may dwell in our land. . . . Yea, the Lord will give what is good, and our land will yield its increase. Righteousness will go before him, and make his footsteps a way."

We are called, then, to meet the God who comes to us so that we may go to him. That is the meaning of today's Gospel for the Church and for each of us: to recognize Christ and to go to meet him with great trust, through whatever storms. The Church and each baptized person are always obliged to this. To the extent that he had faith, Peter was able to walk on the waters. Jesus assures us, moreover, that anyone who believes in him will do the works that he, Jesus, does (John 14:12). Jesus even goes on to say, "and greater works than these will he do, because I go to the Father." "Greater works," because we must complete the work of Christ and make it coextensive with the universe. "Greater works," because Christ, seated at the Father's side, sends his Spirit to help the Church without ceasing.

I could wish even to be accursed for the sake of my brothers, the Jews (Rom. 9:1-5)

A certain preparation is evidently needed if a person is to accept and receive Christ. One step in such preparation is to reject idols. What nation could be better prepared than Israel? They have been given the sonship, the glory, the covenants, the law, the worship, and the promises of God. The patriarchs belong to them, and, above all, it is from their race that the Christ has been born. Israel has all it needs in order to understand the mind of God and to become part of Christ's new people. Yet all that has not kept them from not receiving Christ! For Paul, this is reason for an immense feeling of sadness.

The Christian cannot refuse to acknowledge the riches of the Jewish people, whom God has so loved, and to be saddened, with Paul, that they have not believed in Christ. We must be united with them at least through love and prayer.

TWENTIETH SUNDAY

A House For All Peoples

Israel, but all believers as well (Matthew 15:21-28)

To grasp Matthew's intention in this passage, we have only to read it attentively. His intention is to bring out the universality of salvation. Why this emphasis? Because very likely his readers, who would be chiefly Jewish Christians, were jealous of their privilege as chosen people of God.

In the Gospel passage it is a non-Jewish woman who asks Jesus for a miraculous cure. Her request brings a protest from the disciples, who are still too much preoccupied with externals. Jesus' answer to them is evidently important to

Matthew: "I was sent only to the lost sheep of the house of Israel." This harsh answer would content the Jewish Christians of Matthew's day, as it would have satisfied the Jews who were Jesus' disciples.

Immediately, however, the woman makes a humble and moving profession of faith. Jesus is evidently touched by her attitude and persistence, and says to her: "O woman, great is your faith! Be it done for you as you desire."

The gospel is preached even to the pagans, and salvation is theirs if they believe. That is the chief point being made in today's Gospel. Membership in the chosen people is neither sufficient nor necessary, since those who are not members can attain to salvation if they actively believe. Their faith overcomes every obstacle.

For us today, the most important lesson, one that we should receive with gratitude, is to be found in the attitude of the woman who perseveres in her entreaty with all the clear-sighted determination her faith gave her. In her we see a sureness of hope that shames us. This Canaanite woman is willing even to be called a "dog" by comparison with the children of the house, that is, the Jews, but she insists that she too can receive a favor from Jesus if she believes in him, as she certainly does.

A house of prayer for all peoples (Is. 56:1, 6-7)

We may ask why the author of this passage is so concerned with the religious situation of foreigners. The answer is that their vast numbers could not but be a problem for the Jews and also for the foreigners, who felt excluded from the life of Jerusalem, even though they lived there.

The author reminds his readers that salvation depends first and foremost on the person's attitude and not on membership in a people. The important thing is to "keep justice, and do righteousness." But even foreigners can do this if they become servants of the Lord, observe the Sabbath, and accept the covenant. All who do this will be led to the holy mountain of the Lord. They will find happiness in the house of prayer, and their holocausts and sacrifices will be accepted.

This prophetic statement is extremely important, for it witnesses against the popular nationalistic view of salvation with its claim to reserve the covenant and acceptable prayer to the Jews. This is why the prophet has the Lord say: "My house shall be called a house of prayer for all peoples." This text is, of course, not the only such text in the Old Testament or even the first. In the Book of Amos we already find Yahweh bringing, i.e., guiding, the Philistines from Caphtor and the Syrians from Kir. The same prophet, like Isaiah today, makes it clear that if foreigners can be saved, it is on condition that they be subject to the Lord (Amos 1:3–2:3). We see foreigners coming to Jerusalem in order to experience the salvation that comes from God and his law, and, with Isaiah, we see them turning to the living God (Is. 45:14-17, 20-25). Egypt and Assyria are converted (Is. 19:16-25). All nations and tongues are brought into unity by the Lord (Is. 66:18-21).

The Jews as a people, however, were far from accepting this kind of universalist vision; the dangers of corruption that they had experienced during their captivity pressured them into turning in upon themselves. The result was a strong spirit of exclusiveness (see Ezra 9–10); today's stance in Isaiah served in some measure as a corrective.

The responsorial psalm (Ps. 67) voices the same universalism. We Christians sing the psalm while bearing in mind all that the word "catholic" means as applied to the Church. "May God be gracious to us and bless us and make his face to shine upon us, that thy way may be known upon earth, thy saving power among all nations. Let the peoples praise thee, O God; let all the peoples praise thee!"

All peoples can obtain mercy (Rom. 11:13-15, 29-32)

Paul uses forceful language, and we can imagine the deep feeling of the Apostle as he wrote the lines we read today. He is convinced of the divine call accorded the pagans and of his own mission to them, so much so that he utilizes these facts to stir the Jews to jealousy and to conversion. The Jews were in fact in a painful position. They had refused belief and were now rejected; the covenant once given to them has now been given to the pagans. The world has been reconciled to God, and the Lord has not restricted his privileges to the people he had once chosen. But St. Paul also envisages the return of the Jews, a reintegration into the new people of God, a gift of life out of death as God's life is given to those who formerly did not believe.

There is thus a twofold movement reflected in Paul's words. On the one hand, the pagans, who formerly did not share the life of God, now possess that life through faith and conversion. On the other hand, the Jews, who had been chosen, are now dead as far as life in God is concerned, because they did not accept the Word whom God sent; but they too are still being offered a share in the divine life and can pass from death to life.

St. Paul here shows the principle at work in the divine plan of salvation: disobedience gives the Lord the opportunity to be merciful to the pagans and to continue offering that same mercy to the Jews.

This presentation of the plan of universal salvation is very important for us of today. We are, of course, quite ready to deny any spirit of racial exclusivity. We must indeed continue to assert, as a matter of faith, the unqualified necessity of entry into the Church in order to be saved, but we are also aware of how this statement must be nuanced. The result is that we are pulled in various directions. The division which we now — thank God! — realize is a scandal is real, and it cannot be eliminated by simplistic attitudes. We must therefore suffer it and be able to wait in patience.

The kind of patience meant here presupposes an openness and a dialogue that do not seek to jeopardize the truth but rather to understand the other party and to look for expressions of our faith that will not in any way endanger that faith but will make it more accessible to those who have not always understood it or whom we have not always recognized and accepted.

In any accounting, the universality of salvation remains a great mystery, for it expresses the infinite, mysterious will of the God who wants all men to be saved and who looks within each soul to its faith and its longing for him. These interior realities transcend any verification by human means and are known only to the infinitely wise God. Nevertheless, there exists the divine imperative: "Preach the gospel to the whole creation. He who believes and is baptized will be saved" (Mark 16:15-16).

TWENTY-FIRST SUNDAY
Firm Ground

On this rock I will build my Church (Matthew 16:13-20)

The liturgical proclamation of a text from Scripture is not meant as a course in dogmatic theology. It would therefore be out of place here for us to investigate all the implications of Jesus' well-known words to Peter. Nonetheless the proclamation is important and should make us desirous of attaining a better and deeper understanding of words so decisive for the living reality of the Catholic Church. Their grandeur and seriousness are in no way lessened by the fact that they have been interpreted at times in a tendentious way or used for purposes alien to their true meaning.

Two questions of identity are raised in the text. On the one hand, Jesus asks whom the men that meet him take him to be. On the other, Jesus elicits a confession of faith from Peter and, on the basis of it, gives him a new identity.

There are few objections raised against the first part, that is, the confession of Peter. The second part, however — the promise to Peter — has inevitably occasioned doubts. It is easy to imagine the evangelist forcing the words of Jesus in order to give a basis for the actual situation in the early Church and to confirm it by tracing it back to Jesus himself. In addition, there is a fact that must be taken into account: While the confession of Peter is to be found in each of the other Gospels (Mark 8:27-30; Luke 9:18-21; John 6:69), the promise made to Peter occurs as such only in Matthew; similar statements may be found in Luke, but only in other contexts (cf. 22:32, "I have prayed for you that your faith may not fail; and when you have turned again, strengthen your brethren"), and in the passage of the Fourth Gospel in which the Lord appoints Peter as shepherd (John 21:15-17).

Matthew may indeed have introduced this whole account here in order to highlight the promises made by Jesus. This does not, however, prove that the account is fictional and must be attributed to the evangelist himself as an invention for apologetic purposes. Moreover, as we have just indicated, passages of the other Gospels contain the essential elements found here in Matthew. In addition, we must take into account the literary genre of this typically Semitic passage; in the light of it, it seems evident that Jesus gave Simon the name Peter with all the symbolism attaching to the name.

There is a further problem that lies outside the scope of this liturgical commentary: Does the promise apply only to Peter personally or does it extend to his successors? There are two chief reasons for holding that the promise extends to Peter's successors and disciples. The first is that the work of redemption confided to the Church was meant to perdure; how then could Jesus limit to Peter a help that was indispensable for the operation and mission of the Church?

The second reason is the continuous tradition of the Church from the beginning; traces of this tradition are to be found even in the redaction of the Gospels. Far from being inventions to meet current needs, the Gospels reflect the attitude the disciples adopted from the moment when Jesus made Peter head of his Church. Many of the Gospel narratives, independently of the section we are reading today, emphasize the person of Peter and manifest a general conviction that was never to be denied: Peter received the promise from Jesus for his successors as well as for himself.

It is also to be noted that after the death of Peter (of which no text speaks), all went on as before, and there is no evidence that the still young Church fell into disarray when it lost its first visible head years before the composition of Matthew's Gospel. At various times in history, the transition to a successor was not an easy one, but the law of succession and the promises attached to it have never been called into question.

To express the nature of the firm support he intends to give his Church and its visible head, Jesus uses the symbol of the rock. It is a natural enough symbol; it is also typically biblical, and frequent in the Old Testament. It is applied to God himself; he is called Israel's "Rock of . . . salvation" (Deut. 32:15). Jesus applies Psalm 118:22 to himself and thus calls himself a cornerstone: "The stone which the builders rejected has become the head of the corner" (Matthew 21:42).

A further point to be noted is that in the Bible the giving or changing of a name confers a particular mission on the person. It is to this end that God changes the names of Abram (Gen. 17:5), Sarai (Gen. 17:15), and Jacob (Gen. 32:29). So too, when Jesus gives Simon the name Peter, he indicates clearly what he expects of his disciple and what he is bestowing on him. Jesus also makes the meaning explicit: "On this rock I will build my church, and the powers of death shall not prevail against it" (Matthew 16:18).

Peter also receives the keys of the kingdom. The first

reading in today's liturgy explains the meaning of this symbol: Peter is receiving an almost absolute power; there
exists no higher power after God's own (Is. 22:22). It is for
Peter, as God's steward, to judge to whom he will open the
gates of salvation and to whom he will close them. It would
be a mistake to interpret this power solely as the power to
govern; it contains also, and above all, the power to define
and protect faith and morality.

The power to govern finds expression rather in the phrase
"bind and loose," although "government" here is chiefly
spiritual in nature. The point is that there is complete harmony between the decisions of the Church and those of
God. What is bound on earth is bound in heaven, and what
is loosed on earth is loosed in heaven. "Bind and loose"
means to condemn or absolve, forbid or allow. This promise, made here to Peter, will also be made to the other
disciples (Matthew 18:18); it is a power that Peter shares
with his collaborators. Christ's statement in St. Luke, "He
who hears you hears me" (10:16), confirms that this power
belongs to the other disciples and also that its exercise is
ratified by Christ, in whose name it is used.

A peg in a sure place (Is. 22:19-23)

God chooses his servant Eliakim to replace the usurper in
the governor's chair. Each detail in the passage has its
meaning. Thus, God will put a robe and girdle on Eliakim,
and commit the authority into his hand. Such a statement
says the same thing twice, for God gives Eliakim the insig-
nia of power and the power. The governor's basic role is to
be a father to the inhabitants of Jerusalem and the house of
Judah. He is truly God's vicar.

The governor will carry on his shoulder the key of the
house of David. At that period the key was an iron bar that
was carried on the shoulder for practical reasons but also as
a display of authority. The person with the key had full authority to open and shut. The house of David is a name for
the kingdom that has originated in the covenant between

God and his people; the chosen servant is here God's steward.

The servant will be as strong and stable as a peg fixed in solid ground. Why is the image of a peg used? To understand, we must look at another passage in the Book of Isaiah (33:20), in which the prophet describes the return to Jerusalem and compares the city to a tent that will be immovable because its stakes cannot be pulled up.

A primary lesson we may take with us from this Sunday's readings is Peter's faith in Jesus and in his divinity; it was on account of that faith that the promise was given to him. So too the security that the Church has is a gift given not because of any merits on her part but because of her faith. At difficult moments in the Church's life, the passages read in today's celebration should encourage us, not indeed to overlook difficulties or to ignore the human defects of the Church, but to deepen our faith and to pray that the faith of the Church in God's power may grow ever stronger. Her trust is that the Lord is with her and that she has nothing to fear if she really believes in him who can do all things.

The lesson, then, is that the Church is invincible in her very weakness. Her strength consists in her faith in the power of God who is with her. Such faith is the source, too, of the active optimism that should mark every member of the Church in which Christ's Spirit dwells.

From him and through him and to him are all things (Rom. 11:33-36)

St. Paul here provides us with a fine model for the prayer of thanksgiving. In the preceding verses he has brought out all that God has done for the Jew and the pagans, and concluded that if all men have been prisoners of sin, this was in order that he who sets them free and renews them might be able to show his love for them. As we contemplate this

attitude of God, we are lead to understand the depths of his
wisdom and knowledge. His love for us is like an abyss, so
impossible is it to grasp fully its depth and quality.

The riches of God is a theme dear to Paul. He puts us on
guard elsewhere against presuming upon the kindness of
God because it is so rich (Rom. 2:4). In Christ, God has
filled us with the riches of speech and knowledge (1 Cor.
1:5). These riches we must make known to the pagans
(Eph. 3:8). We are never left destitute, for out of his riches
God supplies our every need (Phil. 4:19). The mystery of
salvation, hidden in God through the ages, has finally been
revealed, for God has chosen "to make known how great
among the Gentiles are the riches of the glory of this mystery" (Col. 1:27). Christ's word dwells in us richly (Col.
3:16). God's riches are his possession but are meant to be
poured out on us.

But God's riches are an abyss, and at times they seem
foolishness to us (1 Cor. 1:25). In the last analysis, God's
wisdom is identical with Jesus Christ, for it is in him that
the treasures of divine wisdom are hidden (Col. 2:3). Also
hidden in him are all the treasures of knowledge, since anything we can say about God is already verified in Christ.

Today's passage ends with a short doxology: "From him
and through him and to him are all things." The Letter to
the Colossians contains a similar but expanded doxology:
"In him all things were created . . . all things were created
through him and for him. He is before all things, and in him
all things hold together" (Col. 1:16-17). St. Paul has the
knack of putting in a few words a wealth of theology that
needs to be prayed through and that shows us the kind of
prayer he himself must have loved and practiced.

TWENTY-SECOND SUNDAY

The Suffering Required of the Disciple

Renounce self and follow the Lord (Matthew 16:21-27)

This scene follows upon Peter's confession at Caesarea Philippi. Now that the disciples, through Peter, have manifested their faith in Jesus, Jesus no longer hesitates to foretell his Passion. St. Matthew shows us Christ foretelling his suffering on three occasions (16:21; 17:22-23; 20:17-19). These predictions are clearly climactic moments in the public ministry, and the whole text leads up to them, for in these predictions Jesus is foretelling the paschal mystery of his death and resurrection.

He is not understood, even though he has spoken in such clear terms. He has not simply foretold what is going to happen; he foretells what "must" happen, that is, he speaks of a mission he cannot but carry out. At his baptism in the Jordan, he has been designated by the Father as beloved Son, the one who is loved precisely because he does the Father's will. He is the Son who is also Servant and Priest, the Son who gives his life in sacrifice in order to do the Father's will and save mankind. He cannot escape from this mission that requires so much suffering of him but that is also represented as glorious.

Peter has acknowledged Jesus to be the Son of God and the Messiah, but he does not accept all the consequences of such a faith; he does not yet understand its full implications. His thoughts are those of a mere man; he does not comprehend God's plan of salvation. Herein we see, as it were, Peter's still divided personality: he is a man of lively faith, but he is also weak. When St. Luke (22) and St. John (21) bring out this paradox, they thereby emphasize the fact that Peter's status as "rock" or solid foundation is a gift of

God and independent of the personal weakness of this apostle who must strengthen others in their faith.

Jesus now goes a step further and teaches his followers what a true disciple's attitude must be. We are all familiar with his words, for they have so often been repeated — and so often ignored in practice! St. Matthew may here be assembling statements originally made on several occasions; in any case, their effect is more powerful by reason of the repetition.

"Deny himself, take up his cross and follow me": these are the three fundamental attitudes. "Deny himself" should not be understood to mean simply a moral attitude and an outward change of ways. It implies a complete conversion, a shift in values that takes place not only in the conceptual order but in the depths of the person. Peter had been rebuked for thinking like a mere human being rather than like God. The lesson for us is that we must change our human valuations of the way of salvation and adopt the way of salvation that God wants us to follow. Even our very way of understanding Jesus must change, so that we will see him as he really is and not as we would like him to be. The same applies with regard to the Church in our day; if we are to understand her, we must deny ourselves, stop seeing her as we would like her to be, and see her as she really is in God's plan.

"Take up his cross" is likewise often understood in too narrow a fashion, as though it meant simply accepting poor health, moral and social difficulties. In fact, the phrase seems to have a broader and more positive meaning of sharing with Christ in the work of saving the world. Our attitude must be paschal. We must "follow" Jesus, which means, first and foremost, to share with him the burden of saving the world. This attitude is one we must cultivate each day and in even the smallest matters. Our role is an important one, and we must always bear in mind the greater, paschal meaning of the little "crosses" in our life.

The disciple must also risk his life. To do so for God and the salvation of the world manifests the courage of a true disciple. Here again, however, we should not think solely of risking bodily life or sacrificing the possible successes that attend on other men's lives. The expression "lose one's life" means something more than that. The real point is that one so believes and follows Jesus that one entirely abandons the self, for God's thoughts are not ours. The disciple must be willing to live according to God's plan for him and to work as the Lord wishes him to for the salvation of the world. In other words, we give ourselves — not in the ways we had anticipated but as God wishes; his ways may not be the same as we would have chosen.

All this, however, leads to glory, and Jesus bids us focus our attention on the glory which the Father will give the Son and in which we too will share, each according to his works.

I am insulted and mocked (Jer. 20:7-9)

This passage is part of the "confession" that Jeremias speaks to his Lord. Here we see the prophet "deceived" by the Lord and unable to resist God in the situations in which God involves him. "Thou art stronger than I, and thou hast prevailed." The prophet now finds himself caught up in insurmountable difficulties. He is forced to preach a violence and destruction that do not correspond to his temperament; yet these positions are forced upon him from above. For this reason he has become a laughingstock and the object of mockery.

In these circumstances the prophet experiences discouragement and is tempted to stop following the Lord's commands and speaking in his name. He is no longer his own man but lives a life that is not truly his own; he experiences an alienation from himself. Yet he cannot free himself from God. There is a burning fire within him that he cannot control. The person of the prophet disappears, as it were, and the Lord speaks in and through him, but at the cost of martyrdom to the prophet. Jeremias has become the very model of self-denial for the sake of doing God's will.

What the prophet is really doing is yielding to the love of God. It is of this that the responsorial psalm (Ps. 63) sings. Like David, the prophet thinks of himself as walking "in a dry and weary land where no water is," but he also knows that "thy steadfast love is better than life," and therefore "my lips will praise thee." He clings to the Lord with all his heart, and the Lord sustains him.

Offer one's person and life in sacrifice (Rom. 12:1-2)

Jeremias had been a model for the sacrificial life of the Christian. Now St. Paul in his turn exhorts Christians to offer their lives in self-denial. For him, however, the model of self-denial for the sake of doing God's will is Christ himself. The Christian must set aside his own ways of thinking, not in order to conform himself to the present world but in order to know and do God's will. It is in this course of action that his renunciation of self consists. But that course of action is also authentic worship and adoration of God. There can be no genuine adoration and contemplation without this self-denial, the nature and quality of which we now understand better.

The same love that led the Son to give himself as a fragrant sacrifice to God (Eph. 5:2) should lead God's adoptive sons to the same kind of self-surrender. The Old Testament had, of course, already known this kind of sacrifice acceptable to God (Sir. 35:1-3), and we have just seen in Jeremias' "confessions" a similarly generous and unconditional surrender of self to God. Now it is those who have been transformed by the Spirit in their baptism who are bidden to renounce themselves after the manner of him in whom they have been clothed in the sacrament of rebirth. The Spirit has given them a new birth; now their person and their very mentality must likewise be renewed.

It follows from this that the Christian no longer owns

himself. He has surrendered his own life in order to be a witness to God's will.

Our age is rediscovering the prophetic stature and quality of the Christian. It is important, however, that we not look on this prophetic quality in terms solely of mission and of claims upon others. At the foundation of all truly prophetic action there is, and must be, the denial of self in order to be the messenger of God's will. In other words, there can be no authentic prophetism unless one does God's will in the details of one's own life, just as there is no genuine worship going on in a congregation that is not basically determined to submit to God's plan for it.

The authentic Christian prophet, then, is the person who, despite charges of conservatism and clericalism, does not seek to flatter the desires of worldly men but dares to proclaim the truth and the message as it really is. We saw how Jesus harshly rebukes Peter for seeking to hold him, Jesus, back from his Passion and the doing of the Father's will in an utterly self-denying way. The Christian is sometimes forced to speak, for there are silences that amount to surrender and compromise. In these circumstances a Christian should, like Jeremias and despite his fear of the consequences, feel himself unable to resist the urging of the Spirit given him at baptism.

The period in which we live needs Christians who are prophetic, but prophetism must be inseparable from the attitude of the servant who gives his life. Without fanfare or ostentation, this servant lives a life that is strongly and solidly grounded in truth and wholly given over to God, through renunciation of personal views, for the sake of establishing God's kingdom.

TWENTY-THIRD SUNDAY

Fraternal Correction

Win your brother over (Matthew 18:15-20)

This passage from the First Gospel enables us to enter into the internal life of an early Christian community and to see the practice of that fraternal correction which the great monastic lawgivers would later try to establish in the families they had founded.

If we are properly to understand the duty of fraternal correction, we will do well to begin with the final verses of the passage. They show us that we are dealing with a community, a local Church.

"Where two or three are gathered in my name, there am I in the midst of them." To "gather in the name of Jesus" means, for St. Matthew, to form a Church. Consequently, in his view and in accordance with Jesus' words, a Church is identical with those who have gathered in the name of Jesus. Such a gathering of two or three is assured that Jesus is present in its midst; for the Church this means the presence of the glorified Lord. St. Matthew will later record Jesus' final words: "I am with you always, to the close of the age" (28:20).

It is because he is thus present that Christ can say, in the preceding verse, "if two of you agree on earth about anything they ask, it will be done for them by my Father in heaven." It is because men gather in Jesus' name and because Jesus is therefore present in their midst that God hears and accepts their prayer. Later on St. Matthew will report another saying of Jesus: "Whatever you ask in prayer, you will receive, if you have faith" (21:20).

This local Church, in which the Lord lives and hears the faithful who pray to him, is made up of the baptized. These men and women, however, continue to be human beings, so sin is possible and does occur. This situation requires fraternal correction. The community cannot simply allow one of its members to live a life that is a contradiction to what the community represents. But the primary reaction to the situation is not rejection or reprobation, but brotherly and sisterly love. There can be no evading some decisive action in the name of the body that is the Church.

The action required must be carefully taken. Jesus is fully aware of this and therefore proposes three stages in the fulfillment of the duty of fraternal correction. The first is for a brother to approach his brother privately and try to persuade him. What a joy if the other listens, for "if he listens to you, you have gained your brother"! This, then, is the first step to be taken out of fraternal love.

If the sinner is convinced that he is right and will not admit the real character of what he does, or if he is convinced that the rebuke springs from subjective motives, then the corrector should take one or two other brothers with him. Perhaps this united front will have an effect. The other may be impressed and come to realize the seriousness of his situation.

If the sinner still does not understand and remains obstinate, then out of love for him and for the good of the community, the corrector must appeal to the community. This appeal may in turn lead to a painful but necessary decision: If the sinner refuses to heed the Church, he must be regarded "as a Gentile and a tax-collector." He has no sense of the Lord's presence in the community and is a living offense to God therein present.

The Church has this power of judging, of binding and loosing, as the Lord puts it. His words echo a rabbinical maxim that he is using to establish, not, it seems, the doctrinal power of the Church, but its "disciplinary" power, that is, the power of maintaining order and protecting the community. A judgment of God corresponds to the judgment of the Church when the latter binds and looses. The sinner who is unwilling to change his way of life is con-

demned by the Church but also by the Lord himself, for it
is in the Lord's name that the Church acts. The Church
knows that its decision is matched by God's.

Warn the wicked man (Ezek. 33:7-9)

The Old Testament knows of a similar duty. Thus
Ezekiel understands that the lord is imposing it on him:
"So you, son of man, I have made a watchman for the house
of Israel." Israel has forgotten its obligation of fidelity to the
Lord. A new exile threatens, and Ezekiel is his people's
only hope: he must continue to make clear what justice requires and to rouse his people to conversion. God makes
him a guardian, in fact the last protector who can still do
something to lead his people back to the right path.

God, of course, is always offering his forgiveness, but the
sinner must acknowledge who and what he is. Someone
must warn him of the death that threatens him. That is
Ezekiel's role. If the prophet does not do his duty, he will
be responsible for the sinner's death; if Ezekiel does not
bid the sinner abandon his evil ways, the evil man will die
in his sins. If, however, Ezekiel warns him but the sinner
does not listen, the sinner will die in his sins, but the
prophet will save his own life, for God would have called
him to account for his neglect of his sinful brother.

Love fulfills the law (Rom. 13:8-10)

Love perfectly fulfills the law that requires the Christian
to exercise fraternal correction. This is the conclusion we
can draw from the present reading, which chance has
joined to the first reading and the Gospel. Fraternal correction pays the debt of love we owe the other. The debt itself
is a permanent thing, for we must constantly love our
neighbor.

We are introduced here to the mystical dimension of the

Christian community, where the greatest commandment is the commandment of love. The Gospel for the thirtieth Sunday (Cycle A) will give us the words of Jesus as reported by St. Matthew: "You shall love your neighbor as yourself" (Matthew 22:34-40). When the Christian exercises charity, he brings the law to its fulfillment, as Jesus did by dying for us (Rom. 10:4). To love one's neighbor is thus not only to fulfill an obligation but to enter upon the way of Christ himself, to imitate him, and to live as he did.

The conditions of modern life and civilization do not allow us to imitate exactly the procedure here recommended by Jesus, but the spirit of what he says is incumbent on us all. The reaction of a Christian when confronted with his brother's sin should always be inspired by this passage, for the stakes are the life of our brother. If we divulge his sin without first having tried in a sensitive way to correct him according to the possibilities open to us in our day, we show that we have not understood the meaning of love. On the other hand, if we allow the whole community to be endangered and if we do not accept to be a watchman over the life of the Church, we are refusing to love our brother.

Fraternal correction has nothing to do with playing the informer or with a fanatical righting of wrongs, still less with the deadly habit of prying and being always ready to denounce without an ardent desire to heal above all. Our gigantic institutions, which are no longer human in their scale, make it difficult and often impossible to exercise fraternal correction in a serene way, although such an exercise is a sign of spiritual vitality in a people that is led by the Lord. At least, each of us must ask himself what his own duty is and not be self-satisfied when it comes to his attitude toward a sick brother.

TWENTY-FOURTH SUNDAY

Forgiveness

Forgive seventy times seven times (Matthew 18:21-35)

This passage must be read in the context of the community, that is, the Church. It deals with the forgiveness of offenses and with the Christian requirement of brotherhood and forgiveness, and sees these directly in relation to the kingdom. The pericope is thus not simply offering an exhortation to morality but teaching us what Christian community must be in its relationship to the eternal kingdom.

Jesus begins his parable with the words: "The kingdom of heaven may be compared to a king." It is not our task here to engage in historical criticism of the details of the parable, for a parable has nothing to do with historical truth. The improbability of the amounts of money is unimportant; in fact, the improbability helps give the parable its shock value.

Nor is there any point to giving an explanation of a parable that is quite clear in itself. It is so clear, indeed, that every reader can identify with the wicked steward! In addition, the ending, "So also my heavenly Father will do to every one of you, if you do not forgive your brother from your heart," reminds us immediately of the petition in the Lord's Prayer: "And forgive us our debts, as we also have forgiven our debtors."

Forgiveness and mercy are basic attitudes that every Christian in the Church must have. They are, and must be, characteristic of every Christian who truly wishes to follow Christ. The Church, when all is said and done, is a community of forgiveness and mercy.

Forgiveness of neighbor and forgiveness of sins (Sir. 27:30–28:7)

The Old Testament knew the obligation of forgiving one's neighbor. The first reading for this day is clear enough, and its content may be easily summarized as follows. Anger and wrath are condemned without reserve. Each of us must bear in mind his own fleshly condition and his weaknesses; if he does, he will find it difficult to condemn others and withhold his forgiveness. After all, we are all members of the same community of weak men. Moreover, how can we pray that our own sins be forgiven if we ourselves do not forgive others? Life under the covenant presupposes a respect for the commandments and a willingness to forgive without holding grudges.

We live and die for the Lord. Why judge? (Rom. 14:7-9)

The verses read today from the Letter to the Romans show a fortuitous but real correspondence with the first reading and the Gospel. The main point that Paul is making here is that whether in life or in death we belong to the Lord, since Christ has become Lord of both the living and the dead. In this context more than elsewhere, the use of the title "Lord" underscores the unlimited power Christ has won through his death and his resurrection glory. "Lord both of the living and of the dead" expresses his unconditioned domination of the entire universe. The same formula is to be found in the Acts of the Apostles (10:42), the Second Letter to Timothy (4:1), and the First Letter of Peter (4:5).

If we accept the Gospel, embrace the faith, and receive baptism, we are accepting the lordship of Christ: "we live to the Lord." But then, all of us alike are under the same lordship, and if we are all servants of one and the same Lord, why do we condemn one another? "Why do you pass judgment on your brother? Or you, why do you despise your brother?" says St. Paul in the verse immediately following on today's passage, and he goes on to show why such condemnation of one another is unthinkable: we must all appear before God's judgment seat and render an account of ourselves.

In the community of the Church, then, each person must forgive the others and stop passing judgment on them. In some cases, one individual may certainly wrong another. But we must also remember that a certain pluralism and variety is quite legitimate, and that one person may be trying to serve in one way, another in another. We have no right to demand a uniformity that is cut to our measure and our personal views. We do not have the duty of judging our neighbor, but, on the contrary, must appear, just as he must, before the tribunal of the Lord. It is to the Lord that we have all been subject during our lives and in our death; it is to him that we have promised service.

The responsorial psalm (Ps. 103) sings of the Lord's forgiveness of us: "He will not always chide, nor will he keep his anger for ever. He does not deal with us according to our sins, nor requite us according to our iniquities."

TWENTY-FIFTH SUNDAY

God's Thoughts and Value Judgments

Do you begrudge my generosity? (Matthew 20:1-16)

The phrase we have just used as a title for this section on the Gospel of the twenty-fifth Sunday can be misleading to the reader. It must also be admitted that the Old Testament reading for the day can direct our thoughts along the wrong lines as far as an understanding of the Gospel is concerned.

The workers of the eleventh hour have been a subject of inexhaustible discussion. The exegetes have labored to explain the behavior of a boss who flouts all our social principles; preachers likewise find themselves in difficulty when they must explain this parable of Jesus to people habituated to the idea of social justice. The theologians, for their part, try to avoid having to find a footing on such treacherous ground and seek rather to follow a different line: We cannot comprehend God's thoughts, for they are not the same as ours.

Two points must be kept in mind as we attempt an explanation of this pericope. The first thing to be remembered is the literary genre of parable. In a parable, details are secondary; the primary thing is the main point being made. In the present parable, the main point is that the last will be first. The parable affirms this principle with an illustration that may seem improbable or even be an example of social injustice.

The second point is that the parable must be situated both within the overall teaching of Christ and in relation to the circumstances in which it was spoken. Two circumstances in particular need to be emphasized here.

Jesus often observes that the chosen people has not proved faithful and has refused to accept him. God's choice is therefore now fixed upon a new people: the Church that is in process of being formed. Over against the Jewish people, which had been God's favorite for centuries, the Church, a worker of the eleventh hour, sees itself overwhelmed by gifts from God. St. Matthew is the only evangelist to report this parable, and he may have had good reason for doing so, namely, to bring home to Jewish Christians the importance and unique situation of the Church. The people formerly chosen by God has now been replaced by a new people, a people of the eleventh hour. Thus the last — those who have now accepted the faith and form the

new people of God — will be first, and the first — the chosen people who did not receive Christ — will lose their
primacy and become last.

There is a further viewpoint that Jesus adopts and that St.
Matthew finds opportune to make part of his catechesis. To
understand this further point, we must recall the parable of
the prodigal son, which is a parallel to the present parable
(see p. 361). The real issue is thus the acceptance and forgiveness of sinners. Like Jesus in his time, St. Matthew is
having difficulty persuading his community to welcome pagans, who are treated as though they too had always been
worshipers of the true God.

These two viewpoints — that of the new people which
now takes first place and that of the sinner who is treated
like the faithful servant — seem to me closely connected. It
is along this line that we are invited to understand the parable.

First of all, we must put the parable into its context. It
follows upon Peter's question at the end of the preceding
chapter: "Lo, we have left everything and followed you.
What then shall we have?" (Matthew 19:27). Jesus answers
him by telling him that his disciples will sit on twelve
thrones and judge the twelve tribes of Israel. He then ends
with the statement, "Many that are first will be last, and the
last first" (Matthew 19:30). Jesus is here speaking of the
latecomers, who are the disciples; even though they come
last, they will sit on twelve thrones and judge the twelve
tribes of Israel, who were the first to come. The reason why
the apostles receive this preference is that they have left
everything to follow Jesus.

Yet the words of Jesus (Matthew 19:30) need some further explanation. "Many that are first will be last, and the
last first" is a vision of things that cannot be understood
solely by reference to the apostles. It yields its meaning
only when related to the kingdom of heaven. That is why
the Lord continues with a parable concerning the kingdom.

The liturgical proclamation of today's Gospel begins, unfortunately, with chapter 20 and omits the last verse of

chapter 19, that is, the verse that leads over to the parable of 20:1-16. Note that verse 1 of chapter 20 begins with the connective "for," showing the continuity with chapter 19. Our parable in chapter 20 ends, moreover, with a repetition of the statement in chapter 19, verse 30.

We may now turn to the parable of the prodigal son in St. Luke and relate it to St. Matthew's parable. The parable of the Pharisee and the tax collector (Luke 18:11) should also be related to the first two. By these comparisons we can gain a fuller understanding of the parable of the workers at the eleventh hour.

In the parable of the prodigal son, the elder son complains bitterly at not receiving what his disloyal brother receives, although he, the elder brother, has always been faithful. He does not understand why the prodigal son should receive anything at all; in other words, his anger is not due to the fact that he, the faithful son, has not received enough, but to the fact that his brother, a sinner, should be given anything at all. He does not agree that his brother should be forgiven, and we even sense a certain contempt in his attitude.

This same contempt may be glimpsed in the objections of the workers who had come at the first hour: "these last," as in the words of the elder son: "this son of yours," and in the words of the Pharisee with regard to the tax collector: "this tax collector." It is this contempt for the sinner and for the worker who comes at the last hour that Jesus intends to reprove and correct. The workers are not protesting so much because they do not receive more than the worker of the last hour, but because the worker of the last hour is rewarded at all. They do not want to see this neighbor of theirs welcomed at all.

The parable certainly is not to be understood as justifying what we today see as a form of social injustice. What it does insist upon is the necessity of welcoming the sinner and not condemning him. Contempt for the sinner only makes it impossible to understand the action of the householder and the forgiveness given by God. The parable thus has for its focal point the goodness and forgiveness of God. It emphasizes God's acceptance of those who receive his messenger; among the latter, the disciples take first place, and will even sit and judge the twelve tribes of Israel.

A person who refuses to regard a sinner as his brother, or the converted Jew who feels contempt for the pagans who enter the Church, cannot possibly enter into and adopt the outlook of God. Similarly, the person who is satisfied with his own uprightness and imagines that it gives him a right to privileges cannot understand the thinking of God.

The parable thus is not to be explained in terms of purely human justice. Neither, however, does it offer a theology of some incomprehensible divine justice. Its aim is to bring out something quite different: the fact that Jesus has been sent to save sinners and that those who receive him with faith become the first in the kingdom.

My thoughts are not your thoughts (Is. 55:6-9)

The prophet is not talking about a God whose behavior is arbitrary and to whom we must submit even though we do not understand him at all. This text, like the parable of the workers at the eleventh hour, has frequently served as the basis for commentaries that urge us to accept trials or comparisons we find hard to admit. Yet we need only read the text attentively and we will see that it is not speaking at all of a God who complacently acts in his own peculiar way, so that we cannot possibly understand his decrees.

If we grasp the real meaning of the Isaian text, it will help us gain a better understanding of today's Gospel. These verses of Isaiah have a quite specific context: the prediction of a new Jerusalem and of a new and eternal covenant (Is. 55:1-4). The Lord creates a new people. To enter into that people, a person must be converted: "Let the wicked forsake his way, and the unrighteous man his thoughts; let him return to the Lord, that he may have mercy on him, and to our God, for he will abundantly pardon" (55:7).

What does God mean, then, when he says that his thoughts are not our thoughts nor his ways our ways? Does he mean that his mental categories are alien to ours? That his justice has nothing in common with ours? It does not seem so. We are to read the Isaian statement rather as an assertion that God's mercy is infinite. Our justice condemns, but God's justice pardons, because his thoughts are beyond ours. The responsorial psalm (Ps. 145) expresses the idea well: "His greatness is unsearchable. . . . The Lord is gracious and merciful, slow to anger and abounding in steadfast love. . . . The Lord is just in all his ways" (Ps. 145:3, 8, 17).

For me to live is Christ (Phil. 1:20c-24, 27a)

"Christ will be honored in my body, whether by life or by death." A preferable translation would be: "The glory of Christ will be manifested through me." "In my body" is a literal translation of the Greek text, but "body" stands here for the person or his existence.

Christ's glory is manifested in the Christian's earthly existence, because through baptism and the Eucharist the Christian has been wholly incorporated into Christ. Christ's glory will continue to be manifested by the Christian in the life to come, because then he will share Christ's risen life. The communion of the Christian with Christ is such that whether the Christian is alive or dead (in terms of earthly life), Christ's glory will always be manifested in him.

At the same time, however, while the Christian is indeed incorporated into Christ even while on earth and is already identified with Christ, death will make possible a more perfect communion with the Lord. In his Second Letter to the Corinthians, Paul writes: "We know that while we are at home in the body we are away from the Lord, for we walk by faith, not by sight. We are of good courage, and we

would rather be away from the body and at home with the
Lord" (2 Cor. 5:6-8). Nonetheless, here in the Letter to the
Philippians Paul hesitates when it comes to choosing death
or earthly life, and he ends by choosing to stay on earth,
since his presence is useful to his disciples.

The Christian has an obligation to lead a life worthy of
the gospel that Christ preached, for he is incorporated into
Christ and must show forth in his life the glory of his Lord.

TWENTY-SIXTH SUNDAY

Repent and Live

Sinners are saved by faith and repentance (Matthew 21:28-32)

The passage proclaimed today may seem to be made up
of disparate pieces, with the first part having nothing to do
with the second. In addition, the first part may seem to be
proposing a simple case of morality and telling us that what
counts is not intentions or words but actions. The chief
priests and the elders evidently had no difficulty in recognizing that the man who truly did his father's will was the
one who actually did it, even though he had begun by refusing to do it. This is fine, but such a very simple lesson on
obedience seems a bit disappointing.

We may also feel some dissatisfaction that Matthew
should follow the parable with a conclusion that seems to
have nothing to do with it. The impression of discontinuity
is one many people have; some missals and lectionaries, for
example, leave a space between the parable on the two
sons and the saying of Jesus. These various difficulties bid
us read the text carefully and put it into its context.

Jesus has entered the Temple and is teaching there. The

high priests and the elders of the people question him, asking by what authority he teaches. Jesus answers with a question: "The baptism of John, whence was it? From heaven or from men?" The others were in a dilemma. If they answered, "From heaven," they would be putting themselves in the wrong for not having believed John. If they answered, "From men," they might anger the crowd, who believed John to be a prophet. The highpriests and elders are therefore forced to be evasive: "We do not know." Jesus in turn refuses to answer their question to him (Matthew 21:23-27).

It is at this point that today's pericope begins. Its context, then, is the faith and obedience that Jesus' challengers are unwilling to risk. Jesus does not leave matters there but proposes the parable of the two sons. The one refused to go into the vineyard but then repented and went, the other said he would go but did not go. We can now see the point of the second part of the passage: John came and you did not believe him, but the tax collectors and prostitutes repented and did believe. The Pharisees, on the one hand, and the tax collectors and prostitutes, on the other, are like the two sons with their different responses.

It is clear, then, that if we are to understand today's parable and its conclusion, we must take into account the section immediately preceding. The questioners of Jesus did not believe in John; to this extent they resemble the first son, who refused to obey. That son repented, however, and did obey, while the high priests and elders refused to be converted even after seeing the prostitutes and tax collectors repenting and believing John. Consequently, the prostitutes and tax collectors will go before them into the kingdom of God.

The parable of the two sons sent into the vineyard reminds us of the parable of the murderous vineyard workers, which follows immediately on today's passage in St. Matthew's text. In the latter parable we find the same refusal to accept Jesus and believe in him, a refusal that even involves a hatred and leads to the condemnation of Jesus.

The point being made is that we must receive Jesus with faith. To accept him means not only to accept him with our minds but to act accordingly. Faith and action — that is the lesson of today's Gospel. Faith in action — that is, faith that leads to conversion and a life based on faith.

Turn from your sins and be saved (Ezek. 18:25-28)

This oracle is a call to conversion: "When a wicked man turns away from the wickedness he has committed and does what is lawful and right, he shall save his life"; and again: "Because he considered and turned away from all the transgressions which he committed, he shall surely live, he shall not die."

We are listening here to a dialogue between God and his people. The people find the Lord's ways strange. Why? The prophet has explained God's view of personal responsibility both in sin and in the avoidance of sin. God does not, however, take pleasure in the death of a sinner; he desires rather that the sinner should live, but this means that the sinner must change his ways. Thus, conversion is a possibility offered to man, and at the same time it pleases God. On the other hand, the just man can prove lacking in fidelity, and if he does, he will die. Infidelity is no less possible than conversion. It is precisely here that Ezekiel's hearers find God's ways to be strange. But the Lord answers their criticism: If the just man turns away from righteousness, becomes evil, and dies in this state, then he dies because of his wickedness and because he has not used the means God gave him for attaining to life.

The Old Testament text leads over to the Gospel of the day. Both deal with the rejection of God and the refusal to be converted; at the same time, conversion is always possible. The danger for a man lies in his tendency to be inconstant and to let his dispositions change. The problem of fidelity is thus a very basic one: we can say "Yes," but then not follow up on our decision; or we can say "No," but then be converted.

Our thoughts today, then, should focus on God's offer of salvation to us. What he did in the past, he still does in our time. On the other hand, we must also be concerned with our own constancy in love and fidelity to the Lord if we are really serious about entering the kingdom.

Evidently the just man has no easy path to walk. He must be upright and faithful in his response to God; breaks in continuity are always possible, and against these he must guard. The responsorial psalm (Ps. 125) asks that God would forgive us our sins and grant us the light we need: "Make me to know thy ways, O Lord; teach me thy paths. Lead me in thy truth, and teach me, for thou art the God of my salvation. . . . Be mindful of thy mercy, O Lord, and of thy steadfast love, for they have been from of old. . . . Good and upright is the Lord; therefore he instructs sinners in the way. He leads the humble in what is right, and teaches the humble his way."

Have the mind of Christ (Phil. 2:1-11)

St. Paul continues to emphasize the closeness of our communion with Christ; he tells us here that it is such that we ought to share the thoughts and sentiments of Christ. Communion with Jesus is impossible without an accompanying close union among all who live by and through him. It is in Christ that we must encourage one another. This theme of mutual encouragement is a favorite of Paul's.

In a manner we might think merely diplomatic, but which is in fact spiritual and soundly theological, the Apostle manifests his desire to see Christians solidly united with one another. It would be his greatest joy as an apostle and a pastor to see this unity flourish. Paul was probably aware of dissensions in the community at Philippi; these would be caused by the ambition of some members or by their striving for their own welfare and advantage. The true Christian outlook, however, is to regard others as better than oneself.

In order to make this last-named attitude understandable, Paul appeals to Christ and his attitude. His description will be forever the greatest theological depiction of Christ's self-emptying on the Cross: "Christ Jesus . . . though he was in the form of God, did not count equality with God a thing to be grasped, but emptied himself, taking the form of a servant, being born in the likeness of men. And being found in human form he humbled himself and became obedient unto death, even death on a cross." Paul is here summing up the whole mystery of redemption that began with the incarnation. The expressions "likeness of men" and "found in human form" do not imply that he was only seemingly a man; Paul is simply making the point that while Christ genuinely made the human condition his own, he did not share man's sinfulness.

The mystery of redemption did not stop with the Cross, however. The paschal mystery of Jesus, which is the center of Christian life, is a mystery of death but also a mystery of resurrection to glory: "Therefore God has highly exalted him and bestowed on him the name which is above every name, that at the name of Jesus every knee should bow, in heaven and on earth and under the earth, and every tongue confess that Jesus Christ is Lord, to the glory of God the Father." Paul is here telling how Christ was enthroned in glory, received the name of Lord, and had his lordship proclaimed by the entire universe.

This hymn may have served originally as a liturgical acclamation. In any case, it has been adopted into the Christian liturgy and used on Good Friday and on other occasions.

The description of the course of Jesus' life, death, and glorification has a practical meaning for the Christian who lives in close union with Jesus: the Christian is to imitate in his own life the phases of Jesus' life.

TWENTY-SEVENTH SUNDAY

The Fruitless Vineyard

He will lease his vineyard to others (Matthew 21:33-43)

This passage still confronts the exegetes with some important problems. Some have seen in the passage a narrative composed by the Christian community in order to describe the advances God had made to his people up until the time when he finally sent them his Son. The parable would thus be a way of relating the life of Jesus to the overall history of Israel; it would show the failure of the advances God had made, and how finally he transferred his favor to a new people. In thus making the Christian community the originator of the parable, the exegetes have no intention of denying the role of the Holy Spirit in the redaction of this short history of Israel, Christ, and the new chosen people.

We cannot go into the problems of literary criticism that are involved here, but we may note that other exegetes do not accept the approach just indicated and think rather that we look to St. Mark's Gospel for an earlier and more original form of a parable that St. Matthew then took and elaborated for the catechesis of his own community.

We shall not make a detailed comparison of the accounts of Mark and Matthew, but we must note that there are some important differences. In St. Mark's parable (12:1-12), a single servant is sent on each of two occasions, before the son of the house is finally sent. Each of the servants is maltreated, the second more so than the first; the tenants are becoming exasperated at the owner, and when the son comes, they kill him. In St. Matthew's parable, two groups of servants are sent, the second group being larger than the first; both groups are cruelly treated, and the son pays for his mission with his life.

We may think that St. Matthew wishes to remind his readers of the fate suffered by the various prophets when they came to the vineyard, that is, to the people of Israel. When the Son, Jesus, finally comes, he too is put to death by the Jews. St. Matthew intends, as so often in his Gospel, to emphasize the responsibility of the chief priests and elders of the people, whom Jesus is addressing here, just as he emphasizes the responsibility of the Pharisees.

The general conclusion drawn by both Matthew and Mark is the same: The workers or tenants deserve death, and the vineyard will be let out to others. St. Matthew adds, however, that the new tenants must make the vineyard bear fruit. The former tenants should have had fruits to give to the owner, and they did not; the new tenants will have the same obligation. They must give him the fruits "in their season"; in other words, there will come a time when they will have to render an account of their work.

St. Matthew seems to have wanted to call attention to the way in which Israel had received the prophets and the divine warnings they brought with them. Israel did not produce the fruits God wanted and expected; they were responsible for the death of the Son when finally the Father sent him. St. Mark brings out the same point.

The exegetes think that, as so often when the words "Have you ever read in the scriptures . . . ?" occur, the community is introducing a quotation from Scripture. In this case the Scripture cited is: "The very stone which the builders rejected has become the head of the corner." St. Matthew, in any case, goes on to say: "The kingdom of God [not: 'the kingdom of heaven,' as is his wont] will be taken away from you and given to a nation producing the fruits of it." Here again, Matthew insists that the new people of God must produce fruit.

The Lord's vineyard is the house of Israel (Is. 5:1-7)

This remarkable poem sums up the entire history of God's fidelity to his people and its many manifestations, on the one hand, and the infidelities of Israel, on the other.

The movement of the passage is clear. The owner of the vineyard does everything he can for it, but the vineyard is a failure. The inhabitants of Jerusalem and Judea are asked to pass judgment. What more could the owner have done? All the inhabitants must certainly understand the harsh way in which he will now treat the vineyard. All that is left to do is to indicate the real-life situation that is being reflected in the parable. Finally the prophet does this.

The passage is a poetic description of God's love for his people and of the infidelities that he receives in return. The people are forced to pass judgment on themselves and to recognize themselves in the fruitless vineyard that deserves only to be uprooted: "The vineyard of the Lord of hosts is the house of Israel."

The teaching of this Sunday is important for the Chuch of our day. The great fault of the first workers in the vineyard, that is, the first people of God, was that they did not bear fruit. They did not listen to the prophets; they were unfaithful. Now the vineyard has been let out to a new people, the Church.

But the Church — the community for which St. Matthew is writing and every community — must remember that it too is expected to bear fruit. In the time that elapses between the establishment of this new people of God and the day of the Lord's return, the Church must see to it that it does bear fruit. The fruit consists first and foremost in love and its deeds. The Church must be a docile instrument in the Lord's hand and not act as owner of the vineyard rather than as simple tenant.

The responsorial psalm (Ps. 80) voices the regrets of Israel: "Why then hast thou broken down its walls, so that all who pass along the way pluck its fruit? The boar from the forest ravages it, and all that move in the field feed on it." The psalm also gives fine expression to the prayer of the new people of God who are the new workers and must make the vineyard bear fruit as it should: "Turn again, O God of hosts! Look down from heaven, and see; have regard for this vine, the stock which thy right hand planted."

The God of peace will be with you (Phil. 4:6-9)

In this passage St. Paul is trying to teach the Philippians to acquire peace of soul through prayer and the practice of the Christian virtues. If they are to be at peace, they must pray in a spirit of thanksgiving, while also making their petitions known to God. If they do that, they need not be anxious about anything.

Does it sound as if the Apostle were living apart from the world, or as if he were unrealistic in his approach to actual life? But this very Letter makes it clear that this is not the case. Not only does he remind the Philippians that he is a prisoner condemned to death, but he knows the difficulties at Philippi and the rivalries and disputes in the community. Nonetheless, he tells them they should be enjoying the peace that God gives. It is not an inactive peace; life in Christ is always a struggle, as the very virtues he lists make clear. If they put into practice the instruction he gives them, the God of peace will be with them.

TWENTY-EIGHTH SUNDAY

The Banquet of the Lord

Those invited to the wedding feast (Matthew 22:1-14)

This parable is also found in St. Luke's Gospel (14:16-24), but once again we find Matthew modifying it to meet catechetical needs. The basic meaning remains the same as in Luke, but Matthew's additions make the parable more suited to, and effective for, his catechesis, which is addressed to converts from Judaism. Without going into details, we shall simply point out what is most important for us and indicate what led Matthew to change and amplify the story.

In Luke, the man issuing the invitation is a rich man; in Matthew, it is a king who is giving a wedding banquet for his son. Later on, Matthew will modify the parable so that those who reject the invitation are Jews. In his eyes, then, the king is God himself.

In Luke, the invitation is given when the time for the banquet has come, and the invitation is carried by a single servant. In Matthew, the king repeats his invitation, and on both occasions sends several servants. Matthew wishes here to remind his readers of the prophets, who were sent repeatedly by the Lord and who not only met with rejection but were mistreated (a detail Luke does not have). In the parable of the vineyard (21:33-43), Matthew had already followed a similar pattern in order to bring out the same point, that is, the rejection of the Lord by the people of Israel; in this parable, too, messengers were sent twice.

It is because of the rejection and mistreatment of his servants that Matthew's king grows angry, sends troops to punish, and finally destroys the city. Matthew may here be influenced by the Book of Isaiah (5:1-7) and by his earlier parable of the vineyard workers who did not produce fruit and were punished by the owner.

The second invitation is not addressed to those originally singled out but to everyone on the streets: the poor, the disabled, the blind, the lame. Here, as in the parable of the vineyard, the invitation finally goes out to people who had had nothing to do with the king (the vineyard will be let out to new custodians). Israel has not accepted the invitation or welcomed the messengers of the owner, who was looking for fruit from the vineyard; now the vineyard will be given to others, and others will receive the invitation to the banquet.

There is a part of the story that is found only in Matthew. Here the king comes into the banquet hall and finds a guest who has no wedding garment. The king's displeasure seems strange, since he had invited everyone without exception to come! This sort of inconsistency, however, is of no consequence in a parable. It is due simply to the fact that Matthew wants to get across a new point of teaching. Here again, there seems to be a parallelism with the parable of the vineyard. In the latter, Matthew emphasized the fact that the new tenants must bear fruit. He was warning Christians not to relax and take pride in the fact that they were chosen to replace the Jewish people; like the Jews, Christians too are obliged to bear fruit.

In today's parable, Matthew's concern at this point is the same. The Jewish people have not responded to God's invitation, and after punishing them and destroying their city, the king invites men who had no right to an invitation. But if they accept and enter the banquet hall, they must be wearing a wedding garment, that is, they must do God's will. The invitation by itself is not enough to save, any more than the mere fact of becoming the new tenants.

It seems beside the point to inquire here into the exact meaning of the statement: "Many are called, but few are chosen." When we grasp the general meaning of the parable and understand Matthew's method and purpose, the conclusion proves to represent simply St. Matthew's desire to combat a tendency among his Christians to sit back and enjoy their position as the new chosen people. They are therefore being warned that it is difficult to enter and remain in the banquet hall.

The banquet of the saved (Is. 25:6-10a)

We must not forget that despite the warning at the end of the parable, Matthew's basic purpose is to encourage: All who want to follow the Lord can be saved. No matter how wretched they may be, all are invited to the banquet; all can and must acquire a wedding garment.

The reading from Isaiah also concerns an eschatological banquet to which we are all invited. The poem is part of the section known as the "Apocalypse of Isaiah" (cc. 24–27). In today's passage, the particular subject is the messianic banquet (the last day and the reward it brings are represented in the Old and New Testaments as a banquet).

All peoples are invited to this "feast of fat things, a feast of wine on the lees well refined." But the banquet, though depicted in terms of luxury, has its spiritual aspects too: sadness and sorrow will be no more and death will be forever destroyed; the Lord will wipe away the tears from every face and take away the reproach of his people.

What Isaiah is describing is the new Jerusalem, the long hoped for banquet of salvation: "Let us be glad and rejoice in his salvation." "Thou preparest a table before me in the presence of my enemies; thou anointest my head with oil, my cup overflows" (Ps. 23, the responsorial psalm).

We Catholics must, of course, keep in mind that it is for the celebration of the Eucharist that we gather on this Sunday. Consequently, both the poem of Isaiah and the parable of St. Luke have a special connotation for us. Each of us has received a call to which he had no right. If he is to share the Eucharistic banquet, which is a sign and foretaste of the eternal banquet in the kingdom, he must have a wedding garment. This does not mean only that he examines his conscience with regard to serious sins he may have committed. He must also not be over-confident; he must see how open he is to others. Has he by his manner of life or by his self-centeredness rejected an invitation being offered to him? This is quite possible, even after he has entered the banquet hall to share in the feast.

Bear with everything by the power of Christ (Phil. 4:12-14, 19-20)

These lines describe the detachment that should mark the life of every Christian. Detachment does not mean, however, that we should not help others in their need. Paul

thanks the community for having done so; God will reward
them for it. The passage ends with one of the beautiful
doxologies we find so frequently in the Letters of St. Paul.

TWENTY-NINTH SUNDAY

The Primacy of God's Service

Give to Caesar what is Caesar's (Matthew 22:15-21)

The teaching of this Sunday touches on religion and politics, a subject of vital interest to many today. It is important,
therefore, to show the relevance of the readings. We shall
be brief, but shall also try to help the reader reflect on the
problems raised. The answer suggested by the readings is
not always the one some would like to hear.

"Render therefore to Caesar the things that are Caesar's,
and to God the things that are God's" is often understood as
an answer that fits right in with today's world: two separate
domains, each self-enclosed, with the parish priest staying
in the sacristy and the politician in the assembly chamber.

As a matter of fact, the two halves of the statement are not
treated as of equal importance in the Gospel. Jesus is indeed saying that Caesar must be given what is his. He also
says, however, that God must be given what is his, and it is
this second half that the evangelist concentrates on and
emphasizes.

For the contemporaries of Jesus, his statement was an invitation to see in him the Messiah and to acknowledge the
presence of the kingdom of which he is Lord. Those who
questioned him, however, did not understand that the one
they were questioning was the Lord of the kingdom, the
one to whom everything belonged.

But even while asserting that in him the kingdom is

present, Jesus also makes it clear that his kingdom is not of this world and is not to be compared with the kingdom over which Caesar rules. Jesus' kingdom is spiritual: "My kingship is not of this world" (John 18:36). Jesus is not a political Messiah, and his rule is not of the political order; he is thus not a competitor of Caesar. On the other hand, Caesar is not independent but must be subject to Jesus, now that the latter's divine rule has been established. This is so because God's plan is one and undivided, and all created things have their place in it.

Against this background, Jesus' statement, "Render to God what is God's," is an invitation to believe in and submit to this Messiah, Jesus, who has come to establish a kingdom of a kind his contemporaires cannot understand. He will establish his kingdom by fleeing any takeover of political power and by handing himself over to his enemies that he may suffer and die and sacrifice his life and rise gloriously from the dead. His victory thus won over sin and death will be the foundation of the kingdom that all believers are called to enter.

"Render to Caesar what is Caesar's" is evidently not on the same level as the second half of the statement; it does not express one half of reality, with the statement about God expressing the other half! In bidding his hearers give Caesar what is Caesar's, Jesus is simply recognizing that every man must have a certain concern for the political and social well-being of his country. At the same time, however, he is stripping political authority of any claim to be divine; it must simply exercise a responsibility that is from God. God wills that men should organize the life they live during their time on earth.

Rendering to Caesar what is Caesar's is also a manifestation of fidelity to God himself, since God wills that we be concerned for our society. Consequently, rendering to Caesar what is his becomes a partial fulfillment of our more basic duty, which is to render God what is his. The fulfillment of the latter duty has an influence on the measure and manner in which we fulfill our duty to Caesar.

The focus of attention in this passage is evidently on the acknowledgment of the only ultimately true kingdom — that which Jesus inaugurated.

I am the Lord, and there is no other (Is. 45:1, 4-6)

This reading is of interest on two counts. First, Cyrus is a pagan, and yet he receives a commission from God. This means that the Lord can distribute his gifts and missions to whomever he wishes, and not only to men of the Jewish nation. It also means that the Lord is interested in the human and political life of his people. The second point is that the mission given to Cyrus by God should lead men to realize that there is no other Lord beside the God of Israel. Cyrus has become a mighty king, but his power is entirely from God.

The text is important and helps us understand today's Gospel. "I am the Lord, and there is no other." This divine claim, uttered at the moment when God is choosing and consecrating Cyrus as political leader, shows that nothing in human history is independent of God. If Cyrus is to be obeyed, it is not because of any merit in him, but because he is invested with power by God, because his power is derived from a God who is not unconcerned with the earthly and political life of men. This earthly and political life must, however, lead men to justice, peace, and salvation.

The teaching of the gospel is thus not indifferent or neutral toward the political order, but neither can the political order be neutral toward God. Giving to God what is God's requires fidelity to social and political duties, but according to the spirit and requirements of the gospel, since everything ultimately depends on God. Every man must live his life as a human being in the social context in which he finds himself, but he must do it in obedience to gospel precepts.

On the other hand, the Church, in proclaiming the gospel, must remind those in the political sphere of the primacy of God and the need of walking in the way of his commandments, if only for the sake of the human happiness of the community whose well-being is entrusted to them. The two halves of Jesus' statement are thus complementary to each other, but the "Give to God . . ." takes priority, for from it flows the second obligation, "Give to Caesar. . . ."

A life of faith, love, and hope (1 Thess. 1:1-5b)

Paul is here addressing "the church of the Thessalonians," or, as he might equally well have put it, "the church in Thessalonika." It is worth our while to dwell on the expression for a moment. We modern Christians tend to think of a local church as a part of the universal Church, the latter being the sum total of these local churches. The Apostle thinks of things quite differently. In his view, each local church is a presence of the universal Church, and that is the view the Second Vatican Council took in its *Dogmatic Constitution on the Church* (no. 26).

The Church is the assembly of those who have been called by God, and it is to this assembly, as found at Thessalonika, that Paul speaks. He addresses Christians whose unity is attained precisely in the form of the Church — their local Church, which is an embodiment of the universal Church. He thanks God for them, for his gifts to them in the past and in the present. They had received God's word, and that word is now active in them, leading them forward in hope toward the return of Christ. The word has not been received in vain but is efficacious; its proclamation has mediated divine power and the action of the Holy Spirit, and has produced conviction.

As we hear Paul's words of thanksgiving, we should reflect on how we ourselves receive God's word. Those whose office it is to proclaim the word should thank God for making it such a powerful instrument.

THIRTIETH SUNDAY

Love of Neighbor

Love your neighbor as yourself (Matthew 22:34-40)

It seems pointless to dwell on Jesus' answer to the law-yer's question and on the two commandments of love that are so closely intertwined. A few remarks are nonethe-less necessary. The two commandments were well known to the Jews, and in answering, Jesus had only to quote the Book of Deuteronomy (6:5) and the Book of Leviticus (10:18).

Yet not all the Jews listening to Jesus would have thought of these two commandments as summing up the whole of the law. In fact, we can be sure that many of them did not and that the question, "Which is the great commandment of the law?" was put to Jesus as a way of trapping him. It rep-resented another attempt to embarrass him. St. Matthew records several such attempts: "By what authority are you doing these things [teaching in the Temple], and who gave you this authority" (Matthew 21:23-27; see page 146); "Is it lawful to pay taxes to Caesar, or not?" (Matthew 22:15-22; see page 158); "In the resurrection, therefore, of which of the seven will she be wife?" (Matthew 22:23-33). It is after his reply to the last-named question, a reply that won the admiration of the crowd, that a new trap is now laid for Jesus.

Everything in the law and the prophets, that is, in the whole of Scripture, depends on these two commandments of love. In Matthew's eyes, the two commandments are on an equal footing, and one cannot put one of them into prac-tice without also observing the other. All other precepts depend on these two. Jesus is not the only one to assert the necessary and unalterable connection between them. St. John, for example, will write: "If any one says, 'I love God,' and hates his brother, he is a liar; for he who does not love his brother whom he has seen, cannot love God whom he has not seen" (1 John 4:20).

The Gospel is here setting forth the essential basis of Christian life, for this life can be authentic only when these two commandments are observed. In the Fourth Gospel, Jesus will say: "By this all men will know that you are my disciples, if you have love for one another" (John 13:35). The New Testament frequently reminds its readers that love of our brothers cannot be separated from love of God, and vice versa; the unity of the two is a hallmark of the new covenant.

Love the orphan, the widow, the foreigner, and the poor (Exod. 22:21-27)

The Old Testament is very demanding when it comes to love of neighbor, and God shows that he is offended when men fail to attend to, and show love for, their neighbor. God is especially angered at a lack of love for the weak. To this group belong the foreigners in Israel; special concern is owing them, because Israel itself had once been in the same position. The widow and orphan are also among the weak; if Israel fails in love for them, the Lord will make those neglectful of them perish by the sword, leaving their wives widows and their children orphans.

An Israelite must show compassion to his fellow Israelite. Today's passage instructs him on how to act when he lends money: he must lend it without interest and must quickly return any pledge given against the loan.

The striking thing in all this is the way in which God enters the picture as soon as the neighbor is harmed. Without saying so explicitly, the text makes it clear that when a man does wrong to his neighbor, he is also insulting God, and God will soon make his wrath felt.

The New Testament goes further, even if along the same general lines. In the New Testament view, the neighbor is the Lord himself. Once Jesus has accomplished his paschal

mystery, Christians will share the same baptism and the
same Eucharist. Everything that increases and deepends
our membership in the Body of Christ provides further
motivation for fraternal love.

It would, then, be incongruous to ask whether today's
Gospel has a lesson for us in our day! But while we acknowledge that Jesus' teaching here is the necessary basis
of our Christian lives, we can grasp and apply that teaching
more fully.

The love of God is and must remain the major concern of
Christians today as in every generation. Today's Christian
must, however, also make use of the means that will enable
him to enter more deeply into the mystery of God and his
plan of salvation, as revealed in Scripture. The Christian
should pray more, preferably in the form of communal
prayer, where Jesus says that he is present. The Christian
should also make an effort to intensify his liturgical life,
since the liturgy, while not being the exclusive means of
union with God, is at least the greatest of these means.

In contemporary society and civilization, love of neighbor
takes many forms that drew less attention in the past. Thus,
scientific research in behalf of human advancement, politics, and social work are certainly forms of service that can
and should be inspired by love of neighbor. Working for the
advancement of cultural values and even of material values
that serve man's welfare is also a way of loving our fellow
man; contributions to the spiritual advancement of mankind
are all the more a way of loving our neighbor. It is therefore
inconceivable that there could be a practice of the Christian
religion that would claim to exemplify love of God without
also embodying, in one or other form, a love of neighbor. At
least such love would have to be shown in prayer for the
neighbor and in a concern for his needs.

We can never overemphasize the importance of these two
commandments for the Christian life. To forget them or to
be mindful of them only fitfully is to risk worshiping God in
an utterly inauthentic way and receiving the sacraments
without any regard for their true meaning.

Turn from idols and serve God (1 Thess. 1:5c-10)

To understand this passage, we must go back and reread the first five verses proclaimed on the preceding Sunday. Paul's thanksgiving in those verses may be summed up as an utterance of joy at seeing a Christian community that was so obviously chosen by God.

His thanksgiving now continues and expands in a way that may astonish us. He seems to forget humility completely when he says: "And you have become imitators of us and of the Lord, for you received the word in much affliction, with joy inspired by the Holy Spirit." This text is very important for a theology of the ministry, for it seems to imply a certain fatherhood on the part of the apostle, who brings sons forth into the light of faith. God gives life, and man becomes God's collaborator by using his sexual powers; so too God gives life through his word, and the herald of the gospel is his collaborator in this new and higher gift of life. The parallelism seems evident.

Paul gives thanks because the Thessalonians had received the word, but also because their reputation for faith has spread abroad. He is grateful, too, that his own coming among them was the starting point for their conversion, their "turning" from idols to the true God. Now they await the coming of the Son who delivers us from the wrath of God.

Every Christian community should meditate on this passage. We have turned away from idols, but there is always danger that we may turn back to new ones that will keep us from hearing the word of God objectively. Our age is quite familiar with such idols: luxury in all its forms; sexual excess; vague notions of freedom and of human liberation.

THIRTY-FIRST SUNDAY

The Law and Obedience To It

They speak but do not act (Matthew 23:1-12)

The people to whom Jesus is referring here are people in important positions. In Judaism, they were the people in authority, and Jesus acknowledges their position as teachers. The Jews believed that on Sinai Yahweh had given Moses a commission to teach, so that henceforth "to sit on the seat of Moses" meant to belong to the esteemed line of men who had been charged with teaching the people.

Others must therefore do as these teachers told them to; Jesus emphasizes this duty. He also insists, however, that others must not act as their teachers act. His words contain a serious accusation that must be backed up by facts. Jesus has no hesitation about going into details and specifying the major sins of the teachers.

He reproaches them on two counts that must have been subject to easy corroboration by those who were able to observe the lives of these teachers. First of all, he accuses them of leading a double life, because they demand various observances of others that they do not fulfill themselves. Jesus uses the image of a burden tied to a slave's back; he must carry it, while those who put the burden on him do not help him at all.

The second accusation is that they are preoccupied with themselves and trying to draw attention to themselves. That is why they wear very large phylacteries (a kind of amulet, which was not, however, an expression of superstitious belief but was intended to remind them of God's law and their duty of observing it). They also wear long fringes on their garments (at the four corners of his cloak a Jew tied a kind of cord, which again was to be a reminder of the commandments of the Lord). They covet places of honor and the respectful salutations given to them. Above all, they love to be called "rabbi" or "teacher."

Jesus lists these faults in a straightforward and not un-ironic manner; he does so in order to inculcate in his disciples an attitude diametrically opposed to that of the Pharisees. St. Matthew may be reporting the words of Jesus as a lesson to those who exercised some authority in his community. Jesus himself is putting his disciples on guard chiefly against the last of the faults that he lists: the desire to be called "rabbi," with all that the title implies. Jesus' disciples are not to let themselves be called rabbi, because they are all brothers and have only one true teacher, Christ, just as they all have but one Father. In consequence, the greatest among them is to be the servant of all (see page 271). The passage ends with a saying we have already met: "Whoever exalts himself will be humbled, and whoever humbles himself will be exalted."

Watering down the law (Mal. 1:14b–2:2b, 8-10)

Once again, the liturgy of this day chooses a text, not for its own sake and on its own terms, as an exegete would who takes into consideration the whole rich context of the passage, but in order to highlight what the Gospel of the day teaches concerning those who have authority in the Church.

From the opening words, the passage is a stern reproach to the priests who do not observe the law but impose it on others. But if they do not take seriously their obligation of glorifying the name of the Lord, the Lord will turn his very blessings into a curse. These men have made of the law, not a guide that would help men to live aright, but a stumbling block for the multitude; by so doing, they have perverted the covenant. The prophet Osee had earlier uttered the same reproach against the priestly caste: "Because you have rejected knowledge, I reject you from being a priest to me" (Osee 4:6; cf. vv. 4-6).

God alone is Father, and sole Father of all, because he created all. His fatherhood is the basis of unity with God and each other in the community that is the people of God. Brothers and sisters must not be faithless to one another. The text is probably alluding to divorce, or marriage with a woman who worships pagan gods, or something of the kind. The liturgy today simply reads the text in the light of the Gospel and is uninterested in such allusions.

Give the Good News and your very self (1 Thess. 2:7-9, 13)

The whole of Paul's teaching has the Good News, the gospel, for its focus. The man who teaches must communicate not his own teaching but that of Jesus. This teaching, moreover, cannot remain purely conceptual; an apostle must give himself along with the Good News, putting his own person on the line both by practicing what he preaches and by showing great concern for the members of his community.

The Letter to the Thessalonians uses a number of expressions that are rather rare elsewhere in St. Paul's writings. We sense that he is filled with enthusiasm and tender affection for the Thessalonians, who probably have shown a great change in their lives since their contract with him. He reminds them that he gave himself to them without reserve in his preaching and how he treated them as would a nurse that is wholly concerned for the children she must nourish and educate. He even goes on to say explicitly why he is so happy with the Thessalonians: they received the word of God from him for what it really was — not a man's word but God's word at work in them. But in all this Paul feels no personal elation or pride, since all the good he accomplished has been the work of God's grace.

In the ecclesial community all have priestly responsibility, but of different kinds and degrees. The layperson as such is responsible for the reign of brotherly love in the community and for the advancement of each and all. The responsibility requires laypeople to be upright and not to lead a kind of double life in which, on the one hand, they follow Christian practices, but, on the other, show a lack of charity and mutual love as they push their way to the first places, even in Christian organizations that are devoted to work for the good of the community. The temptation to Pharisaism exists even there!

The teaching of today's liturgy is, however, addressed first and foremost to those who are appointed to teach others and have a priestly responsibility in the narrower sense. The sometimes very harsh and often unjust attacks upon the Church with regard to these people are a trial indeed, but they can also be for her the occasion of a searching examination of conscience. None of us live lives that are perfectly in accord with what we teach or profess; that will doubtless be the case until the end of time, and we cannot require that a priest or catechist be perfect. But the people do have the right to expect that their spiritual leaders will at least be seeking holiness, not so much for their own sake as for the sake of those whose welfare has been entrusted to them.

The service of the community should come before everything else. Ostensibly people look less for honors nowadays, and persons of rank are less concerned about titles, yet pride evidently makes its way in by other and more subtle paths. Many have no desire to be called "rabbi," but they do claim to be teaching "their own" doctrine, and it is not always the doctrine of the gospel and the Church. This kind of self-assertion often lurks behind a façade of democracy or even bohemianism and an external attitude of hail-fellow-well-met; it is simply a new kind of pride and self-sufficiency.

It is not always easy to preach the gospel objectively and to be faithful to teaching that makes its authoritative demands upon us. The lesson of today's liturgy is that we must all honestly review our inner attitudes and not be too ready to believe that the reproaches of Jesus are irrelevant to us moderns.

THIRTY-SECOND SUNDAY

Watch and Wait

Watch, for you know not the day or the hour (Matthew 25:1-13)

The parable contains only the essential points needed for the story. Thus Jesus has deliberately omitted any description of a wedding as celebrated in his day. Doubtless, in accordance with almost universal usage, the bridegroom would come to the young girl's home in order to claim her and take her to his house.

In what sense is one group of virgins "foolish" and the other "wise"? The first reading helps us to an answer. The "wise" virgin's wisdom is not primarily a human wisdom but a wisdom born of meditation on the mysteries of God and, in this context, specifically on the mysteries of the kingdom. The lamp symbolizes this wisdom that must be cultivated by meditation, reflection, and one's way of life.

Such wisdom does not come in a day. The person must know how to wait (the bridegroom does not come immediately), to store up wisdom, and to keep her lamp properly trimmed. The symbolism of the parable is crystal-clear.

The bridegroom comes at night. In the Scriptures, the night is the time of God's comings, according to a tradition that reaches back into earliest Hebrew history. Thus it is in the night that the Lord liberates his people (Exod. 11:4; 12:12, 19). To some, the night and the Lord's coming bring salvation; to others, such as the Egyptians, they bring death. When the New Testament looks forward to the return of Christ, it regularly thinks of it as occurring in the night (Luke 12:39-40; Matthew 24:43-44; Mark 13:35-36; Luke 12:20).

Those who wait must not sleep but keep vigil, for the bridegroom comes unexpectedly (Matthew 24:27; Luke 17:24).

The theme of the "door" is also full of meaning. We know how the New Testament makes use of the theme: it tells us that we must "enter by the narrow door" (Luke 13:24; cf. Matthew 7:13). We recall, too, that when the destroying angel passed over Egypt, a mark was left on the doorposts of the Hebrews so that they might be spared.

Vigil, night, door — these are paschal themes, connected with liberation and entry into the kingdom. In today's parable the door is closed against the virgins who did not keep vigil and did not trim their lamps properly. Their cries are usless; the hour for the feast has come, and they are excluded. The moral admits of no exceptions: "Watch, therefore, for you know neither the day nor the hour."

Watch, and find wisdom (Wis. 6:12-16)

The first reading describes wisdom in poetic terms. Its theme is that our entire lives should be spent in pursuit of wisdom.

Wisdom is easily discerned by those who love her, and she may readily be found by those who seek her, because she is radiant and visible. It is worth looking for her, because she is unfading. Such are the fundamental attributes of wisdom. This wisdom is not an esoteric doctrine reserved for an elite, but something within the reach of all, provided they are willing to seek her out. When men do search for her, she takes the initiative and presents herself to them; they will find her sitting at their door if they rise early to seek her. The quest of wisdom should be the main preoccupation of a human being; we should think only of her and be watchful on her account.

Without going so far as to regard this wisdom as a person,

the Church has seen in her a prefiguration of Christ and his grace. It is not hard to see the justification for such a transposition. Wisdom, Christ, grace — all three seek out those who are worthy of them; all three graciously appear to men and meet them at every point; all three present themselves whenever we think of them.

Psalm 63, the responsorial psalm, sings of God as the object of man's desire and search: "O God, thou art my God, I seek thee, my soul thirsts for thee. . . . I think of thee upon my bed, and meditate on thee in the watches of the night; for thou hast been my help, and in the shadow of thy wings I sing for joy."

The Church uses this same passage of the Gospel for the Common of Virgins. We may note, too, that the symbolism of the Gospel passage reoccurs elsewhere, inasmuch as the Church gives the newly baptized a candle that they are to keep lit in their lives.

During vigils, and especially during the Paschal Vigil, the Church thinks unceasingly of Christ, her Spouse, who will come to lead her into his kingdom. The chief concern of the Church, therefore, is that the faithful should keep their lamps lit and never be caught by surprise at Christ's coming to them. The chief concern of the faithful should be to seek the wisdom and light of Christ and to keep ever alight the lamp they received at baptism so that with Christ they may enter the banquet hall of the kingdom.

God will bring forth those who have fallen asleep in Jesus (1 Thess. 4:13-18)

St. Paul is trying to instill hope into the Christians of Thessalonika. His message, in brief, is that the resurrection of Christ is what gives meaning to every Christian life, and that God will take to himself those who have died with Christ. We died with Christ in baptism; we shall also share his resurrection.

The confusion in the minds of the Thessalonians provides Paul with an occasion for describing what will happen at the end of time. He works with images, but his point is clear. His essential teaching is that all, whether already dead or still living when Christ comes, will be taken up with Christ into glory.

This teaching will evidently be comforting only to those who have a deep faith in Jesus and his resurrection. It is a source of strength to those who are trying to live in union with the Lord and who want to reach the goal of all human life: perfect union with God. Quite often people think of the resurrection simply as a matter of personal survival and turn it into an end in itself. They forget that we put on Christ in baptism in order that we might glorify the Father by being restored to what his creatures were intended to be, and more.

The resurrection of all mankind and their appearance before the Lord will put an end to the history of the world. St. Paul looks upon this great event without fear and even regards it as the greatest possible source of strength to man in his earthly life as he sees his dear ones die and is compelled to ask himself what life is all about. Paul's answer to the questions of the Thessalonians is permanently valid.

THIRTY-THIRD SUNDAY

Fidelity To Duty and Work

You have been faithful in small things: enter into the joy of your Lord (Matthew 25:14-30)

If we look to the basic meaning of the first and third readings for this day, it is difficult to connect them, even in a broad fashion. Why, then, was this particular reading from the Old Testament selected? If, on the other hand, we allow the first reading to determine what the major point of the third reading should be in the context of this celebration, the connection is much clearer. We have here, then, another example of a liturgical reading of the Scriptures as distinct from a strictly exegetical reading.

Were we to approach the Gospel pericope as exegetes and situate it in its context in St. Matthew's Gospel, we would have to say that the central point being made is the need of watchfulness and the need of making the money produce interest before the master returns. Yet the first reading has nothing to say about watchfulness or the Lord's return. In that reading, the main concern is with the fruits produced by the toil of a worthy wife. It seems then that on this Sunday the emphasis should be on fidelity and on dedication to duty and work. This does not prevent us, of course, from putting this fidelity and dedication into the perspective of the Lord's return and of watchfulness in preparation for the last day.

The evangelists at times report a parable of Jesus but interpret it to meet the needs of their faithful who find themselves in a new situation. Why should not the Church be able to do the same in the liturgy of the word, so as to meet the needs of today's faithful?

There is no point in discussing the details of the parable; the main lines of it alone are of interest to us. Certainly the parable is as rich in instruction for the Church of our day as it was for the first Christian communities. The entire emphasis is on the service every Christian owes to God. Because he is a servant, it is his duty to make profitable use of the gifts given him for the good of the community and the kingdom. The parable makes it very clear that it is not enough simply to give the gift back to God in the form in which we received it.

At times we run into Christians who think of their Christian life in terms of a strict contract between God and themselves: "I observe strictly what the commandments require of me; I do not see why I should do more." This attitude is perhaps more common than we think, even if it is rarely expressed in such a cold and forthright way. There is a kind of Christian minimalism that takes refuge in the commandments of God and of the Church. Again we find people at times who are willing to develop only a favorite talent, and then for their own sake, not the sake of the community.

The master's answer prevents all possibility of misunderstanding: We are all servants and have no choice in the matter. It is not enough for us to preserve what was entrusted to us; we must make it bear fruit in the service of God and others. The baptismal grace that has made us adopted sons and daughters must grow and may not simply be left in its original state; we may legitimately aspire to intensify it, because that is our duty.

Such an attitude is inspired by love and gratitude. It springs also from our awareness that we are called to collaborate in spreading God's kingdom and preparing for the unexpected coming of Christ.

A worthy wife is a precious jewel (Prov. 31:10-13, 19-20, 30-31)

Our contemporaries should not be displeased by this fine portrait of an ideal woman, and yet the liturgy is not interested in the advancement of women. What the liturgy concentrates on is the skills the woman places at the service of the community; it is for these that she wins the praise of all who experience the fruits of them. Her foresight, her ability, her charity to others make her a model of these qualities; she does not let her talents lie fallow but uses them for the good of all.

Although it is not entirely easy to interpret the readings within the overall framework of the Sunday, today's liturgy of the word has its value. It urges persevering work upon those to whom the Lord has given talents for the good of the human community and the Church. Above all, it reminds every Christian of his duty to rise above a trades-

man's ideal of the Christian life. A Christian cannot be
satisfied with the minimum required of him but should
seek to make his gifts bear as much fruit as possible.
Otherwise he may see taken from him the minimum he
sought to preserve with little effort and little love.

If we are watchful and sober, we will not be taken by surprise (1 Thess. 5:1-6)

The expression "Day of the Lord" has become unfamiliar
to the modern Christian; he may never even have heard it.
Yet it is a word with specifically Christian connotations and
should be a source of specifically Christian attitudes.

The Gospels have made us familiar with a day of the
Lord (Amos had spoken of it long before: 5:18-20) that is
terrifying and will, according to Jesus, come suddenly like a
thief in the night (Matthew 24:43; Luke 12:30). The world
goes its way unthinkingly, as though the Day of the Lord
would never come. St. Paul reminds the Thessalonians of
what Jesus had said before him. But a true Christian needs
no reminder; he will not be taken by surprise, since his
whole life is a vigil, an expectation of Christ's return. The
baptized person no longer is part of the world of darkness;
he is a child of the light and the day. As such, he must
always be vigilant, and this watchfulness requires detachment so that he may be ready for Christ's coming.

St. Paul's teaching here moves beyond anything our imaginations might suggest to us about the last day and the
parousia. It speaks of the true meaning of Christian life,
which is wholly directed toward the Day of the Lord. Because we do not keep this Day in view, we concentrate
rather self-centeredly on our own death. Because we do not
keep in mind the final victory that Christ will share with his
disciples, we get distorted value judgments about the
things of this world and give them an undue importance.

THIRTY-FOURTH SUNDAY

Christ, King of the Universe

The Son of Man, the shepherd who will separate the sheep from the goats (Matthew 25:31-46)

The liturgical year ends with a vision of glory. The final retribution of man's deeds is part of the picture, and it may be, at times, that the inclusion of the judgment hides somewhat the glorious splendor of the coming of the Son of Man.

Let us leave aside the literary problem posed by the description of the Son of Man's triumph and go directly to what St. Matthew wishes to teach us in this passage. If we read the text in an objective manner and if we listen to it proclaimed in the Lord's behalf or, more accurately, by the Lord himself today, it seems clear that the judgment rendered by the King of glory is based solely on love. His norm of judgment is: "As you did it to one of the least of these my brethren, you did it to me." Here the Lord sets down only one requirement for entering his kingdom: love of neighbor.

How are we to take the expression, "the least of these my brethren"? The meaning of the love required for entering the kingdom depends on the object of the love, and Christ here seems to rank the object quite low, as it were. It is difficult to identify these "least" who are Christ's brethren. In St. Matthew, as in the other New Testament writers, the term "brother" is applied to members of the ecclesial community (Matthew 18:15, 21, 35; 23:8). However, the word is also applied in a much broader sense to include all human beings (Matthew 5:22-24; 7:3-4). Finally, the disciples, too, are called "brothers" (Matthew 12:50; 28:10).

In our text the expression is even more specific: "the least of these *my* brethren." In this case there can be no

doubt that the disciples are meant. This is confirmed by
other passages: "And stretching out his hand toward his
disciples, he said, 'Here are my mother and my brothers!'"
(Matthew 12:49); "Go and tell my brethren to go to Galilee,
and there they will see me" (Matthew 28:10).

In what sense are they "the least" or "the little ones"?
The expression is one used elsewhere of the disciples, although it can also be applied to Christians generally. It may
help to look quickly at the other texts in which St. Matthew
uses the expression. "He who is least in the kingdom of
heaven is greater than he [John the Baptist]" (11:11). Jesus
is here speaking of John the Baptist, whom he calls the
greatest of those born of woman. In this greatest-least comparison, the reference is really not to the person of the Pre-
cursor himself. Rather, two situations are being compared:
before the coming of the kingdom and after the coming of
the kingdom. The person — any person — who belongs to
the kingdom is in an entirely new situation; the time of the
kingdom is superior to all that went before. "I thank thee,
Father, Lord of heaven and earth, that thou hast hidden
these things from the wise and understanding and revealed
them to babes" (Matthew 11:25). In this context "babes" or
"little ones" evidently means the poor and the lowly. (In
another context — "Do not despise one of these little ones.
. . . It is not the will of my Father who is in heaven that one
of these little ones should perish": Matthew 18:10-14 —
"little ones" clearly means "children.")

There is another text that will prove even more en-
lightening: "whoever gives to one of these little ones even
a cup of cold water because he is a disciple . . ." (Matthew
10:42). The sense is clear. We are at the end of the missionary discourse, and Jesus has just said to his disciples: "He
who receives you receives me, and he who receives me receives him who sent me. He who receives a prophet because he is a prophet shall receive a prophet's reward, and
he who receives a righteous man because he is a righteous
man shall receive a righteous man's reward" (10:40-41). As
in the text of today's Gospel, the context is one of retribu-

tion and of attitudes to envoys. "And whoever gives to one
of these little ones even a cup of cold water because he is a
disciple, truly, I say to you, he shall not lose his reward"
(10:42). The equivalence of "little one" and "disciple" is
evident. Men are to welcome the disciples in the name of
Christ.

It is clear that a homily which emphasizes exclusively the
requirement of love and the need of openness to others is
leaving out some important factors and is likely to give a
false impression. The point of the passage is that we must
receive the messengers of Christ, who are in fact other
Christs; it is to Christ that we give the glass of water when
we give it to his messenger. The attitude being inculcated
is not only one of charity but one of receptivity that is based
on faith. We are to receive not only the person sent by
Christ but his word and teaching as well.

The Lord will judge between sheep and sheep (Ezek. 34:11-12, 15-17)

We must not lose sight of the purpose of today's readings.
All deal primarily with a king who comes to judge. He is
however a king and a judge who has no match on earth. He
is not content to acquit or condemn, but is concerned
chiefly to save and give rest. He is a judge who searches for
the lost sheep; he cares for the wounded sheep and restores
the strength of the sheep that has grown weak. Such a
shepherd is the Lord who comes on the last day; he is the
truest of all shepherds. His judgment justifies men and establishes justice once more.

We Christians know that our sacramental life is preparing
us for the judgment that the King of shepherds will render.
God has prepared a place for us, and we advance toward it
without fear. "The Lord is my shepherd, I shall not want;
he makes me lie down in green pastures" (Psalm 23).

The final reign of the glorious Christ (1 Cor. 15:20-26, 28)

This passage is part of St. Paul's instruction on the resurrection of the dead. In it he speaks of a kind of great apocalypse. We are given a grandiose fresco of the resurrection in which, in Christ, all rise, but in proper order. Then comes the grand finale, when Christ hands over his royal power to the Father, after having finished his work by destroying the last of the enemy powers. Now God is all in all.

This handing over of power to the Father does not mean that Christ's kingship is a temporary condition and ceases when history comes to its end. These statements of Paul are rather a way of saying that all of Christ's activity and even his paschal mystery have no other purpose than to make God the head of all creation once again. The kingdom of God is now fully established.

We may not be well prepared for understanding today's readings; their style may be unfamiliar to us. Nonetheless, the teaching of Matthew and Paul to their communities remains relevant to us today. The time of the Church and the historical time allotted to each of us derive their meaning from the judgment that will come at the end of time, when all things will finally be subjected to God's royal power. We must spend the time given us in loving God and man, in receiving his word and those who proclaim it, and living in expectation of the final judgment. We must also bear in mind, however, that this final judgment is primarily a justification of man and the act by which the world's reconstruction is completed, and not primarily a condemnation of the wicked. We must endeavor to live with loving faith, heeding those whom Christ sends us and putting their words into practice.

SUNDAYS NINE TO THIRTY-FOUR
IN ORDINARY TIME

CYCLE B

Years 1979, 1982, 1985, 1988, 1991

TABLE OF SUNDAY READINGS

In the following table, the general theme of each celebration and the particular theme of each reading are indicated. If the second reading is connected with the general theme of the day, it will be commented on together with the first reading and the Gospel (these second readings are marked by an asterisk in the following list). If the second reading does not fit in with the theme of the day, a heavy line separates the commentary given from the preceding.

Comment on Sundays one to nine in ordinary time may be found in volume one, pages 308-311; 332-432.

CYCLE B
Years 1979, 1982, 1985, 1988, 1991

Sunday 9   The meaning of the Sabbath
           Mark 2:23–3:6   Jesus, Lord of the Sabbath
           Deut. 5:12-15   The Sabbath, a holy day
           2 Cor. 4:6-11   The life of Jesus manifested in our bodies

Sunday 10 Evil overcome
           Mark 3:20-35   Satan conquered
           Gen. 3:9-15   The promise of victory
           *2 Cor. 4:13–5:1   We believe, and so we speak

Sunday 11 Growth of the kingdom
           Mark 4:26-34   The seed sprouts
           Ezek. 17:22-24   The tree planted by God
           2 Cor. 5:6-10   Pleasing the Lord

Sunday 12 Lord of the world
           Mark 4:35-41   The wind and the sea obey him
           Job 38:1, 8-11   Here shall your proud waves be stayed
           2 Cor. 5:14-17   A new world

Sunday 13   God, Author of life
Mark 5:21-43
Wis. 1:13-15; 2:23-24
2 Cor. 8:7, 9, 13-15

     I say to you, arise
God did not make death
Give what you have received

Sunday 14   The prophet rejected
Mark 6:1-6
Ezek. 2:2-5
2 Cor. 12:7-10

     A prophet without honor
A people impudent and stubborn
Strength in weakness

Sunday 15   Chosen and sent
Mark 6:7-13
Amos 7:12-15
*Eph. 1:3-14

     The Twelve are chosen and sent
Prophesy to my people Israel
Chosen before the creation of the world

Sunday 16   The flock gathered
Mark 6:30-34
Jer. 23:1-6
*Eph. 2:13-18

     Sheep without a shepherd
The shepherd gathers the remnant of the flock
Brought near in the blood of Christ

Sunday 17   We are filled with the bread of God
John 6:1-15
2 Kings 4:42-44
Eph. 4:1-6

     The multiplication of the loaves
They shall eat and have some left
One body, one Lord, one faith, one baptism

Sunday 18	Believe, then hunger and thirst no more	
	John 6:24-35	Go to Christ and you will not hunger or thirst
	Exod. 16:2-4, 12-15	A rain of bread
	Eph. 4:17, 20-24	Live as a new man

Sunday 19	The bread that has come down from heaven	
	John 6:41-51	I am the living bread
	1 Kings 19:4-8	In the strength of that food
	Eph. 4:30—5:2	Walk in love, as Christ loved us

Sunday 20	Eat the Bread, drink the Wine, and live forever	
	John 6:51-58	My flesh is food indeed and my blood is drink indeed
	Prov. 9:1-6	Come, eat of my bread
	Eph. 5:15-20	Understand what the will of the Lord is

Sunday 21	Live with the Lord whose words are spirit and life	
	John 6:60-69	To whom shall we go?
	Josh. 24:1-2a, 15-17, 18b	Die rather than abandon the Lord
	Eph. 5:21-32	This is a great mystery, Christ and the Church

Sunday 22	Keep the commandments of the Lord	
	Mark 7:1-8, 14-15, 21-23	Commandments of God and traditions of men
	Deut. 4:1-2, 6-8	Observe the commandments of the Lord
	*James 1:17-18, 21b-22, 27	Act on the word

Sunday 23   The messianic age
            Mark 7:31-37   He makes the deaf hear and the dumb speak
            Is. 35:4-7a   The ears of the deaf shall be unstopped, and
                                  the tongue of the dumb shall sing for joy
            James 2:1-5   The poor shall inherit the kingdom

Sunday 24   The sufferings of the Servant of God
            Mark 8:27-35   The Son of Man must suffer much
            Is. 50:5-9a   I gave my back to the smiters
            James 2:14-18   Faith without works

Sunday 25   The Son of Man handed over to men
            Mark 9:30-37   The Son of Man betrayed to men
            Wis. 2:12, 17-20   Condemned to a shameful death
            James 3:16–4:3   Peacemakers

Sunday 26   Preach and heal in the Lord's name
            Mark 9:38-43, 45, 47-48   Cast out demons in the name of the Lord
            Num. 11:25-29   May the Lord make everyone a prophet!
            James 5:1-6   The corruption of riches

Sunday 27   The unity of the human couple
             Mark 10:2-16   Let man not separate what God has joined
             Gen. 2:18-24   The two shall now be one
             Heb. 2:9-11   Men made holy are the brothers of Jesus

Sunday 28   Abandon all you have
             Mark 10:17-30   Sell what you have and follow Jesus
             Wis. 7:7-11   Regard riches as worthless
             Heb. 4:12-13   The living word of God

Sunday 29   The life of Christ, a ransom for the many
             Mark 10:35-45   The Son of Man gives his life for the many
             Is. 53:10-11   The Servant will justify many
             *Heb. 4:14-16   Jesus, the High Priest, has been tested

Sunday 30   Messianic signs and faith
             Mark 10:46-52   Lord, let me see!
             Jer. 31:7-9   The blind and the lame will be consoled
             Heb. 5:1-6   Jesus, a Priest for ever

Sunday 31	The great commandment	No greater commandment than love of others
	Mark 12:28b-34	You shall love the Lord with all your heart
	Deut. 6:2-6	The eternal priesthood of Christ
	Heb. 7:23-28	
Sunday 32	Give what you have to obtain life	
	Mark 12:38-44	The poor widow has given more than all the others
	1 Kings 17:10-16	The widow gives what food she has
	Heb. 9:24-28	The unique sacrifice of Christ
Sunday 33	The last days	
	Mark 13:24-32	The elect, gathered from the four quarters of the world
	Dan. 12:1-3	He comes to save his people
	Heb. 10:11-14, 18	Having offered his sacrifice, Jesus leads to perfection those he has sanctified
Sunday 34	Christ's rule over the universe	
	John 18:33b-37b	As you say, I am a king
	Dan. 7:13-14	To him was given dominion and glory and kingdom
	*Apoc. 1:5-8	Ruler of kings on earth

NINTH SUNDAY

The Meaning of the Sabbath

Jesus, Lord of the Sabbath (Mark 2:23–3:6)

The evangelists found it necessary to take up the question of the meaning of the Sabbath, since at times (as is the case with St. Matthew, for example) their readers were Jewish Christians. The latter, while celebrating Sunday, also observed the Sabbath, at least in the early days of the Church. (We should not forget that down to the fourth century all Christians worked on Sunday; the day of rest for them, as for everyone else, was Saturday.) The evangelists were also addressing gentile converts to Christianity, for whom the Jewish Sabbath observances would be of little if any intrinsic interest; yet the question of the Sabbath was in fact of concern even to them, inasmuch as they, no less than the Jewish Christians, could slip into a legalistic mentality when it came to outward observances.

St. Mark's position is quite clear: The Sabbath is made for man, not man for the Sabbath. He would find no difficulty in coming out with such a straightforward statement, since his Gospel was meant for converts from paganism, not for Jewish Christians. Some exegetes have maintained that Jesus himself did not utter these words about the Sabbath; they could be more easily uttered at a later date, and especially in a community of former pagans.

The two stories told in today's pericope — the disciples plucking grain on the Sabbath, and Jesus curing the man with the withered hand on the Sabbath — create a conflict between Jesus and the Pharisees. Consequently, they provide an opportunity for him to voice his mind about the Sabbath and the Jewish attitude toward it.

We must not, however, exaggerate the difference between the position of Jesus and that of the Pharisees. Nowhere does Jesus show contempt for the Sabbath; nowhere does he tell men not to observe it; nowhere does he speak of celebrating some other day of the week. Moreover he tells us that he came to fulfill the law, not to abolish it. In fact, when we read the present passage from St. Mark's Gospel, our impression is that it is telling us of something far more important than a conflict between Jesus and the Pharisees.

"The Son of man is lord even of the sabbath" (Mark 2:28). The Lord, however, is above the law. Consequently, while the Sabbath was instituted so that man might honor the Lord while contemplating the Lord's great deeds at leisure, and while the weekly rest was instituted for that same purpose and so that work might be interrupted and the family strengthened, the Lord himself is above this law that he instituted in man's behalf. In fact, anything bearing directly on the very life of man himself is more important than the law. Where healing is required or charity is called for, the law can and should be set aside.

This amounts to saying that Christ is not destroying or abolishing the Sabbath law; he is simply telling men how it is to be applied. Did those present on this occasion understand what Christ meant by calling himself Lord even of the Sabbath? Did they understand that life is more important than the observance of the letter of the law? It seems they did understand, and yet could not accept Christ's principles. Instead, they go off to find the Herodians and plot the destruction of Jesus.

The Sabbath, a holy day (Deut. 5:12-15)

It is evident from this text that a social and religious law was being established. The Jewish people had experienced enslavement in Egypt. Now that they were free, they were being given a weekly opportunity to recoup their strength at two levels or in two ways: as weak human beings, by enjoying a weekly rest they had not known in Egypt; as a chosen people, by strengthening the bonds of a community that had God for its center, and this by adoring him for his wonderful deeds and for all he had done for his people. The new institution was thus both social and cultic.

The Sabbath and its observance has always been a distinguishing mark of Judaism. At times we outsiders have been overly critical of the Jewish Sabbath observances. The observances are a fact and the pious Jew respects them, but the important point for the Jew is not the observances as such, but the worship of God, the development of community and family, and respect for the poor, whom the Jew visits on the afternoon of the Sabbath. The biblical theology of the Sabbath, as understood by the devout Jew, is altogether admirable and can be totally integrated into our theology of Sunday, even though the Christian Sunday is in no sense simply a transposed Jewish Sabbath.[16]

To the Jew, the Sabbath is the feast that celebrates his liberation. It is a kind of weekly Passover and recalls the Exodus from Egypt and the liberation from bondage. The Sabbath is the day of the man who has been freed.

The texts read on this Sunday are extremely important. It is a paradox that in our day the people with the most legalistic attitude toward the weekly observance are the Christians. Observant Jews have a very rich theology of the Sabbath. They are not content to abstain from work but engage in fervent public and private prayer, and do works of mercy, such as visiting the sick. The Sabbath reminds them of how they became a people after the liberation from Egypt and the re-establishment of the nation.

Some Christians tend to be much more legalistic, seeing only the obligatory practices. And yet Sunday is not simply a transposition of the Jewish Sabbath; in fact, as we have already pointed out, Sunday rest was possible and prescribed only in 357, under Emperor Constantine. What Sunday should be for the Christian is a summons to center his life once again on the fact that he has been freed by

Christ's resurrection, on the building of a new world and of God's kingdom, and on the expectation of the last day.

The celebration of the Eucharist, which actualizes the paschal mystery, does not exhaust the positive side of Sunday. To the Eucharist must be added the effort to perfect the domestic community, the parish community (or the group), and our awareness of others, of the sick, the poor, the lonely. Sunday has unfortunately lost much of its meaning for the Christian. The Christian ought not be described by others as someone who "goes to Mass," but as someone for whom Sunday is a day of prayer, a day of community, a day of charity.

—————

The life of Jesus manifested in our bodies (2 Cor. 4:6-11)

We are familiar by now with the difficulties Paul met in his relations with the Corinthians. He found in them a kind of pretentious intellectualism and a quite pronounced philosophical pride. This was serious enough, but it was accompanied by a pride in relation to faith and to preaching. In short, the whole community of Corinth was permeated by a pride that Paul wished to correct. It is this situation that accounts for the somewhat pessimistic tone of his Second Letter.

We carry a treasure — the light that the Lord has given us — but we carry it in worthless earthen vessels. The preacher, then, is simply a spokesman for the Lord. Yet, as a spokesman and authentic witness, he should make the life of Jesus manifest in his very body. The Corinthians, however, were tempted to focus their attention entirely on the resurrection and glorification of Christ, and to reject everything else. They were tempted, that is, to move apart into their own world, but it was an illusory world without weakness, temptation, and suffering. They thought of themselves as a group of chosen souls who lived solely by the Spirit and the resurrection of Christ. They ended up making the world of the Cross and the world of the resurrection contradictory to each other.

St. Paul puts things into proper perspective. The preacher bears witness in his very body to the *kenosis*, or "emptying," of Christ, to the humiliation of the Cross and Passion and suffering. But it is this Passion, this suffering, that actually gives life. That is why Paul can say to the community of Corinth: You seem to be rich, and think you are already living in the kingdom and by the Spirit; I, for my part, live in weakness and poverty, but through the suffering of Christ I bring life, I even bring life to you.

We must not, of course, turn the letter into something it is not meant to be, and require that every preacher of the gospel bear all the marks of suffering of which Paul speaks. On the other hand, we ought to read the passage in the light of the community and the Church today. As it confronts the modern world, should not the community and the Church show that it bears the marks of Christ's sufferings and that it is a life-giving community and Church? The contrast between world and Church can only be where Paul puts it: I (community, Church) am weak, suffering, and afflicted, but I actively accept this lot in order to bring you life.

There are many conclusions to be drawn from such an attitude on the part of the Church, and it would be worthwhile for contemporary society to draw them. But it can do so only if the Church does manifest the signs Paul lists and in which he sees the source of life for the community at Corinth.

TENTH SUNDAY

Evil Overcome

Satan conquered (Mark 3:20-35)

Two incidents, unconnected in themselves, come together in this pericope. Jesus' friends and family come to
seize him; there is an interruption as Jesus is forced to answer those who accuse him of expelling demons by the
power of Beelzebul; finally, the incident of the family's
coming is concluded. But though the two incidents seem
unrelated, there is in fact a certain link between them, as
we shall see.

Obviously, the miracles that Jesus worked could not pass
unnoticed, and the publicity disturbed the scribes and the
family of Jesus himself. He was increasingly surrounded by
crowds of people, so much so that he and his disciples
could not even eat in the house of which Mark often speaks
and in which Jesus lived when he was at Capharnaum. It
was especially the exorcisms Jesus practiced that drew the
attention of the religious leaders. In Jewish thinking, authority over demons, such as Christ possessed, could come
either from God, as a power given by him to one of his
messengers, or from the devil. The crowds are more credu-
lous and incline, without thinking much about it, toward
the first solution: A man who expels demons and works so
many miracles can only be sent by God. The leaders and
scribes are of another mind, and they show it in this passage.

Jesus' answer amounts to an assertion that he has been
sent by God. He does not answer the question directly, but
his argument leads indirectly to a description of what he
truly is. In his reply he uses two examples: the kingdom
divided against itself, and the strong man's house.

The kingdom and the family divided. The answer, Jesus
is saying, is quite simple: If Beelzebul, the prince of de-

mons, expels demons, then Satan's kingdom is at odds with itself, and he has lost the struggle. If the enemy is at odds with himself, he will surely lose the battle. Satan's "house" or family, according to the scribes, is bent on destroying itself!

The strong man's house. No one can enter a strong man's house and steal his possessions without first binding the strong man. That is what Jesus is doing. Satan is the strong man who has taken possession of the world, and Jesus is binding Satan so as to recover the world from him. As of now, Satan's rule is coming to an end; that is the point of the exorcisms. The Messiah is now here, and the new kingdom, foretold by John the Baptist, has begun.

The scribes, for their part, are "guilty of an eternal sin," because, despite the various proofs Jesus has already given of his being sent by God, they refuse to believe. Not only do they refuse to believe, but they accuse Jesus of doing what he does with the help of an impure spirit. They thus commit a serious and unforgivable sin of blasphemy. For by refusing to accept God's messenger, they refuse salvation. Such a refusal, springing as it does not from weakness but from a perverse heart and bad faith, cannot be forgiven; it is an eternal sin.

At this point Mark returns to Jesus' family, which is looking for him. His mother, Mary, is there. St. Mark names her first, as he always does when the Blessed Virgin comes on the scene with others. We need not put any special emphasis on the phrase "your brothers," since it is a known fact that among the Semites, "brothers" could be cousins or other relatives as well as blood brothers. Thus, in the Gospel itself, St. Matthew calls James and Joseph the brothers of Jesus (Matthew 13:55), although they are the sons of a Mary who is not the mother of Jesus (Matthew 27:56).

Jesus' reply with regard to his mother and brothers might suggest that they do not do the Father's will. In fact, Jesus is saying nothing of the sort. They are not excluded when he looks around and says: "Whoever does the will of God is my brother, and sister, and mother." He thus shows how close a bond is forged between himself, the Father's messenger, and those who do God's will.

Is this passage relevant to us today? It is, for though we may think quite differently of the devil today (short of denying his existence), it is certainly not possible to ignore the forces that are constantly assembled in the struggle against the Church. It is a struggle in which the Church can hold her own because she knows Christ is with her; she knows that hell itself cannot triumph over her. This does not mean she enjoys a triumphalistic kind of security. She must always be on guard and she must purify herself each year (as one of the Lenten prayers says). In her sacramental ministry the Church carries on the work of Christ, but she is by no means to be equated *per se* with Christ.

The Church explicitly rejects all triumphalism. She is engaged in a constant struggle with the powers of evil. In that struggle she knows she can win; each of her members knows that at his side in the conflict stands the Leader who himself conquered temptation during the forty days he spent in the wilderness. What the disciple must do is live close to Christ; in order to do this, he must believe that Christ is God's messenger, and he must do the Father's will so that he too may be worthy of having Christ call him brother or sister.

The promise of victory (Gen. 3:9-15)

Everyone is familiar with the text and sufficiently knowledgeable about its literary character and about the essentials of its teaching. The account is a psychological and religious analysis of the phenomenon of temptation and sin, but it also contains a promise of victory. The victory will be God's victory, but it will be shared by man as well. A man may yield to the devil's tempting, but he will always receive the grace to overcome, with the weapons of Christ, the very demon who earlier led him astray. That statement describes the history of salvation in the constant experience of the Church. The Lord conquers sin through the action of sinful man; he conquers the forces of evil through man's very weakness.

The account in the Book of Genesis is grounds for optimism, once we read the Genesis story in the light of the Apocalypse, which describes the victory of the Lamb and the victory we too hope for at the end of time. The Church attributes to the Blessed Virgin a special place in the struggle and in the winning of the victory. Christ's incarnation, to which she gave her consent, brought us a Savior who shared all our struggles and sufferings, except for sin itself, and who conquered death by rising from the dead.

The response to the psalm (Ps. 130) sings of the victory over evil: "For with the Lord there is steadfast love, and with him is plenteous redemption" (Ps. 130:7).

We believe, and so we speak (2 Cor. 4:13–5:1)

The second reading, as we know, was not deliberately chosen to fit in with the other two readings. Nonetheless, it can, without forcing the meaning, be related to the others if we think of the major theme of the latter as being the victory over evil.

St. Paul tells us of his struggles and sufferings and weakness. The thing that keeps him going amid the trials that he accepts and offers up for the Corinthians is his faith in Christ as the risen Lord who has conquered death and evil. Paul believes that he himself will rise as Jesus did; both Paul and the readers for whom he offers his struggles will be with the Lord.

At the same time, Paul tells us, we must have a clear vision of what our present life means. Even if our outward self is undergoing decay, the interior man is being renewed each day. It is Christ — the Christ who while on earth expelled demons and conquered them for good through his Passion and death — that daily renews us interiorly. St. Paul is here sharing his own experience with us, and it is a valuable lesson for us.

Our basic need is the faith that will enable us to pass an

untroubled judgment in the discernment of true values and to see that the trials of the present time are little in comparison with the eternal glory for which they are preparing us. We must fix our gaze, not on what is visible, but on what is invisible and eternal. Christ's victory over the devil and evil is so great that our very bodies, though they are corrupted by sin and must be destroyed, will rise up and live forever.

It is this experience based on faith and this unshakable optimism that St. Paul wants to communicate to us.

ELEVENTH SUNDAY

The Growth of the Kingdom

The seed sprouts (Mark 4:26-34)

In today's Gospel reading, Jesus tells us two parables: the parable of the seed that a man sows and that grows without his knowing how; and the parable of the mustard seed, which is tiny yet produces a great tree. Then Jesus explains why he uses parables.

Two points in the parable of the seed call for our attention. One is that the seed in the ground develops through stages. The other is that when the sower has done his work, he pays no further attention to the seed but goes about his ordinary business; the seed grows without his intervention, which is called for again only at the harvest.

The lesson of this parable must have been clearer to Jesus' contemporaries than it is to us. For the image of the sickle would immediately remind them of Joel's prophecy concerning God's judgment (Joel 4:12-16).

While the seed is growing, the sower is inactive as far as

the seed is concerned; time passes without his paying any attention to the seed. What was Jesus' point in telling this parable? On the one hand, he wished to proclaim the judgment of God, which is evoked in the image of the sickle; he is saying that the kingdom is near. On the other hand, however, there is nothing in the parable itself to indicate this nearness. It must be, then, that in using the example of the sower, who, after sowing, patiently waits for the harvest, Jesus is putting us on guard against a wrong interpretation of the seeming silence of events as regards the kingdom. The seed indeed grows without the intervention of the sower, but the growth is a sure sign that the harvest is coming. The period in which the Lord seems disinterested in what he has sown is precisely the period preceding the harvest and the sudden coming of the kingdom.

The second parable, that of the mustard seed, is also found in Matthew (13:31-32) and in Luke (13:18-19). We are not interested here in the question of which account was historically the first. The way in which Mark presents the parable bids us attend to one point in particular: the fact that the tiniest seed becomes a shrub which is larger than all the others in the garden and in which the birds can make their nests. The tree is a sizable one if it can shelter the birds and their nests.

The tree has been taken as a sign of the kingdom and of the powerful king who protects his subjects. Thus the Book of Daniel speaks of a vision of a great tree in whose branches the birds of the air dwell; the tree represents King Nebuchodonosor (Dan. 4:9-27). The Book of Ezekiel likewise describes a great tree in which the birds of the air dwell; this tree represents the Egyptian Pharaoh (Ezek. 31:6). The point of Jesus' parable would thus be that the kingdom already prepared has a king and offers refuge to all who enter it. The kingdom of God grows slowly but is moving toward its majestic completion. The hearers of Jesus must grasp the importance of the time in which they are living. They are seeing the kingdom being prepared; the kingdom is growing, though the seed and the growth are hardly visible; for all its small beginnings, the kingdom is indeed coming in majesty.

But why does Jesus teach with the aid of parables? Mark tells us that in public Jesus spoke only in parables, but that in private he explained everything in detail to his disciples. This means that the parable differentiated what Jesus wants to say to others from what he wants to say to his disciples. Why so? Because the people of God have not accepted God's messenger and Jesus does not want to further blind a people who reject the light. Therefore he communicates God's message in such a way that only they who possess the key to the parables can understand it. This key Jesus gives only to the disciples, because they have followed him.

St. Mark is writing for the Church of his own day. The chosen people have by now rejected both the message and the messenger; it was this situation that led to the use of parables. In the prophet Isaiah, Mark finds evidence that such was God's will: Jesus speaks in parables "so that they may indeed see but not perceive, and may indeed hear but not understand; lest they should turn again, and be forgiven" (Mark 4:12, citing Is. 6:9-10). In other words, for Mark the use of the parable is a form of punishment inflicted by divine Providence, and a measure provoked by the attitude of the chosen people, who refuse to see. Because they refuse to see, everything is presented to them in parables that only those who have accepted Jesus in faith can understand.

The tree planted by God (Ezek. 17:22-24)

We mentioned this passage above as a parallel to the parable of the mustard seed that becomes a great tree. We need only read the whole passage in Ezekiel to see that the image is of a king who will come and protect his subjects. Is it worth the trouble of trying to pinpoint the precise identity of this king? Identifications have in fact been attempted, but it is not clear that the terms of the prophecy really apply to any of the persons selected. In any event, our concern is to look beyond the historical reference and see the prophecy of the Messiah and of a new kingdom.

The image of the tree is not used much in the New Testament, and yet when St. Mark does use it, we must think that he does not do so by chance. He chose it deliberately, and it serves very well Jesus' purpose in speaking to the crowds only in parables, whereas he was able to speak openly to his disciples.

Does the text have any meaning for us today? Yes it does, provided we take the parables as wholes and not get lost in details. An example of getting lost in a detail would be to emphasize the majestic size of the tree and to see in it the power of the Church; to think proudly of how the Church has developed and grown through the centuries and become a powerful body.

Two points about the parables seem of primary importance to me. One is the divine initiative in the extension of the kingdom; the other is the patience we need and the spiritual vision of events that occur in the Church.

Once the seed is planted, it develops. It is the Lord, however, who sustains and stimulates this development. He is the Sun who makes all plants germinate and grow. There are lessons to be drawn from the parable by the Church of today and each of us. The lesson is not, of course, that we are to neglect missionary activity and wait for God to do everything. The lesson is rather that we must have faith in the divine initiative, and look upon prayer and contemplation as more important than the effectiveness of our works. We have developed catechetical activities and techniques; the various works of the apostolate have made use of the modern means of communication. Yet the use of all these means has not produced spectacular results. Perhaps the fault is in our lack of the contemplative mentality and in our excessive trust in human means that are not supported by prayer.

The parables also invite us to wait patiently for the time of growth and for the harvest, and to learn how to judge aright the events that affect the Church. We sometimes get the impression that the Lord is not concerned about his Church, that he is absent. Our judgments on events are usually quite subjective; we are incapable of properly interpreting our experiences. And yet if we are indeed unable to read the meaning of events, the reason is simply that we are insufficiently contemplative. We are not spiritual enough, and so we interpret the difficulties the Church faces and the needs that must be met if the kingdom is to grow, as a politician or a businessman would interpret them. But the kingdom of God does not depend for its extension solely on our methods; divine Providence often judges things quite differently than we do. Only a humble, contemplative vision of reality can lead us to a proper judgment on what divine Providence is doing in the events God is using for the extension of his kingdom.

Pleasing the Lord (2 Cor. 5:6-10)

This reading tells us how we should conduct ourselves in our present life of faith. We walk in faith and do not see. We are, in fact, both far from the Lord, because we are still in the body, and near to him, because we believe.

Our aim must be to please the Lord. St. Paul links this intention of pleasing God with the final judgment, when everything will be revealed and each individual will receive what he has deserved by his actions while he was still in the body.

A text like this helps us to properly understand what Paul means when he says that we are saved by faith alone and not by works. We refer the reader to our earlier explanation on the ninth Sunday of Ordinary time. That we should be irreproachable on the day of judgment is another favorite theme of Paul's (see 1 Thess. 3:13; 5:23; 1 Cor. 1:8; Phil. 1:10). We must work for our salvation while being ever mindful of the judgment (Phil. 2:12), at which the Lord will reward each person according to his works (Rom. 2:6).

Paul presents the life of the Christian as lived in view of the last day. It is a life lived in the darkness of faith, a life in which, knowing as we do the real meaning of our existence, we seek in all things to please the Lord.

TWELFTH SUNDAY

Lord of the World

The wind and the sea obey him (Mark 4:35-41)

We would considerably subtract from the lesson contained in this reading if we were to see in it nothing but a demonstration of Christ's power over the elements. There is far more to the passage than that.

If we are to understand what the passage is saying, we must reflect on how the Scriptures think of water and the sea. In the Book of Genesis, the primeval waters must be tamed before the world can be created (Gen. 1:6-10). The Lord himself made the sea and all that is in it (Ps. 95:4; cf. Ps. 146:6; Amos 5:8; Jonah 1:9). He established its boundaries and shut it in with doors (Job 38:8); he assigned the sea its limits (Prov. 8:29).

The people of the Bible, many of them fisherfolk, loved the thought of the water which the Lord causes to exist and out of which (according to the cosmogony of antiquity) so many animals emerge; the water that the Lord causes to part, in the Book of Exodus; the water in which so many great living things dwell, including Leviathan, "which thou didst form to sport in it" (Ps. 104:26). They loved especially the thought of the sea and had a grandiose idea of it. Psalm

107, which provides the responsorial psalm after the first reading, is a fine poem about the sea; it brings home to us the splendor of the sea, but also the sacred fear it inspires.

Against this background we can perhaps better understand the amazement of the disciples when, amid their terror at the storm, they see Jesus calm the waters. They express this amazement in the form of a question, but it is really an exclamation of praise: "Who then is this, that even wind and sea obey him?" If we bear in mind the associations that the sea must have had for them, we can better understand their stupefaction.

The story is valuable to us in our day. We are quite ready to give theoretical acknowledgment of Christ's divinity and God's power, but are there not circumstances when our instincts get the upper hand and we become distrustful and unbelieving?

The fact that Jesus is asleep while the storm rages plays an important part in the story. To these men, a storm at sea is the greatest danger they meet in their work; nothing could make them more fearful, even despairing. And yet the Lord lies there asleep in the stern! They wake him and cry out in their fear: "Teacher, do you not care if we perish?"

Here again, the story has a very modern ring to it. Jesus sleeps; God seems unconcerned with us as we try to ride out our storms. How can God allow the abominations of the past and present? How can we put up with his failure to intervene, especially since, being God, he is supposed to be good? These are the angry questions we hear every day, even from Christians. God is sleeping!

Christ's answer is a harsh one: "Why are you afraid? Have you no faith?" As a matter of fact, when Christ is undergoing his Passion, the faith of his disciples will be so weak that Peter will not have the courage even to acknowledge that he knows Jesus. Even at the resurrection Jesus will find his disciples still hesitant to believe in the saving event and the new life it brings. The Fathers of the Church in their time will see the Church shaken by storms within as well as without. And it is certainly true, is it not, that at times we are tempted to think that Jesus is asleep in the boat that is his Church and pays her no heed? There is indeed a problem here, but Jesus tells us here that it is a problem of ,faith. We shall come back to this point and endeavor to answer the questions we ask ourselves, or others ask of us, about the apparent sleep of Christ amid the storms of our day.

Here shall your proud waves be stayed (Job 38:1, 8-11)

Job is the very model of the man who is tried by sufferings of every kind. His friends, however, do not grasp his situation and stir him up to rebel against the Lord. The Lord then appears to Job amid the storm, and reminds him that he, the Lord, created the very oceans. This vision gives us a better understanding of what sea and storm meant to biblical man; but the passage is admirable as well for its literary quality and its theology.

The Lord tells us that he created the sea and assigned it its boundaries; but he sets limits to the flow of the waves: "Thus far shall you come, and no farther, and here shall your proud waves be stayed." He can do all this because he is Creator of the universe in its entirety. But we must not stop here, with the material world. God also directs the course of each individual's life; everything that happens to us is controlled by his providence.

But it is precisely for this reason that the questions mentioned earlier arise. Why does a child suffer? Why does the young father of a family die? Why are dishonest people rich and good people impoverished? Everything seems to say that God is asleep and has no concern for men.

There can be no answer to these questions except one inspired by faith, and faith is what we lack. God knows what he is doing. He knows what it is he allows to happen, and why he does not intervene visibly, here and now, to check the ill will of men. Time belongs to him; he is the one who sees justice done and who sanctifies men. By permitting trials and suffering, he gives his followers the opportunity to deepen their faith and detachment. Faith alone, then, supplies an answer. Can faith disappoint? If any believer is disappointed, it is because he does not trust in God.

Psalm 107, which supplies the responsory psalm, gives fine expression to God's power: "He made the storm be still, and the waves of the sea were hushed. . . . Let them thank the Lord for his steadfast love, for his wonderful works to the sons of men!" (vv. 29, 31).

A new world (2 Cor. 5:14-17)

St. Paul here shares some of his personal religious experience with us. He tells us of the emotions that well up in him when he thinks of how one man has died for all and how all have therefore overcome death. All men are so linked to Christ that they die with him in order to rise from the dead with him. This reality ought to become the focus for every Christian's life.

If a man is to be truly alive and a real Christian in Christ, he must receive the life Christ gives us, which is Christ's own life as one who has died and been raised from the dead. This life in turn becomes the basis for the Christian's entire conduct: he is a man who ceases to live solely for himself, fettered by his instincts and his self-centered way of judging everything, and must instead ground his life in the dead and risen Christ. Christ must live in him.

In light of this truth, all of Paul's human experience fades into the background. He must now see things differently. He cannot judge his neighbor as he did before but must look on him as one who has died and been raised up in Jesus Christ. The same can be said for his way of knowing Christ: his relation to Christ is a relation to the Christ who died and was raised up and now communicates a share of his own life.

In short, we find ourselves in a new world. The old world has passed away. This idea of the old being gone and having been replaced by the new is a favorite of Paul's. We see, in faith, a new creation (2 Cor. 5:17; Gal. 6:15; Col. 1:19-20) that has Christ for its center (Eph. 2:15). Like Isaiah before him (43:18; 65:17), St. Paul urges us to put the former things out of mind.

Such is the enthusiastic vision Paul offers us on the basis of his own religious experience. It is a grandiose but also a demanding vision: the world, man, man's judgments, man's behaviors — all these are to be new. That means that everything in our life must be reviewed and revised, for the past is dead; it must be forgotten so that we can build anew in Christ.

THIRTEENTH SUNDAY

God, Author of Life

I say to you, arise (Mark 5:21-43).

There are several points of interest in today's Gospel, but all can be subsumed under one heading: faith gives life. In order to show the necessity of faith, St. Mark reports two miracles: the cure of the woman with the flow of blood and the raising of Jairus's daughter.

These miracles are responses to faith, and yet we may at first sight be dubious about the quality of that faith. Jesus' reputation has spread abroad. Does not the woman with the flow of blood take him simply for a famous and powerful wonder-worker? Does the ruler of the synagogue, forgetful of his position because he is distracted by the impending death of his child, really believe in Jesus?

To us and our way of thinking (which has something to say for it), it is not very clear that there is genuine faith. We tend to distrust the kind of confidence these people show. We might think, of course, that Jesus is here satisfied with the remote beginnings of faith and wishes to clarify and confirm it by working miracles. This is often the case in the Gospel of St. John, where a cure does not always follow upon faith but sometimes precedes and leads to it.

To the evangelist, however, the faith of the woman and of Jairus can be regarded as of the right kind. To the woman, who had defied the prescriptions of the Jewish law for someone in her condition, Jesus says: "Daughter, your faith has made you well; go in peace, and be healed of your disease." His statement says two things: faith has saved the woman, and she is cured. That is, there are two healings, one bodily, one spiritual. We should note, too, that St. Mark has already said that the woman was healed at the moment she touched Jesus' garment, because "power had gone forth from him." But this observation is of little moment. The important thing is that Jesus wishes to give salvation and life to those who believe.

Jesus manifests the same will in regard to Jairus's daughter. The ruler asks for the healing of his daughter; news is then brought to him that she has died, but he does not lose faith. Jesus enters his house and raises the child. Then, as so often in Mark, he bids the bystanders say nothing about the miracle.

God did not make death (Wis. 1:13-15; 2:23-24)

The Book of Wisdom has its own vision of death: death is an accident, for God is the author solely of life. The thought is the same as in the Book of Genesis, where death, we are told, entered the world because of the devil's jealousy, or, as St. Paul would put it later on, because of man's disobedience (cf. Rom. 5:12; 6:23; 1 Cor. 15:21).

It is not too difficult for us to see the relevance of these two readings to our own situation. The miracles reported by St. Mark have two lessons for us: one is that faith saves; the other is that Christ wants to make men new and indeed to create a new world in which, as the Apocalypse tells us, there will be no sicknesses and no tears.

What is the quality of the faith we find, not only in others, but in ourselves? We know what we should believe about the person of Jesus. But when we pray, does our faith touch him as he really is? Do not many of us find ourselves reaching for some "pure" faith when we pray? Do we think that our faith is less pure if we look for some blessing from God? Do we think that the prayer of petition is less noble than the prayer of praise, and do we find ourselves practicing only the latter? If we do, we are forgetting that to expect something from almighty God is a way of praising him. We must therefore avoid proudly seeking a "pure" faith and realize that God can draw men to him in various ways that are not always as direct as we might think.

The second point that concerns us in these readings is that the Lord wants to give life and to build a new world. Do we as Christians look upon death differently than they do who have not received the gift of faith? Jesus' words about Jairus's daughter, "The child is not dead but sleeping," are repeated elsewhere in the New Testament. They show us that from the very beginning, Christians understood death to be a passage to a new life. When St. John recounts the raising of Lazarus, he tells us that before going to Bethany, Jesus said, "Our friend Lazarus has fallen asleep" (John 11:11). In what may be a fragment of an early Christian hymn we read: "Awake, O sleeper, and arise from the dead, and Christ shall give you light" (Eph. 5:14).

St. Paul elsewhere speaks of "those who have fallen asleep in Christ" (1 Cor. 15:18). Moreover, when Jesus raises someone from the dead, Mark habitually uses the word "awaken" (Greek *egeirein*) for "raise up"; the risen are those who have been "awakened" (Mark 6:14; 12:26). Other writers of the apostolic age use the same verb for the resurrection of Christ himself. It seems clear that from a very early point Christians thought of death as a passage to a new life.

This, then, is the second lesson of the day: Death is a passage to life; Christ is the Author of life and wants to communicate life to us.

Give what you have received (2 Cor. 8:7, 9, 13-15)

The occasion for the Second Letter to the Corinthians was a material need: the Church of Jerusalem was in serious financial straits. In the verses that precede the present passage and in verse 8, which is omitted from the reading, Paul asks the Christians of Corinth to contribute to the collection that will be made, but he accompanies the request with numerous reservations. In addition, the community at Corinth had its problems, as we know, and Paul had had to reproach the Christians there; now, to encourage them, he looks beyond the immediate question of the collection and speaks of the many graces the Corinthians have received. He mentions them: the faith, the word and knowledge of God, and the fervent love communicated to them by Paul himself.

These blessings should encourage the Corinthians to be generous in turn and to show love for the community at Jerusalem. But St. Paul also appeals to the example of Christ, a spiritual example that has nothing to do with money but that nonetheless will encourage the Corinthians to see where their duty lies. Christ emptied himself; being rich, he became poor for our sakes so that his poverty might enrich us.

Applying this spiritual example to the present problem, Paul speaks of the generosity the Corinthians should show in material things. The point is not that they should burden themselves but that they should do what the equality existing between brothers requires. They should give what they can spare; the favor may well be returned in other circumstances. Such a brotherly exchange of material goods is not isolated from the sharing of spiritual blessings that the various communities should likewise exchange. Solidarity among the communities relates to both the spiritual and the material goods that each shares with the others.

The passage is very relevant to us today. It can give our generosity in material things a new dimension. It tells us that a complete openness to others, both spiritual and material, is essential to genuine poverty; that authentic poverty is not a matter simply of giving away material goods and being detached from them, but also of being spiritually open to others and sharing with them what we have received. The passage thus encourages us to reflect on what we mean by the "equality" of which Paul speaks and which our contemporary world applies too exclusively to social and material conditions. If Christianity is to collaborate in building an egalitarian society, it can do so only by adding a necessary corrective, that is, by making the sharing spiritual as well as material. The Christian knows that by reason of his baptism he now lives a new life that requires value judgments different from those of this world.

FOURTEENTH SUNDAY

The Prophet Rejected

A prophet without honor (Mark 6:1-6)

The account is not one to make us optimistic, but we must accept it as a faithful reflection of the situation that will eventually bring Jesus to his death. St. Mark shows that despite Jesus' miracles and teaching, his mission is apparently a failure. Jesus expresses this in a proverb of the day: "A prophet is not without honor, except in his own country." Those who heard him did not get beyond the outward, human facts about him: he is the carpenter's son, Mary's son, and brother to James and Joses and Judas and Simon. The opposition to his new way of life and the scandal people take at the change in him are such that Jesus is unable to work miracles in their midst. He is astounded at their lack of faith and resigns himself to preaching elsewhere.

A people impudent and stubborn (Ezek. 2:2-5)

Can the first reading give us a lead as to how we may understand the Gospel better?

Ezekiel is being sent to a rebellious people who have turned their backs on the covenant and whom the Lord is attempting to convert. Ezekiel himself later on describes (in chapter 20) the disordered state of Israel. Today's passage shows that the most serious aspect of the whole situation was the impudence and stubbornness of this people whom God loved.

Ezekiel will bring God's word to the people; in addressing them, he will use the familiar prophetic opening: "Thus says the Lord." Even if the people do not accept God's word, they will at least know that a prophet has been sent and is among them. They will know it, whether they end up by listening to and heeding his word, or whether they will be converted only by the punishment sent them for being unwilling to listen and remaining obstinate.

The circumstances in which Ezekiel carried out his mission were the very ones Jesus later met. He was there in the midst of his people, but his words and deeds did not make them see that he had been sent to them with a mission. Thus Jesus had the same experience as all the prophets before him.

This drama is still going on. Do men accept the Creed

without changing it? The works of Jesus as recorded in the Gospel and the works he now accomplishes are plain to see, but there are eyes that do not see and subborn hearts that are closed to God's word.

This tragedy of the failure to understand goes on in various forms. To refuse Jesus' teaching as mediated by the Church is not the only way of failing to understand him. Men also reject Jesus by identifying the Church with its form at a particular period of history and refusing to let the Church adapt and be what she should be in today's world. Men reject Jesus by closing their ears to criticism that may admittedly take an excessively bitter form and yet may be inspired at bottom by the Lord, who wishes his Church to change some of her ways. The failure of his own to receive Jesus is repeated more often than we think.

Strength in weakness (2 Cor. 12:7-10)

St. Paul here alludes to revelations he had received. These could have made him proud, but the Lord prevented him from yielding to pride by humbling him with a "thorn" in the flesh that might have led people to think of him as under Satan's influence rather than as a messenger of God. In Paul's day, nervous disorders, like many illnesses, were regarded as caused by the demon. That is why Paul thanks the Galatians for not spitting at him (that is the literal meaning of Gal. 4:14) in a gesture meant to exorcize a person who was sick or blind and therefore regarded as under demonic influence.

There is no point in trying to determine just what the "thorn" was of which Paul speaks. It has been suggested, without proof (what proof could there possibly be?), that the "thorn" consisted in sexual temptations. In all likelihood, it took the form of some humiliating, chronic illness that upset those who listened to Paul and might well cause them to refuse him a hearing. They would ask themselves: Is he really from God (the Galatians received him as an angel of God: Gal. 4:14), or is he under the influence of Satan?

The Lord refuses to free Paul from this "thorn" that causes him to share the Cross of Christ by humiliating him and then making him strong in his very weakness. For amid his weakness, the power of Christ dwells in him. He is strong because he is weak, since his weakness leaves room for the very power of God who is in him to exercise itself. The humiliated, crucified Jesus had the full power of the Spirit within him, and at the very moment when he was suffering and seemed powerless, he was lifting the world from its sin into the life of God.

A life marked by persecution, coercion, and suffering of every kind is not regarded by the Christian as reason for discouragement or despair; rather, it is a life that draws strength from the indwelling Lord. Weakness and suffering enable the Christian to clear a space within himself where the power of Christ can dwell.

FIFTEENTH SUNDAY

Chosen and Sent

The Twelve are chosen and sent (Mark 6:7-13)

The theme of choice recurs several times on the Sundays of Ordinary Time. On the fourth Sunday (Cycle A) we are told that God chooses the weak (1 Cor. 1:26-31); on the eleventh Sunday (Cycle A) we read of the choosing of the priestly people and of the twelve apostles (Matthew 9:36–10:8; Exod. 19:2-6). The theme was evidently an important one to the early Church, and we should go back to the Sundays just mentioned for further discussion of the points that will be made briefly here.

What is it that characterizes today's pericope as compared with the others on the same subject? The first reading, and the second as well (which happens to fit in with the other two), tells us that the main point being made by the liturgy in its use of this Gospel passage is that God has the initiative when it comes to choosing men. He chooses them, and he does it before the creation of the world; he does it, too, without taking into account the qualities we men judged indispensable.

The first thing, then, that we ought to emphasize in the passage is the fact of the choice, together with the delegation of authority and powers. Jesus speaks as one with authority and not like the scribes (Mark 1:22), but the same cannot be said of the Twelve. Their mission and their activity depend on their having been given power. It is in the name of Jesus that they do what they do.

The purpose of their mission is to proclaim the gospel and to call men to conversion. This short statement sums up the Church's real mission, and we must reflect deeply on it. The Second Vatican Council was very much aware of the fact that the Church is by its nature missionary; though the Church possesses a permanence, it is nonetheless always on pilgrimage and must not acquire too much baggage. The bishops must be concerned about all the Church and make sure that they all carry out their mission of preaching conversion.

Prophesy to my people Israel (Amos 7:12-15)

This reading will enable us better to understand why the Gospel pericope was chosen. Amos is preaching at Bethel and has caused a scandal by attacking the immorality, the sacred prostitution, and the social injustice that he finds at the shrine and that have even infected the cultus itself. Amaziah, the priest of the shrine, asks Amos to leave.

The prophet's answer is the most important part of this little passage. In it he tells of his calling: he is a simple herdsman, but the Lord has taken him away from his regular tasks, from "following the flock." He has had no preparation for his mission; the Lord has come and taken him nonetheless. "I am no prophet, nor a prophet's son; but I am a herdsman, and a dresser of sycamore trees."

Despite this background and lack of preparation, the Lord calls him and tells him: "Go, prophesy to my people Israel."

Chosen before the creation of the world (Eph. 1:3-14)

This passage from St. Paul does not directly take up the theme of the other two readings, but it does deal with the same subject to a certain extent. "He [the Father] chose us in him [Christ] before the foundation of the world, that we should be holy and blameless before him. He destined us in love to be his sons through Jesus Christ."

The passage is the hymn with which the Letter to the Ephesians begins. It reminds us that we have been blessed in Christ, who is the source and center of all grace. We were predestined, not because of any merit on our part (cf. 1 Cor. 1:27-29), but simply because God so willed it for his own glory. He has revealed to us the mystery of his will and purpose, and we are given a knowledge of his plan of salvation. A "mystery," as St. Paul uses the word, is thus quite the opposite of what we are accustomed to mean by it. As we use it, it means something hidden and incomprehensible; for St. Paul, on the other hand, it means a revelation of God's plan, which is eternal and has been hidden till now but has been revealed by Christ and taught to men so that they can experience its reality.

Concretely, the mysterious plan of God is to bring everything together under one Head, Christ. God wishes to rescue the world, which had been created in unity, and to restore it to an even greater unity.

The lesson being taught us on this Sunday is clear. The

apostles are chosen, but so are we all chosen, and the choice in every instance is a manifestation of God's merciful love. He chooses us for his own glory and predestines us to be his children. He also chooses us for the great mission that he initiates and that consists in uniting the world under the headship of Christ. To proclaim the gospel is to proclaim the kingdom, that is, the unification of the world under one Head, Jesus, for the glorification of the Father. No one is worthy of undertaking such a work; God chooses those whom he wishes, independently on their preparation, and even takes them away from the place of their habitual labors.

The fact that God chooses even men who are unprepared does not mean that we should neglect the human and theological potentialities of those who feel themselves called. It simply means that God's choice is utterly free. Consequently, our judgment of those who are called should be prudent; the judgment requires great spiritual discernment.

SIXTEENTH SUNDAY

The Flock Gathered

Sheep without a shepherd (Mark 6:30-34)

The narrative is quite brief. The disciples return from an apostolic journey; Jesus takes them into solitude so that they can rest, but the crowd seeks them out. When Jesus sees the crowd, he is filled with pity for them because they are like sheep without a shepherd, and he begins to instruct them in detail. The theme of the passage as read in the liturgy is: sheep without a shepherd, whom Christ wishes to evangelize.

The passage tells us, then, of the anxious concern Jesus feels for the crowds. The evangelists like to point out that the crowds follow Jesus (see Matthew 4:25; 8:1, 18; 12:15 and parallels; 13:2 and parallels; 19:2; 20:29; Mark 1:33, 45; 2:2; 3:20, 32; 4:36; 5:21, 24; 9:14; Luke 7:11; 8:45; 11:29; 12:1; 14:25; 19:3; 23:48; John 12:18). We read that Jesus is moved by the sight of the crowd (Mark 9:36; 15:32) and that the crowd is struck by wonder at Jesus (Matthew 12:23; 21:9; Mark 12:37; John 7:12, 40) and has a great desire to hear his teaching (Mark 11:18; 12:37; Luke 5:1, 15). This desire for teaching, along with the desire to be cured and to see miracles, is what draws the crowds after Jesus.

Jesus' mission is to teach. He teaches in the synagogues (Matthew 4:23; Mark 1:39; Luke 4:44) and in the towns (Matthew 11:1). He himself can say at the end: "Day after day I sat in the temple teaching" (Matthew 26:55; cf. Mark 14:48-49; Luke 22:52-53; John 18:20).

What is the character of his teaching? He teaches with authority (Matthew 7:29) and says that the Father has told him what he is to teach (John 12:49). All those who are of good faith must acknowledge that he teaches truly the way of God (Matthew 22:16; Mark 12:13-14; Luke 20:21). However, he also teaches in parables (Matthew 13:3, 35; Mark 4:2; Luke 8:4). His teaching is new and is confirmed by actions: He commands the unclean spirits and they obey him (Mark 1:27). His hearers ask themselves where he gets this teaching of his and what the wisdom is that has been entrusted to him; they exclaim in wonder at the mighty deeds he accomplishes (Mark 6:2).

The reason why St. Mark says so much about the teaching of Jesus is that his Gospel is meant as a catechesis, perhaps for use during the Eucharist of the Jewish-Christian community. This purpose explains Mark's care throughout the Gospel to show Jesus confirming his teaching by miracles.

When Jesus is moved at the sight of a crowd that resembles sheep without a shepherd, his first reaction is to teach them. In his eyes, the primary function of a shepherd is to communicate the Father's teaching.

This attitude of Jesus should make us stop and reflect. In our day we are tempted to assign the Church's shepherds many roles that often do not leave them time to teach and to prepare themselves for teaching. St. Mark, on the contrary, sees teaching as the first and foremost task of Jesus the Shepherd. What Jesus teaches has, moreover, been entrusted to him by his Father. In fact, what Jesus teaches is precisely that God is a Father and that he loves men and wants to save them. At the same time, today's passage from Mark shows that Jesus was especially concerned to teach his disciples, who would themselves later become teachers of others. He explains his parables to them because they accept him with faith.

It is by teaching the sheep that Jesus gathers them together. This is an aspect of his teaching that must be emphasized. He does not give an abstract religious instruction that stimulates the hearers to discussion. Rather, he teaches with authority and confirms the teaching received from the Father by miracles. His teaching is filled with power and creates a new people. The crowds gather around him and share his teaching with one another by telling one another of their impressions; slowly they form a united flock on which Jesus bestows his love and for which he prepares future shepherds.

The shepherd gathers the remnant of the flock (Jer. 23:1-6)

The theme of the shepherd occurs frequently in the Bible, and this is only to be expected when we recall the kind of life led by many of the writers and readers of the Scriptures. The patriarchs were shepherds; King David himself was called from tending the flocks. Today's text from the prophet Jeremias was written against the kings who misgovern the people of God. Evidently, then, "shepherd" must be taken in a wide sense to include prophets, kings, and even those who misused their authority. Jeremias is not the only one to write against evil "shepherds"; both Isaiah

(56:10-12) and Ezekiel (24:2-10) attack them vehemently. The Lord's basic reproach to such rulers is that they neglect his people and are not really concerned about them. Isaiah speaks of these rulers as blind; Ezekiel speaks even more strongly, accusing them of the selfish abuse of their power: they act as shepherds to no one but themselves.

God himself intends to act as the shepherd of his people, for he is deeply concerned about them. His work will consist first and foremost in gathering the scattered sheep and bringing them to pastures where they will become fruitful and multiply. This divine intervention for the sake of gathering the scattered sheep is a theme that is also to be found in Isaiah (31:8-10; 40:11) and Ezekiel (34:11-16).

In order to effect this gathering, God will provide his people with shepherds. In this promise we have a prediction of the Messiah whose name will be "The Lord is our righteousness" (Jer. 23:6). The same idea may be found, expressed in almost the same terms, in the prophet Ezekiel (34:23-24). Another name, "a righteous Branch," is used of the Messiah in the Book of Jeremias (33:15) and is repeated in the prophet Zechariah (3:8; 6:12) and the New Testament (Heb. 7:10; 1 John 3:9).

The model shepherd, so fully described in the Old Testament, reappears in the New and is concretely embodied in Jesus. The tenth chapter of the Fourth Gospel develops the theme. The Letter to the Hebrews mentions it (13:20) in the context of Christ's high priesthood. The First Letter of Peter speaks of Christ as the shepherd who continues to lead his people and sees him coming on the last day as the great Shepherd (2:25; 5:4). In the Apocalypse we find a strange mixing of themes of lamb and shepherd: "The Lamb in the midst of the throne will be their shepherd, and he will guide them to springs of living water" (7:17); we also see the Lamb, in his role as shepherd, being followed wherever he goes (14:4).

The First Letter of Peter describes us as scattered sheep whom the shepherd gathers: "You were straying like sheep, but have now returned to the Shepherd and Guardian of your souls" (2:25). The theme of the shepherd naturally calls to mind the theme of gathering, for the shepherd makes his voice heard, and the sheep follow him. It is under this image that Zechariah anticipates the gathering of the nations: "I will signal for them and gather them in."[17]

The responsorial psalm for today is inevitably Psalm 23, the song sung by the newly baptized when, after their baptism and confirmation, they go in procession to the Eucharistic celebration for the first time. Consequently, there can hardly be a homily on the Good Shepherd that does not speak of the Eucharist, to which he leads us in order to feed us and to form us into a single people.

Psalm 23 was the subject of frequent patristic commentary.[18] For St. Cyril of Jerusalem, the psalm is a prophecy of Christian initiation:

> Blessed David, too, tells you of the power [of this mystery] when he says: "You have prepared a table before me, in the face of those who persecute me." . . . To what does he refer but to the mystical, spiritual table that God has prepared for us? . . . "You have anointed my head with oil." He has anointed you on the forehead with oil, in the form of the seal you have received from God, so that you are imprinted with the seal and are now consecrated to God. "And your cup intoxicates me like the best wine." You see here mention of the chalice which Jesus takes in his hands and over which he gives thanks and says: "This is my blood."[19]

St. Ambrose offers the same explanation in his commentary on the psalm when addressing the newly baptized:

> Learn again what kind of sacraments you have received. Listen to what holy David says, for he, too, under the impulse of the Spirit, foresaw these sacraments. He rejoiced and declared that he lacked for nothing. Why? Because one who has received the body of Christ will never again be hungry. How often have you not heard Psalm XXII and failed to un-

derstand it! See how well it applies to the heavenly sacraments.[20]

The Fathers thus regarded Psalm 23 as a synthesis of sacramental catechesis, and the psalm had an important place in the ritual of Christian initiation in the early Church. We shall limit ourselves here to two further passages from the Fathers that bring out their pastoral concerns. St. Gregory of Nyssa writes:

> By all these means he [Jesus] teaches the Church that you must first become a sheep of the Good Shepherd through a good catechesis and through initiation into the pastures and springs of Christian teaching so that you may be buried with him and die with him in baptism, and yet not fear such a death. For this death is not death proper but a shadow and likeness of death. . . . Then he prepares the mystical table. . . . After this he anoints your head with the oil of the Spirit and brings the wine that rejoices the heart and fills the soul with sober intoxication.[21]

St. Cyril of Alexandria says that in this psalm

> converts from paganism, having been taught by God and spiritually fed, acknowledge the giver of the salutary food and call him their Shepherd and Nourisher. . . . They have for leader not a mere saint, such as Israel had in Moses, but the Prince of shepherds and the Teacher of teachers, in whom are hidden all the treasures of wisdom and knowledge.[22]

Brought near in the blood of Christ (Eph. 2:13-18)

Today's second reading can be considered along with the other two. It tells us that this Lord who is a shepherd has united Israel and the nations into a single people; in his own flesh he has destroyed the walls that separated them.

It is in a baptismal context that St. Paul says this, for earlier in this second chapter of the Letter (vv. 1-10), he shows us that the baptized have been raised to new life in Christ.

Now he adds that although at one time they were far from God, they have now been brought near to God and to each other through the blood of Christ. Christ the Shepherd has made the two peoples one, and the one people has become a single new man. Peace now is a reality for the people of Israel as well as for the converts from paganism. The two peoples who have become a single new man can draw near to the Father in the power of the one Spirit.

We had gone astray, but now we are led by a Shepherd who has given his life for us. We have become a single people and have access to the Father in the one Spirit.

Today's entire liturgical celebration is thus endowed with a special unity. The Lord stands before us who have gone astray and need a guide; he stands before the peoples of our time as they seek for some unity to their lives. Each individual wants unity within himself; human groups seek for unity; the peoples of the earth are looking for common ways of thinking and for a common life. There is only one hope of succeeding in this manifold quest for unity, and that is to find unity in Christ, who as Shepherd has shed his blood in order to bring the peoples of the world together in unity and peace.

We must not delude ourselves: Without faith in this one Shepherd, there can be no unity and no peace. All other ways are illusory. Every Christian, certainly, must be convinced of this truth. Moreover, when faced with our lost and groping world, each Christian has the responsibility, in some measure, of a shepherd; he must show others the way. But at this point we must be on guard: the world is not looking for our theories, any more than it wants an "easy" religion. It wants the true way, and there is only one true way that leads to lasting life, the way shown us by Christ's Cross. Only the blood of Christ can give peace and unite men on a common road.

The problem of unity among Christians and, more generally, of unity among the nations has but one answer: Christ. It is to be found only in one source: the blood of Christ. There is no getting around the fact that human life will achieve fulfillment only by passing through the crucible of trials accepted with joyous love. The Christian, in his shepherding of his fellows, has no other solutions to offer. If he were to show them another, humanly more acceptable path, he would be creating a costly illusion. We have many examples of such false guidance. When "shepherds," unwittingly acting in an evil manner, point men toward other ways, they are dooming these men to failure, for they are pointing them toward false joys and a false unity. The only true peace and unity are those to which the Spirit of Christ leads us.

SEVENTEENTH SUNDAY

We Are Filled With The Bread of God

The multiplication of the loaves (John 6:1-15)

In the B Cycle, the continuous reading of St. Mark's Gospel is interrupted, and from the seventeenth to the twenty-first Sundays, the sixth chapter of St. John, on the bread of life, is read instead. It will be of great interest to see how the understanding of this sixth chapter is conditioned, Sunday after Sunday, by the accompanying reading from the Old Testament.

In this first pericope the crowd follows Jesus, and the evangelist tells us the reason: they had seen the signs Jesus gave by healing the sick. This opening statement already gives the ensuing narrative a messianic dimension. It is followed almost immediately by a further observation that hints at the sacramental character of what is to follow: "Now the Passover, the feast of the Jews, was at hand." We must bear in mind, of course, that John's catechesis is addressed to Christians; the latter could not but think of the Eucharist when they read that the multiplication of the loaves was thus so closely linked in time with the Passover.

We observed a moment ago that the reference to the healing of the sick gives a messianic coloring to the events and discourses to follow. This messianic dimension is further accentuated by the way John concludes the multiplication, for while the synoptic Gospels pass directly to the event of Jesus' walking on the water, John reports the crowd as saying: "This is indeed the prophet who is to come into the world!" They wish, therefore, to make him their king.

Even before the discourse on the bread of life, John insinuates that the miracle of the multiplication was an anticipation of the Eucharist and part of the progressive revelation Jesus was undertaking. Thus he notes, before the miracle, that Jesus "himself knew what he would do."

It has been claimed that in this passage of his Gospel, John intends to evoke in a systematic way the memory of episodes during the Exodus. In any case, the evocation does not follow the chronology of events as recorded in the Book of Exodus but rather the chronology adopted in the Book of Wisdom, when the latter speaks of the manna (16:20-26). John's narrative also refers to the Book of Numbers (11:13), from which there will be some citations in the following verses.

The situation of God's people in the desert is not the only reference to the Old Testament. Surely the story of the loaves being multiplied by Eliseus was also in St. John's mind. In that story (2 Kings 4:42-44), as in St. John, the loaves were of barley. In addition, Eliseus' servant raises an objection almost identical with that of Philip: "How am I to set this before a hundred men?" (2 Kings 4:43). Finally, as in St. John (6:12-13), there is a reference to bread being left over: "They ate, and had some left" (2 Kings 4:44).

In telling the stage-by-stage story of the journey through the desert, the Book of Numbers emphasizes the fact that the people could not possibly save themselves; the Lord was the one who saw to that. Moses, for example, objects that he cannot feed six hundred thousand people (Num. 11:21-23); he estimates that all the fish in the sea would not be enough to feed such a multitude. In the Book of Exodus (ch. 16), enough manna falls to feed each and all.

It would be an exaggeration, of course, to say that John's account of the multiplication of the loaves is a tissue of allusions to the Eucharistic celebration. At the same time, readers who had read the accounts of the institution of the Eucharist and were participating in the Eucharistic gatherings must inevitably have seen in the account as a whole a desire on John's part to present the story of the multiplication as a prophecy of the Eucharist. Here, as in the Eucharist, Jesus takes bread, gives thanks, and distributes it.

When Jesus performs the miracle of the loaves and fishes, the food he supplies proves to be too much, but at his bidding the disciples gather up the remnants. Does John intend some symbolic meaning when he says that twelve baskets of fragments were collected? If so, what was this symbolic intention?

The crowd fails — tragically, we might well say — to understand the deeper significance of the miracle. They see only a sign that their nationalistic messianic longings are to be satisfied.

They shall eat and have some left (2 Kings 4:42-44)

We have already referred to this passage in commenting on the Gospel pericope. It is useless to go further and try to determine the locality of the wonder and the details of the event. Its meaning is the important thing. There was evidently a disproportion between the twenty loaves and the hundred men who were to eat them, just as in the Gospel. It is not clear whether the author of the text wanted to glorify Eliseus and create a legend about him, or whether he sought rather to emphasize man's impotence and God's ready intervention.

The two passages read today do not lead us to a proxi-

mate meditation on the bread of life. The accent is rather on
Christ's mysterious preparation for the discourse, as he stirs
in the crowd a desire for a more than material nourishment.
More specifically at this moment he wants them not to go
astray by thinking of salvation in nationalistic terms when
they are forced to recognize the power of God's messenger.
Jesus is not the messiah imagined by the Jewish people of
his day, but the crowd does not see this. He therefore withdraws into the hills by himself. For the evangelist, this
means that Jesus withdraws to pray in solitude and silence.

The readings for this Sunday already show us the true
Messiah who heals and the true Prophet who has power to
feed the crowds. Since we have faith, we are prepared to
take the next step and accept the consequences of what
Jesus does here, for we already know the sequence and its
teaching. But even if we stay simply with the first fifteen
verses of chapter 6, we are already being invited to enter
upon the ways of God and to acknowledge his power and
his determination to share the life of men.

The responsorial psalm (Psalm 145) after the first reading
bids us sing: "The eyes of all look to thee, and thou givest
them their food in due season. Thou openest thy hand,
thou satisfiest the desire of every living thing." The rest of
chapter 6 will spell out what is meant by these words of the
psalm, but we already think of the Eucharist as we sing it.

――――

One body, one Lord, one faith, one baptism (Eph. 4:1-6)

Life in Christ is not a matter simply of receiving the sacraments. On the contrary, the sacraments point us to a way
of life. We must live and act in accordance with what we
have received. The unity that exists in Christ's Body is not
only the result of moral activity but an epiphany or manifestation of what each individual has become, an outward ex-

pression of the radical inner transformation of his person by the sacraments, a manifestation of what the new creature really is. Humility, gentleness, patience, mutual loving support, the desire for peace — these are not simply virtues plastered on to life, but the normal expression of the person who is now part of a single Body due to the action of one and the same Spirit.

This splendid text, so clear but also so theologically profound and solid, deserves frequent meditation. Without this solid base, a Christian's life becomes weak; he is in danger of succumbing to mythical thinking and to the superstition of ritualistic magic. The sacraments have nothing magical about them, however; they require of us a real commitment, as baptism evidently does in linking us to the one Body by the power of the one Spirit. Only one kind of life and action is possible thereafter.

EIGHTEENTH SUNDAY

Believe, Then Hunger and Thirst no More

Go to Christ and you will not hunger or thirst (John 6:24-35)

In this continuation of chapter 6 of the Fourth Gospel, we read the beginning of the discourse of the bread of life. Jesus delivers the discourse in the synagogue at Capharnaum (6:59), where the crowd has found him, across the lake from where the miracle of the loaves had occurred.

As is usual with St. John, the discourse begins with an ambiguous statement: the crowd seeks Jesus because it has been filled, not because it has seen signs. In other words, what draws the crowd to Jesus is not the proclamation of

the kingdom, but the fact that he gave them their fill of material food. The ambiguity proper is in the word "eat." The
crowd has eaten bodily food but has not understood the further "eating" of which the bodily food and the bodily act of
eating were meant to be a sign. To put it another way, the
crowd has failed to perceive the ambiguity, or the deeper
meaning behind the surface meaning, in Jesus' taking bread
and distributing it.

As far as the crowd is concerned, the food that Jesus gave
them disappeared once they ate it. Consequently, they ate,
saw, touched the sign, but they did not understand the sign
or what they were doing. Such is the crowd's state of mind.
Jesus takes advantage of the fact that they have at least
come after him to tell them that in addition to the food that
perishes, there is another food that does not perish but endures to eternal life. He thus enunciates the theme of his
discourse.

The first part of the discourse continues as far as verse 34.
In the pericope for Mass, verse 35 is included. It clarifies
what has preceded, but it also begins a new development
that will not be read until the next (nineteenth) Sunday.

With the opening words of Jesus, we pass from perishable earthly food to a food that endures to eternal life. The
latter is linked to the person of Jesus; it is a food "which the
Son of man will give you; for on him has God the Father set
his seal." Does the crowd understand who this "Son of
man" is? It seems not, since later on in the Gospel (12:34)
they will still be asking, "Who is this Son of man?" But
whether or not the crowd realizes it, Jesus is the Son of man
who has been appointed by the Father to carry out his will;
the Father has set his seal upon him through the intervention of the Spirit (John 1:32).

The crowd evidently does not grasp the full implication
of Christ's statement. They do, however, sense that Jesus is
speaking of some sacred reality in which they are to share
through their activity; that he is pointing a way to them and
telling them of something God wants done. But, for the
Jews, "the works of God" mean chiefly actions that have a

material, visible dimension: prayers, fasts, ascetical practices, proselytizing, etc. For this reason their response to Jesus' opening statement is a question about external activities: "What must we do, to be doing the works of God?" Jesus' answer is direct and to the point: "This is the work of God, that you believe in him whom he has sent." He proposes here an activity that his hearers were surely not expecting, since it is entirely interior. At the same time, however, Jesus does not speak in abstract concepts but shows the concrete form this interior action must take: believe, and believe specifically in the one God has sent.

The crowd now realizes that there is a connection between Jesus and the messenger who bears God's seal. They ask for a sign; that is, they have failed to grasp the meaning of the multiplication of the loaves. Another point they instinctively grasp, however, is that there is a connection between the messenger and the eternal food. That is why they remind Jesus of the manna in the desert. Their forefathers had been given a food from heaven; what sign can Jesus offer?

The mention of the manna allows Jesus to advance a step and to mention the true bread. The bread Moses gave was a perishable bread and a prefiguration of something further. Jesus offers the true bread that the heavenly Father gives.

At this point Jesus goes further and speaks of the true bread as identical with himself. "The bread of God is that which comes down from heaven, and gives life to the world." Then, when the crowd cries, "Lord, give us this bread always," he makes the identification completely explicit: "I am the bread of life." Anyone who comes to Jesus and eats will never be hungry or thirsty again. Jesus is referring to the messianic banquet, and his hearers probably had some inkling of his meaning. They knew the prophecy, "They shall not hunger or thirst" (Is. 49:10). This imagery had often accompanied God's declarations that he would send a Messiah to liberate his people (cf. Is. 55:1-3; 65:13). St. John would later use the same language in his Apocalypse (7:16).

Thus does the discourse unfold, through a series of ambiguities. We must accustom ourselves to John's way of structuring the discourses of Jesus. There is a food that perishes, but there is another that endures to eternal life. The manna is not truly a heavenly food; it is the Father who gives the heavenly food; he gives his Son who is the bread of life. Men must believe in the person of the Son; to do so is to do the work of God. He who believes in the Son will not hunger or thirst.

A rain of bread (Exod. 16:2-4, 12-15)

This account is not the work of a single author but has undergone important revisions. The scholars have seen the Yahwist source behind verses 4-11, while they regard verses 12-14 as the work of the Priestly source. As far as the liturgical proclamation of the passage is concerned, the fact that the account unites two different traditions is of no particular significance.

For our spiritual understanding of the passage and our understanding of the Gospel, the points we should bear in mind can be summed up rather briefly. The situation of God's people in the desert is desperate and leads them to a complaint that is proof of their lack of faith. And yet, even while the people murmur because they lack confidence in him who brought them out of Egypt and through the Red Sea, they still have a lively hope in God's goodness and action in their behalf; this hope is almost a subconscious reflex with them. The manna falls from heaven, and the quail cover the ground. Now this gift of God also brings a further test of faith: Will the people accept what God gives on his terms? He intends to "prove them, whether they will walk in my law or not." God is giving them this bread from heaven as bread for their journey toward the Promised Land.

It would have been impossible for St. John, addressing as he was a believing community, to recount Jesus' words about the bread of life without recalling the manna.

The responsorial psalm, Psalm 78, recalls the manna and praises God for it: "He commanded the skies above, and opened the doors of heaven; and he rained down upon them manna to eat, and gave them the grain of heaven. Man ate of the bread of the angels; he sent them food in abundance. . . . And he brought them to his holy land, to the mountain which his right hand had won."

Live as a new man (Eph. 4:17, 20-24)

We continue here the reading of the Christian charter as contained in the Letter to the Ephesians (the reading of which began on the fifteenth Sunday). Chapter 3 of the Letter to the Colossians (3:5-15) closely resembles this fourth chapter of the Letter to the Ephesians. Both are concerned with unity among the baptized. We who are baptized have taken up a new way of life and must not live like the pagans. At this point (Eph. 4:18-19), St. Paul gives a list of the attitudes characteristic of the pagan, but these verses are omitted from the liturgical selection: hardness of heart, religious ignorance, etc. St. Paul sums it up as "futility" and warns us not to be led astray by it.

We must, then, put aside the old self that still exists in us and be guided instead from within by a renewed spirit. In this last phrase Paul is clearly alluding to baptism, which has utterly transformed the life of the person who has received it and who has become a new man through rebirth from water and the Spirit. The Letter to the Colossians voices almost an identical idea: "You have put off the old nature with its practices and have put on the new nature, which is being renewed in knowledge after the image of its creator" (3:9-10). The Christian has been created as one who is holy and just in truth, after the image of God; he must therefore lead his life under the guidance of the renewed self.

All this is perfectly obvious. How sad to think, then, of what the world could be if Catholics remembered, in act as well as in thought, what they truly are and are meant to be. What power they would have in the present situation to remove the burden of the new enslavements we are constantly accepting! No truly good and viable civilization can be built apart from the spiritual renewal of outlook that should be exemplified in and promoted by the baptized in Christ.

NINETEENTH SUNDAY

The Bread That Has Come Down From Heaven

I am the living bread (John 6:41-51)

This time the Jews have understood Jesus' statement about himself and the heavenly bread. They realize that he is identifying himself with the heavenly food he offers. This scandalizes them, however: "How does he now say, 'I have come down from heaven'?"

Jesus is clearly aware of the question in their minds. How could they — or we — help asking it? There are, of course, the miracles Jesus does, the healings, and especially this most recent miracle of the loaves. But the crowd does not really understand. They look upon Jesus as a prophet who is to restore their kingdom; they cannot locate what has happened at the level where it belongs.

Jesus then goes on to say: "No one can come to me unless the Father who sent me draws him; and I will raise him up at the last day." To understand Jesus and move toward him is a gift from the Father, and the person who receives this gift of faith and does come to Jesus will be raised up for eternal life. The gift of faith requires a responsible attitude on man's part: he must listen to the Father's teachings, since "every one who has heard and learned from the Father comes to me."

It is important to emphasize at this point that as Jesus speaks to the crowd, the context is that of the desert in which the manna fell and the crowd complained (Exod. 16). The crowd in those days did not follow the Father who drew them to him with signs and teaching. Now they complain against the Son, in whom they are willing to see only the son of Joseph. The drama is thus repeated — a drama of unbelief and refusal to follow the paths of salvation opened by God. This time Jesus sharply rejects their attitude and declares himself to be what he truly is: the bread that has come down from heaven.

Jesus now explains what he has been saying. In his explanation he begins with the manna that had prefigured the Eucharist and explains that while the Father gave manna to the Hebrews when they complained against him in the desert, the manna was nonetheless only an earthly food, and, consequently, those who ate it eventually died. The same holds for the people who have eaten the miraculously multiplied loaves, for these too are but a prefiguration of the true bread that is yet to be given. Whoever eats this last will live for ever, but it is a bread that is only foretold, not given as yet. The reason for the delay is that the bread is the flesh of Christ, and this he does not and cannot give here and now. But he will certainly give this flesh in the future, and therefore he will give the bread as well, for he will one day give his life, his flesh, himself, for the life of the world.

In this last statement we see the condition required if the promised flesh is to have its saving power. It is Christ's flesh and must be handed over, given up, for the life of the world. The reference is to the sacrifice of the Cross, as in the account of institution in the First Letter to the Corinthians: "My body which is for you" (11:24).

At this point in the discourse on the bread of life, we have passed from the bodily food that secures bodily life — the manna and the multiplied loaves — to that which such bodily food signifies: the everlasting food, the flesh of Jesus that gives eternal life.

In the strength of that food (1 Kings 19:4-8)

In this passage Elias is the very model of a man who is discouraged and beaten down by opposition and persecution. He is fleeing from the outraged Jezebel when an angel appears to him in a dream. On awakening, he finds a meal ready for him: a cake baked on hot stones and a jar of water. This is a divine intervention like those Israel experienced during the Exodus when God fed his people with the manna and the quail (Exod. 16:9-16). The same kind of miraculous food is now given to Elias so that he may continue his journey. With his strength renewed, the prophet walks on for forty days and forty nights until he reaches Horeb, the mountain of God, where he will meet the Lord.

It is odd that patristic tradition did not eagerly lay hold of this tradition as a prefiguration of the Eucharist, since the forty days and the miraculous food were parallel to the forty years in the desert and the manna. In today's liturgy, at any rate, we are evidently meant to see in the story a figure of the Eucharist, no less than in the story of the multiplication of the loaves.

Psalm 34, a psalm traditionally used in the Eucharistic celebration, provides a suitable responsorial psalm for today's Old Testament reading: "The angel of the Lord encamps around those who fear him, and delivers them. O taste and see that the Lord is good!"

Walk in love, as Christ loved us (Eph. 4:30–5:2)

The reading on the eighteenth Sunday reminded us of the new life that is ours in Christ. In this passage Paul continues his exhortation. We must not grieve the Holy Spirit of God, who has marked us with his seal in anticipation of the day of redemption. While the Letter seems to have in mind people recently baptized, it applies just as well to the entire Christian community. St. Paul lists the attitudes and actions that can grieve the Spirit within us, and it is to be noted that these attitudes are chiefly ones that disturb the life of the community: bitterness, wrath, anger, and so forth. We must develop attitudes contrary to these and be kind to one another, tender-hearted, forgiving of one another. We must walk in love like Christ, for the Christian must be an imitator of God.

TWENTIETH SUNDAY

Eat the Bread, Drink the Wine, and Live Forever

My flesh is food indeed and my blood is drink indeed (John 6:51-58)

The Gospel reading continues the discourse on the bread of life. On the preceding Sunday we heard Christ assert his claim to be the bread of life that has come down from heaven. With verse 51 we begin the third section of the discourse, in which the statement just referred to is developed, namely: "I am the living bread which came down from heaven; if any one eats of this bread, he will live for ever; and the bread which I shall give for the life of the world is my flesh."

Jesus' language leads his hearers to question him. In this manner of development we see a characteristic procedure of St. John. It can be seen, for example, in Jesus' conversation with the Samaritan woman, where misunderstandings about the "water" lead to new questions (John 4:5-42). It can also be seen in the conversation with Nicodemus; here the latter misunderstands Jesus and asks: "How can a man be born when he is old? Can he enter a second time into his mother's womb and be born?" (John 3:1-21). At this point in chapter 6, a similar misunderstanding leads once again to a question: "How can this man give us his flesh to eat?"

Jesus did not give a direct answer to the Samaritan woman or to Nicodemus. Neither will he give a direct answer here to the question asked him by the Jews; instead, his answer will take the form of reaffirmation, but with explanations. St. John does not, however, put on Jesus' lips the sacramental explanation of the gift of his flesh, the explanation we find Jesus giving at the Last Supper and Paul repeating in the First Letter to the Corinthians: "This is my body, which is given for you." Had Christ done so, his hearers would not have understood him.

While Jesus does not explain how he will be able to give his flesh to eat, he does explain clearly what the significance is of eating his flesh and drinking his blood. The effect of such actions will be a union with Christ, analogous to that which exists between Jesus and his Father. Jesus will dwell in them, so much so that he who eats the flesh of Jesus will live because of him. In this passage we can, once again, easily see the allusion to the violent death of Jesus. The union with Jesus, by reason of which he lives in us and gives us life, leads finally to our resurrection on the last day.

Here again, as in the account of Lazarus' resurrection, we can see John's method at work, the method whereby misunderstanding leads at last to a grasp of the real meaning of Jesus' words (cf. John 11:23-27). In our present passage, Jesus explains what is meant by the life he gives by referring back to the manna. The manna was a bread for man's everyday life, and those who ate it finally died. The bread that is the flesh of Jesus is a food that gives eternal life. In fact, the dwelling of Jesus in us and of us in him *is* eternal life.

Come, eat of my bread (Prov. 9:1-6)

It cannot be maintained that in the Book of Proverbs, wisdom, concerning which we read some beautiful lines in today's Mass, is a divine person, and specifically Christ. While fully realizing this, the liturgy nonetheless follows the commentaries of the Fathers and sees in this wisdom a prefiguration of the Eucharist. This is why the text has been so frequently used in liturgical celebrations. In the old Office for Corpus Christi, for example, the first antiphon at Lauds was the opening verse of the present pericope.

The house being built is Jerusalem, and it is in Jerusalem that wisdom sets her table. We may recall the words of Psalm 23 (sung during Christian initiation): "Thou preparest a table before me in the presence of my enemies."

The Fathers, as we noted, had a high regard for this passage on wisdom, since they saw in it a prefiguration of the messianic banquet and of the Eucharist. St. Cyprian, in one of his letters, links the passage from Genesis on the prefigurative offering of Melchisedech with our present passage on the banquet that wisdom prepares: "Solomon speaks [in the Book of Proverbs] of the wine mixed, that is, he prophetically announces the chalice of the Lord with its wine and water." [23]

Origen, in his commentary on the Song of Songs, writes:

We said earlier that the friends of the bridegroom are to be understood as referring to the prophets and all who have served the word of God since the beginning of the world. The Church, or the soul that clings to the word of God, asks them to lead her into the wine cellar, that is, the place where wisdom has mixed her wine in the bowl and whither, through her servants,

she invites all who are ignorant: "Come, eat my
bread, and drink the wine I have mixed." This is the
wine cellar and banquet house in which all who come
from east and west recline at table with Abraham,
Isaac, and Jacob in the kingdom of God. . . . Into this
wine cellar the Church, and each soul, desires to
enter by becoming perfect, there to enjoy the teachings of wisdom and the mysteries of knowledge, as
though these were a savory food and a wine that re-
joices the heart.[24]

Finally, St. Ambrose says: "Do you want to eat and drink?
Come to the banquet set by wisdom, who invites all with a
great proclamation: 'Come, eat my bread and drink the
wine I have mixed for you.'"[25]

Psalm 34 has been chosen as the responsorial psalm.
Though less expressive in this context than Psalm 23 would
be, it does tell how nothing is lacking to those who seek
God, whereas the rich go empty-handed and hungry.

We are constantly being invited to this table of wisdom
that Christ prepares for us, even though, because we live
for Christ and share in his suffering, we, like Paul, are considered fools by the world around us. If we eat this bread
and drink this wine, we will, as today's reading from the
Book of Proverbs says, "leave simpleness [foolishness], and
live, and walk in the way of insight." Wisdom invites us to
eat her bread and drink the wine she has mixed for us; in
the light of today's Gospel, we identify wisdom with Christ,
who invites us to eat his flesh and drink his blood. If we
accept the invitation, we will be fools in the eyes of the
wise of this world, but wise with Christ in a world that rejects his invitation.

Understand what the will of the Lord is (Eph. 5:15-20)

St. Paul continues to instruct us on the subject of the new life. He sees it as an ongoing reality situated between the baptism that renewed us and the moment when we enter into glory. He wants us to make the most of this time given to us, for dangers beset us, since the days are evil. New Christians have to live in a pagan milieu, and this brings with it the possibility and risk of slowly and almost unnoticedly falling back into pagan ways.

Paul is accurately describing our situation today. It must be acknowledged that many Christians lead a pagan life, a life tinged by certain Christian practices but unmarked by any Christian wisdom or even any search for such wisdom. It is in such a context as this that we must seek to know God's will. Prayer in all its forms is the means of finding wisdom and of preserving it once found.

St. Paul here presents a picture of what the liturgical gatherings of his day must have been like. Christians must have done a great deal of fervent singing of psalms, hymns, and spiritual songs. Thanksgiving must have been the dominant ethos — thanksgiving offered to God the Father in the name of our Lord Jesus Christ. In this same context, St. Paul states the ideal of constant prayer: pray always and for everything. This means a type and method of prayer that will enable us to be in constant union with God and thus to exist in a pagan milieu yet live according to the wisdom proper to our new life.

If we create such a vital milieu for ourselves, we shall be able to know God's will for us and put it into practice, as we pray we may do, in the Our Father: "Thy will be done on earth as it is in heaven."

TWENTY-FIRST SUNDAY

Live With The Lord Whose Words Are Spirit and Life

To whom shall we go? (John 6:60-69)

In today's Mass we read the end of the discourse on the bread of life. We are made witnesses of the drama and of the division it caused, even among the disciples of Jesus. "This is a hard saying; who can listen to it?"

The passage contains a dialogue between Jesus and his disciples. They had had their part to play in the multiplication of the loaves, but the subsequent discourse had involved chiefly the crowd in a dialogue with Jesus. Now that the discourse is ending, the disciples come into the foreground once again. That is to be expected, since they are in a far better position to grasp the last part of Jesus' address to the crowd and to lay hold of its basic meaning. Even within the group of disciples, however, some are not yet able to believe fully and to accept the deeper meaning of Jesus' words. They really lack an essential faith in Jesus as messenger of the Father. Otherwise, even if they had not fully grasped what he was saying in the discourse, they would have accepted him as did the disciples who elected to stay with him.

The important thing in this concluding section is the introduction of the "spiritual" element; we must, however, understand that this "spiritual" is utterly "real"! In fact, for St. John, there is a very close relationship between the spirit and what is real and true. The realm of the spirit is absolute reality, as opposed to the flesh, which is a secondary kind of reality. In other words, for Jesus and St. John, the spirit — or the spiritual, as we would say — is real *par excellence*, whereas material things — the flesh, for example — exist only in the phenomenal order.

This contrast occurs several times in St. John. In his conversation with the Samaritan woman, Jesus links "spirit" and "truth" (John 4:23). In the dialogue with Nicodemus, when the latter cannot understand how a man can be born again, Jesus explains that it is a question of being born from above through water and the Spirit (John 3:5-7). So now, in the sixth chapter, Jesus says: "It is the spirit that gives life" — the spirit is reality and truth, while the flesh is powerless. If, then, the words of Jesus are life-giving, it is because in them spirit and truth reside. Earthly food is simply material, while spiritual food is reality and truth. The spirit alone can give life. Christ is from above, but he has taken flesh, and this flesh is now a means of union with him. No one can accept this, however, unless he "sees" Christ. But to "see" him and believe in him is itself a gift from the Father.

At this point there arises the dramatic crisis that will separate the other disciples from the Twelve who remain faithful to Jesus. In his moving answer, Peter says to Jesus: "Lord, to whom shall we go? You have the words of eternal life." In other words: We know that you are spirit and life, and that you possess the words of truth. Peter then goes on to express the faith of the Twelve: "We have believed, and have come to know, that you are the Holy One of God." To the Twelve, who remain faithful, unlike the other disciples and the scandalized crowd, Jesus is not only the Holy One of God; his words also give eternal life.

Today is the last of the Sundays (seventeenth to twenty-first, Cycle B) on which the sixth chapter of St. John is read. It seems useful, now that we have seen the whole series, to give a brief overview here.

Verses 1-15 (17th Sunday): Multiplication of the loaves; Jesus is hailed as the great prophet, and they want to make him king.

Verses 26-35 (18th Sunday): The Jews misunderstand; they follow Jesus because they have eaten a perishable food, whereas they should be ask-

ing him for a food that is eternal. The manna
was perishable food; the Father gives a
heavenly bread, which is Jesus himself, the
Bread of Life.

Verses 41-51 (19th Sunday): Jesus is the bread from
heaven? But is he not Joseph's son? — No one
can come to Christ unless the Father draws
him. Men must listen with faith to the teaching of God as transmitted by his messenger.
This means men must also believe in the
messenger who comes from heaven. Those
who ate the manna have since died; those
who eat this bread from heaven will live
forever. The bread to be given is Christ's flesh
for the life of the world.

Verses 51-58 (20th Sunday): Christ is both the bread
and the giver of the bread. Therefore he gives
his very self, his flesh and blood. Eat the flesh
and drink the blood of Christ, and the result is
that he dwells in us and we in him. This flesh
is to be "given" for the life of the world (an
allusion to the Eucharist).

Verses 60-69 (21st Sunday): Conclusion. If a man is to
understand Jesus' message, he must be called
by the Father. The words of Jesus are spirit
and life: the spirit gives life, while the flesh is
powerless. Earthly food perishes, but the food
from above, that is, the spirit, brings eternal
life. The true bread is spiritual food.

Die rather than abandon the Lord (Jos. 24:1-2a, 15-17, 18b)

The people have gathered at Shechem at Josue's summons. Shechem is the place of the covenant, but the gathering in this case does not seem to be for worship. The
people are summoned because they must make a definitive
choice. Josue delivers a lengthy discourse, in which he recalls all that God has done for his people, beginning with

the call of Abraham. His kindness to the people has been great indeed, and he has bestowed on them blessings they did not earn. Now they must choose. The people's answer is clear: to die rather than abandon the Lord. The people in their turn recall what the Lord has done, and they come to the conclusion that they wish to serve the Lord because he is their God.

All this is prefatory to the renewal of the covenant. In his address (which should be read in its entirety), Josue does not gloss over the difficulties the people must face and the many temptations to infidelity that they must overcome. His predictions were in fact to be realized, and the soft life in Canaan would corrupt the people.

We too are faced with a choice. When we celebrate the Eucharist, which is the sacrament of the new covenant, we are forced to choose and to say, with the faithful disciples, "To whom shall we go?" or, with the Israelites, "Far be it from us that we should forsake the Lord." Every sharing in the Eucharist implies such a decision, for each time that the Church celebrates the Eucharist, she renews her covenant with the Lord, protests her faith in him, and draws the faithful with her in her act of unconditional fidelity.

In response to this first reading, we sing in Psalm 34, "What man is there who desires life, and covets many days, that he may enjoy good?"

This is a greaty mystery, Christ and the Church (Eph. 5:21-32)

As he continues his disquisition on the Christian's new life, St. Paul comes to the family and domestic life. In order to give a theological basis for the mutual relations of husband and wife, the Apostle lists the duties of each and bases his statements on the union and relations of Christ and the Church.

It was not difficult for Paul to portray the Church as the

spouse of Christ. When the prophet Osee had wanted to describe the requirements of the covenant, he appealed to the image of God as husband and the chosen people as wife, and he developed the theme in a realistic manner (Osee 2:18-22). As for Paul, he also depicts Christ as husband and the Church as wife, in his Second Letter to the Corinthians (11:2). In today's passage he sees Christ as the Head and the Church as the Body — a new way of expressing the unity existing between God and his people, and an entirely new metaphor. But the new image is not an artificial product of Paul's own imagination. According to the Book of Genesis, the wife is the body of her husband (3:23-24). This is why, after citing a passage from the Book of Genesis (2:24), Paul says that the mystery of the union of man and wife is a great one, for he thinks, as he quotes the Book of Genesis, of Christ and the Church.

The words, "This is a great mystery, and I take it to mean Christ and the Church," are not easy. The Apostle seems to mean that the kind of union being depicted in the Book of Genesis, the reality contained in such a union, prefigures the union of Christ and the Church, while the latter represents the ideal of every marriage. The union of man and wife, as defined in the Book of Genesis, is a "type" that finds its fulfillment in the union of Christ and his Church, while every marriage lives up to its ideal if it resembles the union of Christ and the Church.

The Apostle is thus giving us here one aspect of his theology of the Church. But he also tells us something about conjugal life by comparing it to the union that is the very basis of the Church's life.

The words, "This is a great mystery," have made Christians think of the sacrament of marriage, simply because "sacrament" (sacramentum) was the traditional Latin translation of the Greek word for "mystery" (mysterion). Such an interpretation extends somewhat the real meaning of the text. It is more correct to see in the text an image and ideal of marriage, a way of understanding fully the reality that the Church will later define as the "sacrament" of matrimony.

That is how the Council of Trent interpreted the text when it said that in the passage from the Letter to the Ephesians, Paul "intimated" or "hinted" (*innuit*) that Christ, through his Passion, merited the grace by which the natural institution of marriage is perfected and the spouses are sanctified.[26]

TWENTY-SECOND SUNDAY

Keep The Commandments of The Lord

Commandments of God and traditions of men (Mark 7:1-8, 14-15, 21-23)

It seems quite normal that the new Christian community should find itself in concrete difficulties caused by the opposition between the ways it is abandoning and those it wishes to acquire. The Old Testament and Judaism were not alone in feeling tempted to take refuge in traditional practices and observances, and to soothe the pangs of conscience thereby. Christianity did not have to wait for modern times to experience this temptation; the early Church was quite familiar with it.

St. Paul shows us that legal purity and the observances of the law led to attitudes that needed to be tested. The problem keeps cropping up in the Acts of the Apostles, the Letter to the Galatians, the First Letter to the Corinthians, and the Letter to the Romans.

The Letter to the Galatians shows us that Peter was daunted by the reactions of men. He had been in the habit of eating with Gentiles, but the arrival of some of James's entourage caused him to draw back from the Gentiles out of fear of the party of the circumcised. He chose thus to act like other Jewish converts, and for this Paul opposed him vehemently (Gal. 2:11-14).

Chapter 10 of the Acts of the Apostles shows Peter facing this same problem, but now he learns from a vision how he is to act. He enters the centurion's house, even though, as Peter himself recalls, a Jew was forbidden to do so.

St. Paul finds it necessary to emphasize that traditions concerning food are quite secondary. "'Food is meant for the stomach and the stomach for food' — and God will destroy both one and the other" (1 Cor. 6:13). In his Letter to the Romans he shows balanced judgment with regard to the same problem: "The kingdom of God does not mean food and drink but righteousness and peace and joy in the Holy Spirit" (Rom. 14:17). He goes on, however, to exhort his readers to circumspection for the sake of the "weak." "Do not, for the sake of food, destroy the work of God. Everything is indeed clean, but it is wrong for any one to make others fall by what he eats" (v. 20).

These various problems of the early Church enable us to understand better what St. Mark is teaching his faithful in today's Gospel. In this pericope Jesus finds himself under attack from the Pharisees because of the way he handles human traditions. He insists on the principle that it's not what goes into a man from outside but what comes out of a man's heart that defiles him. What are some of these defiling things? ". . . evil thoughts, fornication, theft, murder, adultery, coveting, wickedness, deceit, licentiousness, envy, slander, pride, foolishness." To those who invert this order of values he says in outraged tones, "You leave the commandment of God, and hold fast the tradition of men."

Observe the commandments of the Lord (Deut. 4:1-2, 6-8)

The commandments and decrees that Moses transmits in God's name are a sign of the Lord's love for his people. They bring out the two major aspects of the covenant he is establishing with the Israelites. On the one hand, God chooses this people, leads them, protects them amid the many difficulties they encounter, and constantly proves his fidelity to them. On the other hand, God's fidelity calls for man's fidelity to him in return; concretely, man must hear and keep the commandments; he must observe them in their entirety without adding or subtracting anything from them.

This, then, is how man should respond to the fidelity of God. If he hears and accepts the law, if he meditates on it and observes it, he will contribute to the carrying out of God's plan of salvation. If and when Israel thus responds, she will show herself to the pagans as a great and wise people. The law is thus not meant as a crushing burden but as a leaven and a source of enthusiasm for Israel, which will find in the law both salvation and greatness.

"O Lord, who shall sojourn in thy tent? Who shall dwell on thy holy hill? He who walks blamelessly, and does what is right" (Ps. 15:1-2).

Act on the word (James 1:17-18, 21b-22, 27)

There is an illusion that constantly tempts us, as St. James points out. It is the temptation to be satisfied with hearing the word and not to put it into practice.

This word is a gift from above, a marvelous present from God: it gave us a new birth. The Christians to whom James writes were the very first to benefit by this gift of the regenerative word. But despite the objective efficacy of this word, it is not enough simply to hear it; a man must welcome and accept it with docility. Since the word is a law, this means that man must put it into practice. Here St. James tells us quite clearly what it means to "practice our religion" and sweeps away all the deliberate or indeliberate illusions cultivated by Christians who think they can take refuge in religious practices and traditions. "Religion that is pure and undefiled before God and the Father is this: to visit orphans and widows in their affliction, and to keep oneself unstained from the world."

The message given us in today's readings is a profitable one and needs frequent repetition. The point made is not that we should be contemptuous of, or regard as hypocritical, all traditions and customs; that would be a puerile attitude. The point is rather that we must be constantly purifying the way we live and practice our religion. Our worship may not be worship in spirit and truth; it may be tainted with legalism, it may have degenerated into a refuge.

There can be a false kind of sacramentalism that unconsciously uses the sacraments as a dispensation from the practice of charity. This description is doubtless too harsh, but it does point to the confused state of mind into which a Catholic can fall. He may come to imagine that the practice of the sacraments and other observances can save him in a magical way and require a lesser love of God and men. No Catholic would put things so baldly, but he may hold this view subconsciously. Christ, however, gives us a means of judging whether or not our worship and observance has a solid basis: What comes out of a man may be corrupt.

TWENTY-THIRD SUNDAY

The Messianic Age

He makes the deaf hear and the dumb speak (Mark 7:31-37)

The whole manner of this healing seems strange to us. It was not an oddity in the time of Jesus, for it reflected practices that were more or less part of the medicine of the day.

Once again we find Jesus forbidding those present to speak of the miracle to others. The crowd is evidently deeply moved. Do they perhaps realize that such cures as this are a sign of the Messiah's presence in their midst? We may think so when we listen to their acclamations, which may well be echoes of popular songs of the kind Isaiah presents to us in the first reading. It certainly seems, at least, that this messianic reference is the reason why Jesus bids those present be silent about the cure. It is to be noted that silence is imposed, if not always observed, with regard to miracles considered to be works of the Messiah who was to come: "The blind receive their sight and the lame walk, lepers are cleansed and the deaf hear, and the dead are raised up" (Matthew 11:5).

Jesus forbids others to speak of the miracle when he cures the leper (Mark 1:44), when he raises Jairus's daughter from the dead (Mark 5:43), when he cures the deaf-mute (Mark 7:36), and when he cures the blind man at Bethsaida (Mark 8:26). The reason for the prohibition is that he does not want to reveal his identity before the appointed time; he still has to undergo his Passion. He wishes to make himself known only gradually and to faith.

In today's Gospel the reactions of the crowd, which St. Mark notes, indicate a certain progress. The crowd exclaims in praise that is directed to what has been done but that says nothing as such about the person of Jesus, although it certainly urges reflection on his identity. We may well ask, however, whether the cry of the crowd is not also the cry of Christians who have been enlightened by the paschal celebration of the death and resurrection of Jesus and who therefore understand the messianic significance of Jesus' action in the light of the later events they have celebrated.

It is to be noted that the rite of baptism at one time made use of the actions Jesus here performs in curing the deaf-mute.

The ears of the deaf shall be unstopped, and the tongue of the dumb shall sing for joy (Is. 35:4-7a)

The coming of the Messiah, which certain cures tell us has taken place in Jesus, was foretold by Isaiah. St. Mark knew of the prophecy and must have thought of it as he wrote, just as his Christian readers must have thought of it. Of course, many stages of history were to pass between prophecy and fulfillment. In addition, now that the Messiah has in fact come and has suffered his glorious Passion, we find ourselves awaiting a new coming.[27] We go our way in company with the Church, and we are witnesses to the presence of the Messiah and the accomplishment of his saving mission.

Only Christ can give us the light to walk in the right path, just as he alone can cure our leprosy and rescue us from death. These spiritual miracles are constantly being worked for us, and they strike with wonder anyone who witnesses them. We know, moreover, that the liberating miraculous deeds of Jesus are still being done, even though we are not always able to see them or put them into words. Our real difficulty, however, is in interpreting the signs that we do see in our own day. It is the same problem as was faced by the disciples contemporary with Jesus, and this even though twenty centuries of ecclesial experience now lie behind us.

The problem of the first disciples was to see Jesus as he really was and therefore to construct a new and different idea of the Messiah than the one that had always filled their imaginations. They had to try to understand what his miracles really meant. We know that when Jesus first spoke of the Eucharistic sign — the eating of his flesh and the drinking of his blood — he met with harsh misunderstanding from many. In our day too, in connection with the sacramental signs that affirm the presence of the kingdom and the Church's progress toward the definitive establishment of that kingdom, there occur many interior miracles as the grace of enlightenment and conversion is bestowed on individuals or groups that now find they must live with eyes fixed on the death and resurrection of Jesus, and for whom human existence takes on a new meaning. Far from despising human life, they work for its advancement, but they also see it as related to an invisible goal that transcends any claims men can make.

The poor shall inherit the kingdom (James 2:1-5)

It can hardly be denied that if James began the second chapter of his Letter in this manner, he did so not in a fit of abstraction but because a real situation in his community required him to do so. In his Jewish-Christian community, he saw favoritism at work, perhaps unconsciously, and a consequent failure to live by the Christian ideal. Respect for persons was entangled with faith in Jesus Christ. And this must have been the case even at the celebration of the liturgy.

The words "For if . . ." are simply diplomatic. Men were certainly making judgments based on a false scale of values. Yet, "has not God chosen those who are poor in the world. . . ?" Paul says the same thing to the Corinthians: "God chose what is foolish in the world to shame the wise . . ." (1 Cor. 1:27-29). The whole of the Old Testament is very much concerned with the poor, and the prophets are constantly lashing out at those who show contempt for the poor. The Gospel shows the same concern, and its "Woe to you rich" and "Blessed are the poor" resound like solemn challenges that sum up the entire Good News.

And yet neither riches nor poverty supply, of themselves, a norm of judgment. The sole norm is love. Those who love the Lord will inherit the kingdom he has promised, for he has made them all rich in faith. Faith is authentic wealth, and love is the passport into the kingdom.

We must all challenge ourselves: What are the values in the light of which we deal with those we must often be with?

TWENTY-FOURTH SUNDAY

The Sufferings of the Servant of God

The Son of Man must suffer much (Mark 8:27-35)

On the twenty-first Sunday (Cycle A) we read, from the Gospel of St. Matthew, the same account of Peter's confession and the prediction of the Passion (Matthew 16:13-20). In the context of the twenty-first Sunday, the emphasis was placed chiefly on the confession of Peter and on the solid foundations of the Church. Today, on the contrary, the emphasis is on the prediction of the Passion and on the necessary suffering of Christ.

Jesus has kept his identity secret, not judging it timely to reveal his messiahship. He has frequently ordered bystanders not to spread the news of a miracle, especially when the miracle could be seen as a clear sign that the Messiah had indeed come. Now, at Peter's confession, the veil is lifted, at least for the immediate disciples.

The prediction of the Passion leads Christ to tell his disciples the conditions that must be met if they are to follow him. Even though Mark's account is the source of the account in St. Matthew, we may refer the reader to our commentary on the latter (pages 129–131).

I gave my back to the smiters (Is. 50:5-9a)

Part of this passage, which is the third poem of the Suffering Servant, was read as a first reading on Palm Sunday.[33] The prophecy is repeated here and brought into relation with Jesus' prediction of his Passion and his invitation to the disciples to follow him in accordance with certain necessary conditions.

The Servant's inner attitude is made clear from the opening lines of the poem: he does not rebel and does not flee from the sufferings inflicted on him. In fact, not only does he not seek to escape, but he even offers his back freely and does not protect his face against blows.

The Servant thus becomes a model for those who want to follow Christ, take up their cross, and not seek to save their own lives. Such discipleship would be impossible if the Lord did not come to the aid of the person who surrenders his life in obedience. Here the prophecy waxes lyrical: The Lord helps his Servant, and the latter becomes invincible, setting his face like flint against his enemies. His strength is chiefly moral; that is, he knows he will not be put to shame, because the One who justifies him is at his side; it is the Lord himself who is his defender.

The Servant sees his sufferings as occurring in a short interval before the last day. The One who justifies him is at hand, and the Servant has no fears about appearing before the Lord's tribunal, along with those who inflict martyrdom on him. It is prayer that enables the Servant to pass safely through all the attacks and to endure them for the Lord. The responsorial psalm (Ps. 116) reminds us of how God helps the person who offers himself in sacrifice in order to do God's will: "The snares of death encompassed me; the pangs of Sheol laid hold on me; I suffered distress and anguish. Then I called on the name of the Lord. . . . When I was brought low, he saved me."

In the readings of this Sunday, the Christian's suffering is transformed, and the self-denial involved in following Christ ceases to appear a mutilation or a purely negative asceticism. Instead, we see it as a sharing in the glorious Passion of Christ as he undertakes the redemption of mankind and the rebuilding of the world. The suffering of the Servant of God, that is, of Christ, is a priestly sacrifice. Consequently, as each Christian follows the lead of Christ, he shares more fully in the priesthood of Christ who offers himself and mankind.

From this we see that the only useless suffering is the suffering we do not accept and offer to God; every other suffering is redemptive. If this were not the case, there would be no reason for insisting on the realism of our baptism as a participation in the death and resurrection of Jesus.

We would also have to shrug off as unreal and mythical that
which constitutes the very heart of Christian life, namely,
the fact that we have put on Christ. To deny oneself, then,
and to carry one's cross is not to mutilate oneself but, on the
contrary, to give one's life a supreme efficacy and thus to win
through to glory.

Faith without works (James 2:14-18)

We must show our faith by the way we act. This passage of
James will protect us against all the illusions that beset
Christian life, for it warns us that the test is not concepts but
concrete actions. As we read the passage, it becomes clear
that it was meant to be read aloud; its sentences strike like a
hammer, and it can leave no one indifferent. The Christian
who hears it must immediately turn to himself and examine
his own life.

St. James supposes that we know what faith is and to what
it is directed. He concentrates on the concrete activity that
faith should inspire and directs his attention chiefly to loving
concern for others. The theme is also a favorite of John's, but
here the style is simpler and more pastoral. A merely conceptual faith does not save, but only a faith that takes concrete form in our lives.

In order to make his point more forcefully, James, like a
good preacher, uses an example. The little scene he describes sounds humorous, and yet we know of "good Christians" in our own day who are fine when it comes to principles but are not too anxious to put them into practice. St.
Augustine once said: "You do not preach the gospel to
people with empty stomachs." A true witness to the faith is
not satisfied with preaching it; he is on the alert for the needs
of others and tries to be of help to them.

For St. James, then, the Christian of his example has only a
dead faith: "Faith by itself, if it has no works, is dead." It is

not enough to have faith; you must also act in accordance with that faith. In this, St. James is not at all in disagreement with St. Paul. When the latter says that faith alone saves (Rom. 3:28), he is only expressing in a theological formula the fact that the Lord has the initiative in the work of salvation and that he exercises this initiative by giving us the gift of faith; our human actions, by themselves, cannot save us. Faith is a gift of God (Rom. 3:27; 4:2-5), and faith is an indispensable condition for salvation (Rom. 3:22-28). At the same time, however, Paul emphasizes the fact that Christ saved us through his obedience (Rom. 5:18-19); it is precisely for that reason that man's own works cannot save him (Rom. 3:28). Yet if a man is to be saved, he must cooperate and live according to the faith he has received: "We are his workmanship, created in Christ Jesus for good works, which God prepared beforehand, that we should walk in them" (Eph. 2:10).

TWENTY-FIFTH SUNDAY

The Son of Man Handed Over to Men

The Son of Man betrayed to men (Mark 9:30-37)

This passage contains the second prediction of the Passion. The first is contained in readings we have already seen (p. 129); the second occurs here, in Cycle B; how Luke presents the message may be seen on the Twelfth Sunday in Cycle C (p. 310).

In the texts parallel to this one of Mark, the Passion is spoken of in the future tense: "The Son of Man is to be delivered into the hands of men" (Matthew 17:22; Luke 9:44). In Mark, however, it is spoken of as a present event: a literal translation of the Greek would be: "The Son of Man is delivered [or: being delivered] into the hands of men," although the slaying of Jesus and his resurrection are put in the future.

As the reader doubtless knows, the word "deliver" is a characteristic verb of the Passion narratives. We also meet it in Jeremias (26:24) and in St. Paul (Rom. 4:25; 8:32; Eph. 5:2). It is also used in Luke and Paul in the accounts of the Last Supper (Luke 22:19; 1 Cor. 11:23).

How are we to take the statement that "the Son of Man is [or: will be] delivered into the hands of men"? It does not imply a constraint placed upon Jesus but simply the fulfillment of God's plan, for it is the Father who delivers his Son — the Son of Man — into the hands of men. Here we have a favorite Johannine theme: "God so loved the world that he gave his only Son" (John 3:16). In words closer to Mark's text, St. Paul writes: "He . . . did not spare his own Son but gave him up for us all" (Rom. 8:32).

The disciples do not understand the prediction of the Passion. So little do they understand it that at this moment, which should have been such a dramatic one for them, they fall into a discussion about who is the greatest among them!

Jesus takes advantage of this discussion to teach them what the ideal of "first place" must be in the community they will constitute. Primacy is first and foremost a primacy in service; to discharge a responsibility will mean that the responsible one makes himself the least and the servant of all the others. It is possible that disputes had already arisen among the disciples about who would possess authority; we have, for example, the incident in which the mother of the Zebedees asks a special place for her sons (Matthew 20:20). It is possible, too, that the evangelist had met with challenges in his own community and wished here to report the words of Jesus, and thus bring home the true meaning of authority and first places in the Church. We may also ask whether, having just predicted his Passion, Jesus is describing himself as the first who is the servant of all by giving his life for all. That is the point he will make again at the washing of the feet, when the Passion is at hand.

Today's pericope continues: "He took a child, and put him

in the midst of them." The connection of this incident with what precedes is not clear. All the hypotheses offered are possible, but they remain simple hypotheses.

Is there a connection between the prediction of the Passion, Jesus' role as servant, and faith in Jesus who insists on accepting the child as the symbol both of innocence and of defenseless weakness? "Whoever receives one such child in my name receives me; and whoever receives me, receives not me but him who sent me."

In point of fact, this final episode of the child hardly forms part of the theme of this Sunday, which is given over to the prediction of the Passion.

Condemned to a shameful death (Wis. 2:12, 17-20)

The text draws a picture for us of Jesus predicting his Passion. Jesus is the kill-joy: "He . . . opposes our actions" (Wis. 2:12). The complaints against the just man are listed. The first is very general: he opposes us. The second is more specific: he reproaches us for our behavior. The third is still more offensive to the Pharisees: he accuses us of betraying our traditions.

This passage, especially the verses read in today's liturgy (vv. 17-20), has been seen as a prophetic prediction of Christ's Passion. This view seems justified. In St. Matthew's Gospel, though without any express reference to the Book of Wisdom, we find the Jews speaking the same language as the persecutors of the just man in the prophecy: "He trusts in God; let God deliver him now, if he desires him" (Matthew 27:43). Whether or not the Old Testament text is prophetic, it presents at least a prefiguration of Christ, who in his suffering will reach the pinnacle of martyrdom.

The responsorial psalm (Ps. 54) expresses the determination of Christ the Servant to offer himself to the Father: "With a freewill offering I will sacrifice to thee; I will give thanks to thy name, O Lord, for it is good."

Peacemakers (James 3:16–4:3)

St. James' thoughts about his Christian community are not totally optimistic, and in this a parish priest of our day could often agree with him. There is a genuine wisdom: it comes from God; its fruits are unmistakable, and the most important of them is justice accompanied by peace. The lack of this justice and peace is disastrous for the Christian community and for the world generally. James sees that the life of the Christians he is addressing is not what it should be. Even their prayer is no help in this regard, because what they pray for is material riches and the satisfaction of their instincts.

TWENTY-SIXTH SUNDAY

Preach and Heal in the Lord's Name

Cast out demons in the name of the Lord (Mark 9:38-43, 45, 47-48)

Today's passage from the Gospel contains several themes that have little connection with one another. It gives an impression of a conversation in which Jesus turns from subject to subject according to the questions his disciples put to him.

John asks a question, prompted by his wonder and concern that someone who does not belong to the group should be casting out demons. The answer Jesus gives is important, because it can and should deepen the disciples' understanding of their own group. Jesus is telling them that there can be people outside the group who believe in him and can perform exorcisms in his name. There is no reason for hindering such a man. The implicit criterion is that he should not speak ill of Jesus. St. Matthew tells us that the mark of a false prophet is that he does not do the Father's will. It is not indispensable that a person belong to the Christian community in order to act in the name of Jesus, provided he believes and observes the commandments.

Jesus is trying to broaden the outlook of his disciples, who may be tempted to seal themselves off as a closed group and to maintain in a spirit of jealousy what they consider to be the exclusive prerogative of the community. This does not mean, however, that it is meaningless to be a disciple of Christ. When someone offers a disciple something as small as a cup of water, he is offering it to Jesus himself. There is a close link between Jesus and the disciples, and this should be further reflected in solidarity within the Christian community. The disciples "belong to Christ" (an expression favored by St. Paul; see Rom. 8:9; 1 Cor. 1:12; 3:23; 2 Cor. 10:7).

The Gospel reading now moves on to another area: the question of scandalizing the "little ones" who believe in Jesus. "Little ones" should not be taken as referring only to children. It can also mean the simpler members of the Christian community, that is, those who are less educated and who belong to a lower social class and are materially or culturally poor.

The passage ends with still a third admonition, this one concerning occasions of sin. To attempt a detailed exemplification of Jesus' meaning would, however, distort his message. He never thought of a catalogue of temptations corresponding to a catalogue of sins. His teaching is concerned rather with the unconditional value of the kingdom as compared with anything and everything else. The important thing is to live by the standards of the kingdom and thus to avoid the fire of hell.

May the Lord make everyone a prophet! (Num. 11:25-29)

The situation of the people of God requires that it possess institutions and that provision be made for its future; there must be continuity between the successive leaders of the people. This is why Moses establishes a council of seventy elders. The Lord takes some of the spirit that rests on Moses and bestows it upon the elders. They begin to prophesy, but this phenomenon is passing.

The spirit also comes to rest on two men who were not present at the meeting at which the seventy were appointed, and they begin to prophesy in the camp. This startles a young man, who runs to tell Moses of it; the reaction of Josue, the minister of Moses, is that the two men should be stopped. Moses' response, on the contrary, shows a fine breadth of outlook: "Would that all the Lord's people were prophets, that the Lord would put his spirit upon them!" In this response we see a desire for openness as opposed to rigid traditionalism.

Moses' response represents a reaction against what in our time we might call a proud clericalism. The responsorial psalm (Ps. 19) supports such a reaction: "Keep back thy servant also from presumptuous sins; let them not have dominion over me!"

The teaching given today is by no means irrelevant and should stir us to reflection in several areas. The readings teach us to be open and to reject all forms of clericalism and ecclesiastical triumphalism. These temptations are real both for the Church at large and for those in the Church who hold authority and exercise power.

A further point is that while the priesthood of Christ is communicated in forms that are essentially and not only accidentally different, nonetheless all the baptized are in some sense prophets. Consequently, just as we must not turn the Church in on herself and deny that great things can be done outside of her, neither must those who have received a higher and more important degree of priesthood prevent the faithful from exercising the priesthood that is properly theirs, even though they should exercise it under the control and authority of the hierarchical priesthood.

The problem of scandal should likewise not be neglected. It relates not only to the temptations each of us experience but to the possibility of shocking those whose faith is not properly enlightened. There is, of course, only one truth; this does not mean, however, that everything should be said and taught to everyone without exception and in every circumstance and without regard for the manner in which it is done. We should review our attitudes on this point as on the others made in today's readings.

The corruption of riches (James 5:1-6)

James speaks harshly; the passage sounds like a homily intended to reawaken consciences. Without regarding it as a party platform, it certainly applies to situations we find today. It has the advantage of avoiding the vulgarity and superficiality to which this kind of criticism often degenerates.

The picture of wealth and the wealthy is unsparing and forthright. Wealth, seemingly so splendid and desirable, unexpectedly vanishes, leaving only a few wretched tatters behind. It seems worthwhile only if we do not put it in the perspective of the last day that is drawing near; if we do view it in this perspective, it proves valueless, and even a source of condemnation, since it is too often derived from injustice: wages not paid and crying for retribution, people slain so that the rich man might live his life of luxury. The rich often kill the righteous without their resisting; they deprive the poor of their bread and thus condemn them to death. Does "the righteous man" refer to Christ? Certainly it was the wealthy and those living luxurious lives who killed Christ, inasmuch as he bore the sufferings and injustices that are the lot of the poor.

St. James is content with this short description, with this reproach whose "peaceful violence" has rarely been surpassed. He doubtless saw in the Jewish-Christian community situations that called for such a harsh attack. Certainly our own age can meditate with humility on this passage and profit from it.

TWENTY-SEVENTH SUNDAY

The Unity of the Human Couple

Let man not separate what God has joined (Mark 10:2-16)

Today's Gospel passage contains two parts, with no visible link between them. St. Mark is recording various teachings of Jesus under the general rubric of revelation and faith, but he is not interested in there being any further logical link between the teachings. Today's first reading is connected with only the first part of the Gospel pericope. We are thus invited to emphasize chiefly the first part, but without wholly neglecting the second. We shall comment on the first part, then go to the first reading, and finally come back to the second part of the Gospel.

Mark is recording a debate between Jesus and the Pharisees. The Pharisees begin with an insidious question concerning divorce. The conversation reminds us of a worldly gathering today at which an attempt is made to embarrass a priest with questions regarding civil divorce. It seems clear that St. Mark is glad of the opportunity to provide his faithful with clear instruction on this matter.

The issue, of course, is the Christian view of marriage, which stood in contrast to both the Jewish and the pagan views of it. Christianity was in conflict with Judaism and paganism alike on the question of fidelity in marriage.

In rabbinic Judaism, a wife could be guilty of adultery toward her husband, but he could not be similarly guilty toward his wife. To this view St. Mark opposes the clear attitude of Jesus: Man and woman have the same duty of fidelity, so that a man who divorces his wife and marries another is an adulterer. Adultery can be a man's sin no less than a woman's. Jesus is here clearly abolishing the Mosaic law on divorce and promulgating once again the law of God, which is timeless, unlike the Mosaic law, which represented a yielding to temporary circumstances.

Jesus is not satisfied to enunciate a principle; he shows that the Scriptures agree with him, as he gives his interpretation of the text of the Book of Genesis: "From the beginning of creation, 'God made them male and female.' 'For this reason a man shall leave his father and mother and be joined to his wife, and the two shall become one.' So they are no longer two but one." He is here stating the permanent and indissoluble unity of marriage.

The two shall now be one (Gen. 2:18-24)

The account of creation in the Book of Genesis shows man and woman to be equal beings with a common origin. Woman is indeed not "created" in the same way as man, since her being is drawn from his. But the point of the description is to show the human beings as being diversified so that the male receives from God the helpmate he has requested. The account is not saying that the second human being — woman — belongs to a different level or order than the first. On the contrary, Adam is able to say: "This at last is bone of my bones and flesh of my flesh." He then gives her her name: "She shall be called Woman." The English here reflects to some extent the relation between the Hebrew words for Adam and Eve: Adam is *'ish*, that is, "man," while Eve is *'ishah*, that is, "woman," *'ishah* being simply a feminine noun formed directly from *'ish*.

The Book of Genesis goes on to explain the consequences of this "creation" of woman from man: "Therefore a man leaves his father and his mother and cleaves to his wife, and they become one flesh." The unity of the couple is being emphasized. However, we must not read too much

into this text. People of early times understood quite well
the role of woman as helpmate to man without concluding
that polygamy was to be practiced. It was not practiced in
the time of the biblical patriarchs. In today's passage from
Mark, divorce is the only issue; Jesus says nothing of
polygamy. The author or authors of the Book of Genesis
were interested only in asserting the equality of woman. In
human terms, she is not a different kind of being from man
and is not inferior to him. She possesses the same nature as
he does; she is "part" of him; she is his partner and equal.

Consequently, from the beginning the Church has felt
bound to transmit a doctrine that is confirmed by her own
experience. In God's plan, woman is joined to man as a
helpmate, but a helpmate who is his equal. The union between them is so great and strong that there can be no question of breaking it. None of the reasons given for permitting
divorce can counterbalance the ontological fact that is manifested in their being "created" together. The unity of the
couple and the requirement of mutual fidelity are not simply moral imperatives required by external convention.
Rather, the demand for fidelity flows from what each of the
couple is ontologically for the other. No one has a right to
act contrary to this ontological relationship, be it individual,
State, or Church. This very fact implies that the requirements of fidelity may demand heroism of the couple.

Surely today's reading will be a subject for salutary meditation by all married people, especially in today's world, in
which pagan and erotic views of marriage are gaining the
upper hand. It is not simply an external moral code that
requires fidelity of spouses, but the way in which God himself has planned the world and set man therein, giving him
a helpmate who is to be another self to him.

To such belongs the kingdom of heaven

We come now to the second half of the Gospel pericope;
as indicated above, it has no connection with the first half.
The words concerning the kingdom and little children

have at times been misinterpreted. Jesus is not recommending a vague and naïve attitude to life nor saying that the irresponsibility of a child will take us into the kingdom. He is simply pointing to a single truth: We must be open to the gift of the kingdom. The child here is a model, not of childish naïveté nor of the supposed beauty of inexperience, but of receptivity; a child is still open to reality much more than an adult. A child has not yet been hardened by selfishness or closed off by pride in his own knowledge and accomplishments; therefore he readily and generously accepts what is given to him.

These dispositions are necessary for the kingdom. Children enter the kingdom easily because they are capable of accepting gifts. It is this candor and openness, which has nothing to do with naïveté, that Christ wants to see in those who wish to enter the kingdom.

Men made holy are the brothers of Jesus (Heb. 2:9-11)

He who sanctifies (Jesus) and those who are sanctified (men) are intimately linked with one another: they "have all one origin." This is why Jesus calls men his brothers. But the perfection of man in Christ is the result of a long and painful journey on Christ's part and on ours. Jesus remains the source of all holiness. But it is God's intention to have a multitude of sons and daughters whom Jesus will lead to glory. This plan required that he who is the source of salvation for everyone else should himself first be made perfect through suffering.

This passage contains expressions that we may find quite strange at first hearing, and they need to be properly understood. All of them bring out the reality of the incarnation; they apply to the human nature of Jesus and in no way derogate from his divinity.

Jesus was made a little lower than the angels, but because he suffered and died, he was crowned with glory. This is one of the themes of the Letter to the Philippians (2:1-11; see twentieth Sunday, Cycle A). In today's passage the writer cites Psalm 8:5 in order to give expression to the humbling of Jesus in his human nature.

Jesus has also been brought to his perfection through suffering. He was, of course, perfect in his divine nature. On the other hand, he took to himself a human nature and everything in it, except for sin; he accepted even the consequences of sin, and therefore he was capable of being perfected. His human nature will be made complete and whole, and in this sense perfected, through suffering. Suffering is not in and of itself the source of perfection, but suffering accepted and offered up in accordance with God's plan is such a source. In the case of Jesus, the "perfection" to which he is brought takes the form of his glorification. If such has been the course of Jesus' life, then it must also be the course of our lives, since he gave his life for us, his brothers.

TWENTY-EIGHTH SUNDAY

Abandon All You Have

Sell what you have and follow Jesus (Mark 10:17-30)

Today's passage from St. Mark offers no special difficulties. Its theme is easily grasped: Wealth makes the attainment of salvation difficult, even when the rich man desires salvation and seems to be seeking it. Jesus then promises a hundredfold, even on earth, to those who leave everything and follow him.

The young man who has great wealth but throws himself at Jesus' feet certainly is desirous of obtaining eternal life. He is eager in his wish to learn from Jesus the means of salvation. He calls Jesus "Good Teacher." Jesus answers him with a question, "Why do you call me good?" but does not wait for an answer; instead, he continues by saying, "No one is good but God alone." Jesus is doubtless here taking advantage of an opportunity to emphasize his own divinity and to open the eyes of the rich man. We may also suggest, however, that the adjective "good" which befits God alone is also introduced because of the commandments that follow and that are a sign of God's good will toward his people, since through his commandments he leads them in the right path.

When Jesus lists the commandments, the rich man says that he has observed them since his youth. Well, then, all he lacks is one thing: to sell all he has, give it to the poor, receive treasure in heaven instead, and follow Jesus. At this point the mood changes: the rich man grows heavy of heart and goes away sorrowful.

Jesus now has occasion to develop his teaching on attachments and the kingdom. The example he gives is so extreme, however, that it discourages the disciples when they realize that it is not enough to have surrendered all their possessions. St. Matthew is thinking, of course, of all Christians, and not all of them were rich people; even for those who are not rich, there are many obstacles along the road, and these must be overcome. But who is capable of that? Jesus answers the disciples' fearful question by saying: "With men it is impossible, but not with God; for all things are possible with God."

This passage has at times been interpreted as referring to "religious life," as we understand this term today, that is, to a special path of perfection. But in fact Jesus is here addressing all Christians, and that is how Matthew understands him. All Christians must renounce what they have and follow the way of detachment, because that is the price of entering the kingdom. Such a teaching confronts the Christian with an immense task, and in the face of it there is only one resource: faith in God who can do all things.

Peter and the other disciples are discouraged; he speaks in their name: "We have left everything and followed." We can guess his anxious implication: What good is it all? Jesus then lists the things men must be detached from, and promises, along with persecutions, a hundredfold reward in this life. This amounts to saying that it is not possessions as such that are an obstacle to salvation (otherwise they would not be given back to us a hundredfold), but our attachment to them. (St. Mark must have had a twinkle in his eye when he added persecutions to the blessings that will be restored!) Detachment will bring eternal life in the world to come.

Regard riches as worthless (Wis. 7:7-11)

The choice of this passage is evidently determined by the Gospel pericope. We may therefore read it in the light of the Gospel, just as we may in turn read the Gospel in the light of this reading. This procedure may not be justified according to the strict norms of exegesis, but we have on several occasions in these volumes explained the nature of a liturgical reading of the Scriptures.

The prayer of the wise man, who is now able to regard riches as worthless, shows that this kind of wisdom is a gift and must be asked for. The detachment that the wise man now possesses is humanly impossible without this gift of wisdom. Like wisdom, poverty and detachment are gifts; but once wisdom is received, all riches become as nothing in comparison with it.

Using the words of Jesus, St. Mark in today's passage teaches his Christians the dangers of wealth, but also the dangers of any attachment to earthly things. The person who wants to follow the Lord must rise above everything that is transient and set his heart on what abides. He cannot do this unless the Lord gives him his grace.

Too often, as we said above, texts like this are applied

only to "religious life," but in fact they refer, in the Gospel, to the life of every Christian. We must apply them to ourselves.

―――――

The living word of God (Heb. 4:12-13)

There is always a danger that we may think of the word of God simply as the expression of concepts or ideas. In fact, however, the word of God is essentially something living and active. The writer of this Letter expresses this aspect of God's word with the help of a striking image: the executioner's sword.

The Old Testament prophets have already made us familiar with the idea that the word is active and efficacious (see Is. 55:11). It is a power that brings salvation. The word always looks to our real selves; it is not deceived by appearances but lays all things bare. The Christian is therefore urged to cultivate honesty in the presence of the word. The liturgy of the word is a time of judgment for him, but also a time when he is helped to greater holiness and courage. We shall have to render an account of the word spoken to us.

TWENTY-NINTH SUNDAY

The Life of Christ, A Ransom for the Many

The Son of Man gives his life for the many (Mark 10:35-45)

In the immediately preceding scriptural title for this commentary on the pericope from Mark, I have deliberately

omitted the words "as a ransom." I am not trying to emend
the Gospel. The fact is, however, that the expression "give
his life as a ransom" needs to be provided with a context
and explained accordingly if it is not to be misinterpreted.
It is misinterpreted when the reader imagines a kind of exchange between God and man or a contract between God
and the victim that he requires if he is to forgive sins. That
kind of interpretation makes God's forgiveness conditional
upon the death of a victim; it is consequently an insult to
the mighty love of God. Yet the expression does suggest
that kind of interpretation and needs therefore to be properly explained.

The petition of the sons of Zebedee seems both strange
and bold. They already know that Christ must suffer, for he
has predicted his Passion three times already. Yet they
seem quite determined: "We want you to do for us whatever we ask of you." The trouble is that though they want to
share Jesus' lot, they want in fact to share only his glory and
not the sufferings in store for him. (James and John were
among the first four disciples whom Jesus called; traditionally, though without any proof, they have been regarded as relatives of Jesus.)

Jesus answers them, but in doing so he uses an unusual
vocabulary, and his whole answer is couched in such a special way that some exegetes think that the episode and
Jesus' answer were introduced later on as a postfactum
prophecy of the martyrdom of James and John. In any
event, the other disciples are indignant at the two brothers
for making such a request to Jesus.

Jesus does not answer their petition directly. He tries to
make them understand more fully the painful reality of his
Passion, for they must endure it in their own way, just as he
must. Jesus knows that they do not really understand what
it is they are asking. He tells them they must drink the cup
that he will drink. "Cup" is a frequent image in the Bible;
thus, "the cup of wrath," "the cup of salvation," "the cup of
blessing" were familiar expressions that pointed to a crucial
moment in the life of an individual or a city.

On the other hand, the image of a "baptism" that Jesus must undergo and that his disciples must share would not have been familiar. In itself, the image might have the same content as the image of the cup: a baptism in suffering, an immersion in pain, under the wrathful hand of God. Psalm 109 speaks of a curse as penetrating like water (v. 18). In Psalm 42 the psalmist speaks of the waves and billows of God that pass over him (v. 7). If today's passage from Mark was indeed introduced into the Gospel later on, as some exegetes suggest, we could relate this baptism to the forgiveness of sins through the Passion of Jesus.

The sons of Zebedee persist in their request and claim that they are prepared to share in Jesus' sufferings. Even so, Jesus grants them only a share in his Passion. The sharing in his glory does not depend on him, but on the Father who prepares places for men. Men can only submit to his decisions.

The indignation of the other disciples gives Jesus an opportunity to give further teaching on authority and service. The other disciples are not as bold as the sons of Zebedee, but they doubtless had similar ambitions. Jesus therefore tells them what authority and service should mean for those who are his disciples. Among them, the attitudes of the world are turned upside down. Here authority is a form of service. The great men of the world make others feel the weight of their power; not so among the disciples. Among them, anyone wishing to be great will serve others, and the one who wishes to be first will make himself the slave of everyone else. ("Servant" and "slave" are two words that mean pretty much the same thing here.)

We may think that this passage was important to Mark in the light of his Church's needs. He wants his Christians to think in terms of service rather than of authority, and to realize that the service in question must be given to everyone in the community and will impose a kind of slavery on the servant, since he will be utterly at the disposal of all. No one can undertake such service by his own unaided powers; it can only be accomplished by God's gift.

Even though there are degrees of service in the Church, with persons at each level putting their talents and gifts at the service of all, all the degrees together form a kind of body of slaves, dedicated to the service of the community at large. In undertaking such service, the disciple will simply be imitating what Christ does before him, for Christ took upon himself the condition of a slave (Phil. 2:5-8). In today's pericope, Jesus sums up his situation with utmost clarity: "The Son of man also came not to be served but to serve, and to give his life as a ransom for many."

We can understand what "give his life as a ransom" means, and yet it sounds strange to us. Some theologians, as I indicated earlier, have gone so far as to postulate a kind of exchange: Jesus surrenders his life so that we might have life. Yet how horrible and even blasphemous seems the idea of a God who wishes that a man should die as a ransom for sin and who demands this death as the means of liberating others! Certainly, when presented dryly and in bare form as we are presenting it here, this kind of trade seems not only repugnant but utterly unworthy of God and of human beings confronted with God. We must therefore avoid the words "as a ransom," while keeping the valid thought that the words contain.

If we are to understand the text correctly, we must turn to historical fact and not let ourselves be hampered by what may be simply a temporally conditioned image that reflects the social conditions of a country or even the larger world at a particular moment in time. Both the Old and the New Testaments are familiar with the theme of a man who suffers and gives his life in exchange — as a ransom — for many. The first reading for today provides us with an example (Is. 53:10-11). The synoptic Gospels (today's pericope, for example) use the theme, and St. Paul will develop it at length. The first Christian communities liked to think of Jesus as the suffering Servant who gives his life as a ransom for many. In short, the ideas of redemption (buying back), ransom, and substitution occur frequently. The question is: Do they express a theology, or are they simply images that try to approach the reality in a particular way?

In an unqualified form, the theology according to which Christ pays a ransom to God for us all by dying, brings us very close to religious myth. It seems more suited to some ancient religion or other in which a god wants an expiatory human victim.

What are the historical facts? By this I mean: What happened in the life of Jesus? We must see his life, not through the spectacles of images, but as it really was. In reality, then, the entire life of Jesus was a struggle — not at the ideological level, but a concrete struggle against all that enslaves man, all the imbalances that have become like a second nature to him. The preaching and examples of Jesus were entirely a manifestation of his will to restore mankind to true freedom — a freedom from sin and guilt. More concretely, we see Jesus seeking to free men from the law. In what sense? Not by abolishing the law (he explicitly says that he does not wish to abolish it), but by showing that it is not *per se* the way to salvation. In so doing, he comes into conflict with the religious establishment of his country.

Jesus refuses to play the political game that is expected of him, for he refuses to let his mission be interpreted as a political restoration of the nation. Moreover, he refuses to let his mission and powers be co-opted for a political miracle that would bypass the responsibility of men and their free will. He refuses also to let men rest in an easy security in relation to God or to employ magic in their dealings with him. He demands, instead, true love of neighbor, forgiveness of others, humble charity, hidden prayer, and unostentatious austerity.

In all these ways Jesus disappoints and shocks others, and his death will be the outcome of his persistence in his ways. He dies as a prophet who has refused to cater to the desires of the people he teaches. He has disappointed them. Worse than that, he has done a disservice to the cause of well-ordered religion, its priestly caste, and its learned men.

Jesus dies, and his death is especially meaningful and efficacious because it is a death endured for the sake of the forgiveness of sins. This forgiveness will free the many and lead them to a new life. We might try to bring out the basic direction of Jesus' life by saying that his Passion began at his incarnation, for it was at that moment of entering upon the human condition that he deliberately accepted death. His death, his forgiveness ("Father, forgive them; for they know not what they do"), and his resurrection — these mediate the salvation that God has intended for mankind from the beginning.

We must be careful not to put our theology into categories that are temporally and culturally conditioned. Can God in his anger require the death of a human being — his Son — so that others may thereby be ransomed? Does such an idea express a truly theological vision, or does it rather represent theology translated into the cultural language of a particular age?

Let us look for a moment at the Trinity. Does not the Father give himself to men, all of them, so that he may win them? He does not die himself, and his suffering at giving his Son is not identical with the suffering of the Son, but the Father does suffer at the death of the Son. When Jesus dies, we do not have the Father standing as a judge over against the Son who gives himself as a victim in place of all the others and pays in behalf of all the price the Father requires. No! Between Father and Son there is a perfect conformity of wills.

Perhaps John best expressed the point we are making when he wrote: "God so loved the world that he gave his only Son, that whoever believes in him should not perish but have eternal life" (3:16). The same evangelist sees the mystery of the Cross as a mystery of the love that is God's very being: "God is love" (1 John 4:16). God is love even at the moment of Jesus' death. At this moment, when Father and Son seem to be so utterly separated, they are in fact utterly united in a single love for the salvation of the world. Bloodshed and death are but the signs that express love; it is not the death that saves, but that which the death expresses. Yet the death was needed precisely so that the love might find expression and convince the world of its reality.

If we go back now to the words "give his life as a ransom for many," we can see better what they mean, and we can without difficulty overlook the commercial overtones of a "swap" or exchange that the words would normally carry. In this context the words are an imaged way of expressing the reality of the love that the Father and the Son have for the world they wish to save. The Son has been sent into the world, and he dies in consequence of a deliberate attitude of obedient self-surrender that has been his throughout his earthly life. In his death he forgives us all, and in his resurrection he brings us all to victory with him. Thus he frees us all for eternal life.

The Servant will justify many (Is. 53:10-11)

The preceding commentary will enable us to read this text from a Christian viewpoint. For an analysis we refer the reader to the commentary on the Good Friday liturgy.[28]

Jesus, the High Priest, has been tested (Heb. 4:14-16)

This reading has likewise already been read on Good Friday; a short commentary on it was given at that point.[29]

The readings of this Sunday require more than passive contemplation. They have consequences for the spiritual life of each individual. Like Christ, we must accept the consequences of our baptism, which puts us in clear opposition to the principles of the world. Baptism makes us strangers and pilgrims on earth, although it does not absolve us of our duty to be concerned about our world.

Like Christ, we are servants, and the more authority we may happen to have, the more we must make ourselves the servants of others. In our service, we must give our lives and we must forgive the offenses of all so that they may believe and live by what they believe. In fact, the thing we must communicate to others is that same desire to serve; then all will share in the kingdom. The divisions among us and the fight to get the first places in the Church are shame-

ful and most unworthy. Each of us should seek to be where
the Spirit wants us to be, according to the judgment of the
Church. And wherever the Church puts us, she wants us to
be servants of the word, to the extent of sacrificing our lives
for all.[30]

THIRTIETH SUNDAY

Messianic Signs and Faith

Lord, let me see! (Mark 10:46-52)

Jesus is on the road, moving toward Jerusalem. A sizable
crowd follows him. Beside the road sits a blind man named
Bartimaeus. These are the circumstances of a miracle that,
like all the miracles of Jesus, is a sign that the Messiah is
now present.

Jesus is moved to act by the blind man's faith-inspired
cries: "Jesus, Son of David, have mercy on me!" The crowd
tries to silence him, for they find his cries embarrassing and
almost indecent; they hardly sense the faith of the man,
moving though it is. But Jesus is touched by it; he stops and
has the blind man brought to him. His act is inspired by
kindness, but he does not go to the man; rather, he has the
man brought to him. His coming, even though he is led by
the hand, is a personal act. The intensity of the man's faith
can be seen by the way he throws off his mantle, leaps to
his feet, and comes to Jesus.

The question Jesus asks seems odd. Why ask a blind man
what he wants done for him when he cries out for pity? But
just as Jesus wanted the man to come to him and thus prove
his good will, so he wants the man to express his faith in
Jesus in a clear way: "Master, let me receive my sight."

Jesus' response is immediate and unhesitating: "Go your way; your faith has made you well." The blind man receives his sight and follows Jesus on his way.

The blind and the lame will be consoled (Jer. 31:7-9)

This passage from Jeremias was chosen for today's liturgy because it contains the words, "I will bring them . . . the blind and the lame. . . . With weeping they shall come, and with consolations." But this consolation is simply one of the signs proving that "the Lord has saved his people, the remnant of Israel." The blind and the lame as such have but a very secondary role in the passage; they are part of a great assembly of exiles returning from Babylon, to whom salvation is being offered. The "remnant" of Israel is returning from a foreign land, and Jeremias lists the various categories of people found in their numbers. All these people went away in tears, but now they are returning amid consolation. The Lord ends his oracle with the words, "I am a father to Israel."

The responsorial psalm (Ps. 126) is indeed a response to this reading, for it sings of the joyous return of the exiles: "The Lord has done great things for them. The Lord has done great things for us; we are glad."

The theme of this Sunday is a broad one. What profit can we draw from it? The cure of the blind man doubtless makes us think immediately of the light that God gives us, but the first reading does not lead us in the direction of such an interpretation. The following remarks may help us make a synthesis of the important points in the two readings.

In the order of salvation, everything depends on God taking the first step, for in the last analysis, it is he who saves. This was true for exiles whom he freed from Babylon; it was true for the blind man whom Jesus healed. God deliberately reaches out in his goodness and establishes contact with man.

At the same time, however, some movement of man to-

ward God is also required. Thus the remnant of Israel
obeys the call and journeys toward Jerusalem; even the
blind, the lame, and the pregnant women take to the road.
So too the blind Bartimaeus leaps up and moves toward the
Lord. This movement is a sign of a deep faith; in fact, the
blind man has already been crying out so loudly that the
crowd tries to silence him. On man's part, this kind of faith
is the basic element unto salvation.

Salvation is not limited to some immediate, personal
cure. The cure of the blind man is a messianic sign; that is,
it is a sign of a final age that is still coming. The remnant of
Israel journeys to Jerusalem, but that holy city is itself only
a sign of an abiding city. In order to enter this abiding city,
this ultimate age, men must be converted and must live by
faith.

We must be on guard, then, not to stop short at immediate
events as though they were an end in themselves. The cure
of the blind man is not a goal simply, but also a sign of the
world to come. Neither must we stop short at the sacramental signs as though the sign were all; the sign is important
because it helps us and our world toward the final day and
the complete reconstruction of the world.

On this Sunday, therefore, we are urged to deepen our
faith by directing it toward the abiding world that is on its
way. Every grace we receive should lead us onward to this
final day.

Jesus, a Priest for ever (Heb. 5:1-6)

In this day and age, a reading on priesthood should not
leave us indifferent but should provide an opportunity for
clarifying our ideas on a subject that is part of our faith. The
priesthood of the New Testament is radically different from
that of the Old, not only because it is not hereditary, as the
priesthood of Aaron was, but also because it comes through
a new mediator, Christ.

"The order of Melchisedech" is only an analogy, and the priesthood of Christ, though prefigured by that of Melchisedech, also transcends it. Much that is said of the high priest in the Old Testament can be said of Christ, but Christ's priesthood is nonetheless fundamentally different: he is the one Priest and need not offer his sacrifice more than once. Because he is both Priest and Victim, he offers but once, and his sacrifice is perfect.

The priesthood given through ordination and the priesthood given through baptism are participations, essentially different among themselves in degree, in the one priesthood of Christ. The priesthood given through ordination is essentially distinguished by its Spirit-given power to make the past mysteries of Christ present and operative.

THIRTY-FIRST SUNDAY

The Great Commandment

No greater commandment than love of others (Mark 12:28b-34)

In St. Matthew's account, the scribe's question was: "Teacher, which is the great commandment of the law?" The question was meant as a trap, for the Jews used to discuss among themselves which commandment might be said to sum up all the others (see page 162). In St. Mark's Gospel, the same question takes a slightly different form, and we have less of a sense that the questioner is trying to entrap Jesus. In fact, the scribe who asks the question even admits that Jesus is right. For doing so, he receives praise and encouragement from Jesus: "You are not far from the kingdom of God."

In his answer, Jesus quotes a passage from the Book of

Deuteronomy (6:4) that speaks of loving God. It is chiefly in
this book that the expression "love God" occurs in the Old
Testament; it is less frequent in the other books, but it does
occur (for example: Jos. 22:5; 23:11; Ps. 31:23; Sir. 2:10;
7:32). Even the word "love" is quite infrequent, for the Old
Testament prefers a related set of terms: fear of God, service of God, seeking the face of God, fidelity. In the passage
from the Book of Deuteronomy, love of God is linked to a
monotheistic faith: "The Lord our God is one God." To this
love of God, Jesus then adds love of neighbor as a commandment closely connected with it.

The response of the scribe to Jesus' answer is itself a
teaching, for it tells us that love of neighbor is more important than offerings and sacrifices.

Jesus' final words are to be noted: "You are not far from
the kingdom of God." They reflect Mark's preoccupation
with the kingdom that has been proclaimed and is at hand.
That kingdom is continually proclaimed when love of God
and neighbor rules the community. Surely, that too is a lesson Mark wants his readers to take with them.

You shall love the Lord with all your heart (Deut. 6:2-6)

This is the passage from which Jesus drew his answer to
the scribe. It is such an important passage that it became
part of the prayer *Shema' Israel*, which the devout Jew re-
cites daily, even in our time. Since the Lord Jesus quoted
the text to express a central point in his own teaching, it
deserves our meditation; it is certainly also an important
point of contact between Christianity and Judaism.

In the Book of Deuteronomy, the Lord promises happiness if the Israelites observe the law he is about to give
them. In the context, this happiness is doubtless the earthly
happiness of Israel as a community. We should not look
down our noses at this, since earthly happiness is a good
thing, and no authentic spirituality can be totally unconcerned about it, to the extent that it does not become a

stumbling block or make a person forget the happiness that will be lasting. This much is certainly true: the observance of the commandments of love for God and neighbor makes a community well balanced and creates in it an atmosphere that is relaxed and joyous.

The love commanded us is love of the one true God whom the text calls "our God." "Yahweh is our God" is a kind of liturgical acclamation that may have been used in various celebrations. Toward the fifth century B.C., "Adonai" had become a favorite title for Yahweh; it was forbidden to pronounce the name "Yahweh", and "Adonai" was substituted for it, although the written text continues to read "Yahweh."[31] In the phrase "our God," Israel prayed to the God it regarded as its own special possession.

If the commandments are obeyed, God promises that the land will be fruitful, "flowing with milk and honey." In many countries, a newborn child used to be given some milk and honey; the practice was medicinal, but also superstitious to some extent. According to the *Apostolic Tradition* of St. Hippolytus of Rome (beginning of the third century), an adult neophyte received a drink of milk and honey at his baptism as a reminder that the promises of God to the patriarchs had now been fulfilled.[32] It is easy to understand how a practice that already existed in handling newborn babies could be given a spiritual meaning and transferred to "newborn" Christians.

The responsorial psalm (Ps. 18) sings of love for God. In fact, it is one of the relatively few psalms that use the verb "love" with God for its object. "I love thee, O Lord, my strength. The Lord is my rock and my fortress."

In our day the Church continues to remind the baptized of the fundamental principle on which her, and our, life is built. In our efforts to live by the principle of love for God and neighbor, we should draw strength from Jesus' response to the scribe: "You are not far from the kingdom of God." A community that puts into practice the love of God and neighbor is already an initial embodiment of God's rule.

The eternal priesthood of Christ (Heb. 7:23-28)

The Letter to the Hebrews continues its teaching on the priesthood (see last Sunday for its beginning). Christ's priesthood is utterly unique, because while death prevented other priests from continuing in their office for ever, Christ lives eternally and has a priesthood that never ends. He lives always and is always making intercession for us.

His priesthood is unique for other reasons: he is holy and utterly without sin, and he therefore has no need to offer first for his own sins, then for the sins of others; and when he did offer for the sins of the people, he needed to do so only once in an offering of himself. Under the law of Moses, the high priests were weak men. In the new covenant, the Son has been brought to his perfection and has been appointed by the Father to be the one authentic High Priest.

THIRTY-SECOND SUNDAY

Give What You Have to Obtain Life

The poor widow has given more than all the others (Mark 12:38-44)

Jesus calls his disciples to him in order to point out the hidden value of the widow's action. The crowd that passes by and puts money into the treasury is contrasted with the humble widow: many in the crowd make their contribution ostentatiously, while she is simply embarrassed that she can give so little, even though it 's all she has.

Today's Gospel begins with Jesus' warning against the scribes, who are so preoccupied with wearing distinctive garments and with getting the first places. The contrast between these men and the widow brings out once again the importance of the interior religion that God finds pleasing and acceptable. The lesson was an important one for Mark's Christian community. St. Luke recounts the same incident, for he too thinks it useful to his readers. In order to make the contrast even stronger, Luke omits mention of the crowd and sets the rich men and the widow side by side (Luke 21:1-4).

All these others gave of their abundance; the poor widow gave all that she had.

The widow gives what food she has (1 Kings 17:10-16)

As we saw earlier, widows are regarded in Scripture as the special targets of social injustice; they exemplify misfortune and poverty in all its forms. In today's reading, two exemplars of poverty meet: a widow and the prophet Elias.

In the story, the widow is inspired by faith ("As the Lord your God lives . . .") to give what she has to the prophet. The miracle is then performed, because the widow has such faith and because she has given, not any extra food, but the last food she possessed.

The responsorial psalm (Ps. 146) reminds us that the Lord "executes justice for the oppressed . . . gives food to the hungry . . . He upholds the widow and the fatherless; but the way of the wicked he brings to ruin."

The Church and the faithful are being urged on this day to examine themselves on two points. The first is their generosity as inspired by faith. All the faithful are members of one body, and all belong to Christ; their generosity should be inspired by a faith that rises above all calculating attitudes. The second point is that they should be so detached from their possessions that they are ready to give even their necessities, if this is necessary in order to save others. This is the kind of openness and readiness that should characterize a community that truly belongs to the Lord.

Today's Gospel also reminds us of the interior dimension in every Christian's life. God's value judgments are not always the same as those of men; he knows men's hearts and can judge them perfectly. It is the intention and manner of giving, not its material value, that makes a gift precious in his sight. Once again, Jesus and the evangelists are calling us to a religion of Spirit and truth.

The unique sacrifice of Christ (Heb. 9:24-28)

This passage throws important light on both the sacrifice of Christ and the Eucharistic celebration. The writer first underscores the superiority of Christ's sacrifice over all others: our earthly sanctuaries are man-made and are but imitations of the true sanctuary — heaven — into which Christ entered in order that he might stand before God and intercede for us. He is our perpetual intercessor.

Christ was able to enter this heavenly sanctuary because he had a sacrifice to offer. It was a perfect and utterly unique sacrifice: it did not have to be offered anew, because Christ was offering his own blood, not another's. Nor did he have to suffer his Passion over and over again, but he offered his sacrifice once and for all, because it was a perfect sacrifice. He will appear a second time, not to offer sacrifice for sin, but to take to himself all those who await his coming.

This unique and infinitely valuable sacrifice of Christ does not prevent the Eucharist from being a true sacrifice. Christ willed that we should offer the Eucharist in memory of him. But this remembering is not simply a psychological act; it is a rendering present and operative of the one historical sacrifice. That sacrifice is rendered present so that the Church and each of the baptized may offer it with Christ, who is always interceding for them. To "renew" the sacrifice of the Cross is not to begin it again (it was offered once and for all), but to render it present, in accordance with Christ's own will, so that we may actively share in it.

THIRTY-THIRD SUNDAY
The Last Days

The elect, gathered from the four quarters of the world (Mark 13:24-32)

This and similar passages from the Gospel are bound to prove disconcerting to a modern listener. They are so alien to our way of thinking and speaking, and their images are so naïve and fantastic, that we can hardly keep from thinking that we are listening to an unusual poem or to a vision of some gigantic catastrophe as conceived by a genius of the theater. There is danger, then, that the Gospel pericope and the passage from the Book of Daniel may have no effect on us and that their teaching may pass us by.

There are other difficulties. The exegetes debate the authenticity of the passage in the Gospel. More specifically, they ask to what extent the evangelists, especially St. Mark, expanded a teaching that Jesus may well have given in a less imaginative form and perhaps with greater brevity. We shall not explain the various hypotheses that have been constructed, especially since no one of them can claim wide acceptance. It seems clear at least that here, as in other passages, the evangelists have used the teaching of Jesus to meet the needs of their Churches; they have not invented the teaching, but while leaving its substance untouched, they have expanded it and put into a new framework.

It is difficult, if not impossible, to imagine that we can now determine with certainty all the phrases and expressions that come from Jesus himself. But when everything is said and done, this whole problem should not disturb us. We accept that the evangelists were divinely inspired and that this does not mean that they were automatons in writing their Gospels, but rather that the Holy Spirit is responsible for the teaching of Jesus conveyed in writing to later generations.

Since our interest here is not literary, there is no profit in examining the details of the description. We may, however, dwell briefly on a few expressions.

"They will see the Son of man coming in clouds with great power and glory." This description is taken from the Book of Daniel (7:13). How does the Gospel interpret and make use of this passage from the prophet? In Daniel's vision, beasts are contrasted with a son of man, who belongs to a transcendent, divine world (although he cannot be further identified). The beasts represent the various world empires that must collapse and give way to the kingdom of God. After Daniel, the symbol of "a son of man" continues to be used, but with even greater emphasis on his transcendence. Finally, the expression, transformed now from "a son of man" to "the Son of man," enters the Gospels. We know that Jesus applies the title to himself (Matthew 5:11; Luke 6:22; Matthew 16:13-21; Mark 8:27-31). According to the Acts of the Apostles, the dying Stephen has a vision of Jesus as the Son of man (7:55); and in the Apocalypse, the figure of "Son of man" appears again (Apoc. 1:12-16; 14:14). For Jesus, the Son of man is evidently a person — himself! — who gives his life to ransom the many (Mark 10:45).

"He will . . . gather his elect from the four winds, from the ends of the earth to the ends of heaven." According to Jewish belief, all the Jews of the world would be assembled in their own country. The Gospel refers rather to all the baptized, who make up the new kingdom. The same image will recur in the *Didache*, a Jewish-Christian writing.[41]

"Truly, I say to you, this generation will not pass away

before all these things take place." There will be preliminary signs. Here the fig tree serves as a parable from nature. Are its branches becoming tender and is it putting forth leaves? Then we know the summer is at hand. Similarly, when the predicted signs occur, we will know that the Son of man is at hand. "All these things": the reference is not quite clear; perhaps what is meant is the phenomena described earlier in this chapter, including the destruction of the Temple.

"This generation" would literally mean the generation contemporary with the evangelist, but the reference is nonetheless quite vague. For the first Christians, "this generation" included their Jewish contemporaries and the culture that would vanish with the Temple, the destruction of the latter being a sign of God's judgment. And yet the parousia in its totality was still in the future; Christians awaited it, but its date was not known. Besides, Jesus himself had said: "Of that day or that hour no one knows, not even the angels in heaven, nor the Son, but only the Father." (This text has its own difficulties. How can the Son be ignorant of what the Father knows, especially since, as Jesus himself says, no one knows the Father but the Son? The exegetes solve this difficulty by distinguishing between the Son in his divine nature and the Son as incarnate, who, in his human nature, did not know the day or the hour.)

What this pericope and the whole of chapter 13 presents us with is an attempt of the evangelist to explain the parousia to his community and to awaken both a desire for it and an attitude of deliberate expectancy.

He comes to save his people (Dan. 12:1-3)

The first verse describes, in very general terms, a time of catastrophe. Yet it is at that moment that salvation will come to the people, a salvation that Daniel describes as coming in the form of judgment and resurrection. The dead will awaken, some to eternal life, others to eternal shame and contempt. Among the blessed, the wise men and the teachers of uprightness will shine like the brightness in the firmament. Daniel is once again asserting here an individual resurrection and retribution for man's deeds in this life. This is a theology that is as yet novel in Judaism; it will be accepted and taken over by the New Testament.

The responsorial psalm (Ps. 16) says: "Thou dost not give me up to Sheol, or let thy godly one see the Pit." In these words the psalmist provides the lesson of this Sunday. Our attention should not be absorbed by the frightening details of a great catastrophe; instead, the joy that is to come on the last day should inspire us to hope.

Christians today do not think enough about the parousia, or second coming of Christ; we tend to reflect exclusively on our death and our appearance before the judgment seat of God. This is because we are not sufficiently conscious that we belong to a kingdom that must someday enter its final and definitive state. This does not mean, of course, that we should be uninterested in our individual, personal salvation; it means only that we should view this in the perspective of the final and all-embracing passage of this world to its final state and condition at the last judgment.

The "last judgment" is in any case more than simply a judgment and should not be approached purely in a spirit of fear lest we be punished. It is also God's great act of reconstruction, and we can be sure that God will produce something unimaginably new and great. The Christian expectation of final redemption should take the form of a lively, joyous hope of that great act of reconstruction.

The Eucharistic celebration is a pledge that Christ is coming again and that then the new and lasting world will begin. It is also the efficacious power that causes the world to reach its maturity and thus hastens the coming of the end. Every time we celebrate the Eucharist, we await Christ's coming and advance further toward the moment when the regime of sacramental signs will pass away and we will see him face to face. This whole spiritual outlook has unfortunately been so much forgotten that we even find it difficult to understand many a passage of Scripture. We tend to wrap ourselves up in a somewhat fearful expectation of our own death and fail to connect our lot with that of the whole Church journeying toward the meeting with the Lord.

—————

Having offered his sacrifice, Jesus leads to perfection those he has sanctified (Heb. 10:11-14, 18)

The doctrine of Christ's one sacrifice and its limitless efficacy continues to be the writer's theme. His point of departure is a comparison with the sacrifices of the Old Testament. The repeated sacrifices of the old law could not remove sin, and the priest was forced to stand daily at the altar. Christ offered but one sacrifice and now sits at the right hand of God. The writer is continuing the line of thought we met last Sunday.

There is one statement, however, in today's passage that deserves our attention: "By a single offering he has perfected for all time those who are sanctified." Does such a statement apply to us, when we have daily experience of our own weakness? The answer is that we understand the writer to be speaking of what Christ accomplished *in principle* by his sacrifice. That is to say, he has created a situation in which it is possible for us to be perfect, but we must enter into that situation and lay hold of the gift offered.

There is, then, a tension at the heart of all Christian life: the Christian is already made holy, and yet he must be constantly striving for the holiness offered him. Consequently, though Christ offered but one sacrifice, our weakness requires that it be constantly made present and operative in our lives. There is no need of another sacrifice for the forgiveness of sins, but Christ himself willed that his own sacrifice be made present to us and, with it, his forgiveness.

THIRTY-FOURTH SUNDAY

Christ's Rule Over the Universe

As you say, I am a king (John 18:33b-37)

The scene is the praetorium, where Pilate is questioning Jesus. We can sense that Pilate is interested in, and even disturbed by, this man who stands before him; he is asking himself who this man may really be. We need not read irony into his question: "Are you the King of the Jews?" Jesus alludes quietly to the inner disturbance Pilate feels: "Do you say this of your own accord, or did others say it to you about me?"

Jesus does not intend to hide his true rank any longer; he picks up Pilate's words and applies them to himself. But Pilate may still not see his claim correctly. Christ's kingship is of the spiritual order, not the political. His royal authority is spiritual and comes from God; his kingdom does not originate in this world but is given to him by the Father.

Pilate may think of Jesus as a political king, but he is wrong; he is right, however, in saying that Jesus is a king, even if of a different order than Pilate realizes. The exercise of Jesus' kingship consists in bearing witness to the truth. "Truth" here does not mean a philosophy; it means eternal reality, the reality of God himself, as contrasted with transient things. Jesus has been sent to give men the eternal reality that will set them free from the guilt of sin. That is the essential object of the revelation for the sake which he has become a man.

This scene from Jesus' trial is marked by paradox. Pilate acts as judge of Jesus; in reality, Jesus is Pilate's judge. He is the true King and Judge, because he frees men or condemns them, depending on whether or not they accept his testimony about divine truth.

To him was given dominion and glory and kingdom (Dan. 7:13-14)

In this passage the prophet presents the Lord as the Judge of the last times. For us, this symbolic personage — the son of man who comes before the Ancient of Days — is Jesus the Messiah. We see him exercising dominion and power as the glorious King of all nations and peoples. His rule is eternal and will never be abolished. "The Lord reigns; he is robed in majesty; the Lord is robed, he is girded with strength" (Ps. 93).

Ruler of kings on earth (Apoc. 1:5-8)

We pass here from the apocalypse of Daniel to the Apocalypse of the Apostle John. In it Christ is presented as King, while in his kingdom we are the priests of God his Father.

The passage is a doxology, a hymn to the King who has freed us from our sins by his own blood and who now gives us his peace. He is the first-born of the dead and guarantees our resurrection as well. He is the ruler of earthly kings, and now all acknowledge him, the one they pierced, to be their sovereign Lord.

Christ's paschal mystery has borne its fruit, for he has established a kingdom of priests to serve the Father and glorify him. He has established a great kingdom in which all praise the Lord as the Alpha and the Omega.

Today's liturgy in its entirety conveys a vision of glory. Yet unless we are careful, it may lead us astray. When Jesus admitted to Pilate that he was a king, he meant that he was a king very unlike any earthly king. He does not free nations, as a political king might. Pilate might mistake Jesus' meaning; so may we. But then, even the apostles mistook it! On the very day of the ascension they asked him: "Lord, will you at this time restore the kingdom to Israel?" (Acts 1:6)! It is not surprising, then, that during his earthly life the crowd should have wanted him for their king (John 6:15).

If Jesus is a king, then all Christians belong to a royal race. How easy then to argue: Every Christian is a brother of Christ and a king; the Church is Christ's people and therefore of royal stature; therefore the Christian and the Church deserve social privileges.

It is indeed possible, even if not in such a crass way, to transform Christ's spiritual kingship into a very earthly and transient type of kingship. But in fact our kingship is one of service; every Christian and the Church in her entirety belong to a truly privileged kingdom and therefore have no concern for temporary privileges. Their sole function is to bear witness to the truth, for their kingly rank comes to them precisely as messengers of an eternal kingship and kingdom. They bear witness to the King who frees men from the bondage to sin in which even earthly kings and political rulers live.

On the other hand, the spiritual character of this kingship and the fact that Jesus had no interest in political power do not mean that the Church is to live, as it were, apart from the world and cultivate a spiritualist lack of interest in the life of our contemporaries. No, the very fact that Christ is a king forces all who are engaged in the political order to become aware of the ultimate goal that all politics must serve. The true relationship would be stood on its head if we thought that, because Christ is a king, the Church must have political authority in this world! The Church has been tempted at times to confuse the kingship of Christ with an earthly kingship, when in fact Christ's kingship should have led her to remind earthly kings of the limitations and true purpose of their transient power.

It will always be necessary for the Church to study anew the impact Christ's kingship should have on this world. She is not to seek domination herself, but rather is always to encourage as best she can the concrete efforts being made to liberate the weak and the oppressed. The Church does not do honor to Christ's kingship by seeking any form of earthly supremacy, but by encouraging those engaged in the political order to keep ever before them the one, true, eternal King and his eternal rule.

SUNDAYS NINE TO THIRTY-FOUR
IN ORDINARY TIME

CYCLE C
Years 1980, 1983, 1986, 1989, 1992

TABLE OF SUNDAY READINGS

In the following table, the general theme of each celebration and the particular theme of each reading are indicated. If the second reading is connected with the general theme of the day, it will be commented on together with the first reading and the Gospel (these second readings are marked by an asterisk in the following list). If the second reading does not fit with the theme of the day, a heavy line separates the commentary given from the preceding.

Comment on Sundays one to eight in ordinary time may be found in volume one, pages 308-311; 332-432.

CYCLE C
Years 1980, 1983, 1986, 1989, 1992

Sunday 9 Faith is answered
  Luke 7:1-10   The faith of a foreigner
  1 Kings 8:41-43   The prayer of a foreigner in the Temple
  Gal. 1:1-2, 6-10   Either serve Christ or please men

Sunday 10 The gift of life
  Luke 7:11-17   I say to you, arise
  1 Kings 17:17-24   See, your son lives
  Gal. 1:11-19   To preach your Son among the Gentiles

Sunday 11 Sin forgiven
  Luke 7:36–8:3   Forgiveness and love
  2 Sam. 12:7-10, 13   The Lord has put away your sin
  Gal. 2:16, 19-21   Christ lives in me

Sunday 12 The suffering Messiah and Savior
  Luke 9:18-24   Take your cross and follow Christ
  Zech. 12:10-11   They shall look on him whom they have pierced
  *Gal. 3:26-29   Clothed in Christ

Sunday 13 Follow without delay
           Luke 9:51-62
           1 Kings 19:16b, 19-21
           Gal. 5:1, 13-18

           Do not look back
           Leave everything
           Called to freedom

Sunday 14 Joy and peace
           Luke 10:1-12, 17-20
           Is. 66:10-14c
           Gal. 6:14-18

           Joy springing from mission
           The joy and peace of the messianic age
           Bear in your body the marks of Jesus

Sunday 15 The law of love
           Luke 10:25-37
           Deut. 30:10-14
           Col. 1:15-20

           Who is my neighbor?
           Live by the word of God
           All things were created through Christ and
             for him

Sunday 16 God visits us
           Luke 10:38-42
           Gen. 18:1-10a
           Col. 1:24-28

           Receive Jesus in your house
           God comes and fulfills his promise
           The mystery hidden and revealed

Sunday 17 Ask and you shall receive
           Luke 11:1-13
           Gen. 18:20-32
           Col. 2:12-14

           Learn to pray
           Pray tirelessly against all hope
           Buried and risen with Christ

Sunday 18	The passing and the abiding	Rich in God's sight
	Luke 12:13-21	Leaving one's possessions to an unknown
	Eccles. 1:2; 2:21-23	Seek the things that are above
	*Col. 3:1-5, 9-11	
Sunday 19	Be ready to receive God's glory	Be ready
	Luke 12:32-48	Called to glory
	Wis. 18:6-9	Look for the city of God
	*Heb. 11:1-2, 8-19	
Sunday 20	Signs to be contradicted	Violence for the sake of the kingdom
	Luke 12:49-53	The prophet, a man of discord
	Jer. 38:4-6, 8-10	Hostility from sinners
	*Heb. 12:1-4	
Sunday 21	The whole world at the feast in the kingdom	
	Luke 13:22-30	The last will be first
	Is. 66:18-21	Gather men from all nations
	Heb. 12:5-7, 11-13	To correct is a sign of love
Sunday 22	Humble yourself, and you will be exalted	
	Luke 14:1, 7-14	He who exalts himself shall be humbled
	Sir. 3:17-18, 20, 28-29	Humble yourself and find favor with God
	Heb. 12:18-19, 22-24a	You have approached Jesus, Mediator of a new covenant

Sunday 23   Be free, and understand the Lord
             Luke 14:25-33   Renounce your possessions and become a disciple
             Wis. 9:13-18   Wisdom enables us to understand God's will
             Philemon 9b-10, 12-17   Onesimus is to be treated as a brother, not
                                       as a slave

Sunday 24   The Lord's forgiveness
             Luke 15:1-32   Joy in heaven for a sinner's conversion
             Exod. 32:7-11, 13-14   The Lord relents and does not punish
             *1 Tim. 1:12-17   Christ came to save sinners

Sunday 25   The Christian problem of money
             Luke 16:1-13   The service of God and money are incompatible
             Amos 8:4-7   Greed of the merchants
             1 Tim. 2:1-8   Pray that all men may be saved

Sunday 26   The false security of the rich
             Luke 16:19-31   Final lot of the rich and the poor
             Amos 6:1a, 4-7   A corrupt civilization
             *1 Tim. 6:11-16   Keep the Lord's commandments until he returns

Sunday 27   The dynamism of faith
             Luke 17:5-10   The power of faith
             Hab. 1:2-3; 2:2-4   The just man lives because of his faith
             2 Tim. 1:6-8, 13-14   Bear the hardship that the gospel entails

Sunday 28   Gratitude to God
             Luke 17:11-19
             2 Kings 5:14-17
             2 Tim. 2:8-13

             They have not returned to thank God
             Naaman returns to glorify God
             We have died with Christ and shall live
               with him

Sunday 29   The prayer of faith
             Luke 18:1-8
             Exod. 17:8-13
             2 Tim. 3:14-4:2

             Pray unwearyingly and with faith
             The power of Moses' intercession
             Be inspired by the wisdom of Scripture
               and proclaim the word

Sunday 30   The prayer of the humble
             Luke 18:9-14

             Sir. 35:12c-14, 16-18b
             2 Tim. 4:6-8, 16-18

             The tax collector is justified by his
               humble prayer
             The prayer of the humble man pierces the clouds
             Receive the reward of a winner

Sunday 31   The compassion of a loving God
             Luke 19:1-10

             Wis. 11:22-12:2

             2 Thess. 1:11-2:2

             The Son of Man has come to seek out and
               save what was lost
             The lengthy patience of God, who urges men
               to conversion
             The Lord Jesus, glorified in us

Sunday 32 The God of life
Luke 20:27-38   All receive life from God in the world to come
2 Macc. 7:1-2, 9-14   Raised up for eternal life
2 Thess. 2:16–3:5   The Lord is faithful; he strengthens us
                       and protects us from evil

Sunday 33 The Day of the Lord
Luke 21:5-19   Persevere through suffering so as to obtain
                       life on the Day of the Lord
Mal. 4:1-2a   The Day of the Lord, a blazing oven for the
                       wicked, a sun of justice for the good
2 Thess. 3:7-12   Earn your own bread

Sunday 34 A crucified King
Luke 23:35-43   Jesus crucified, remember me when you
                       come as King
2 Sam. 5:1-3   David, anointed as shepherd and king of
                       Israel
*Col. 1:12-20   In the kingdom of the beloved Son

NINTH SUNDAY

Faith Is Answered

The faith of a foreigner (Luke 7:1-10)

The story of the cure of the centurion's servant is also found in St. Matthew and St. John, though with differences that are not lacking in interest. St. Luke's intention seems to be to contrast the ease with which a non-Jew believed in Jesus and the difficulties the Jews felt in committing themselves to him. In addition, St. Luke sets the stage carefully and in detaiil. As a pagan, the centurion does not himself come to Jesus, for he feels ill at ease and does not dare to approach him. Instead, he sends some Jewish elders for whom he had probably done favors. The elders tell Jesus that the man had built a synagogue for them and was truly a friend of the nation. Finally, when Jesus sets out for the centurion's house, the latter sends word that Jesus should not take such trouble, for he knows that a Jew is not supposed to enter a pagan's house. It is at this point that the man's faith is manifested in moving words that have become part of the Eucharistic celebration in the Latin Church: "I am not worthy to have you come under my roof. . . . But say the word, and let my servant be healed." Jesus' response to this is carefully recorded by St. Luke: "I tell you, not even in Israel have I found such faith."

Perhaps Jesus could say the same thing about us, the new people of God, as he says here about Israel. Does he find the centurion's faith among us? This is a question we ought to ask about ourselves and about the contemporary Church on this Sunday. Is it in the Catholic Church that we find the greatest manifestations of faith? Is it in the Christian Churches that faith in God is always seen to be liveliest?

Christ's words to the centurion might well be applied to our age as a hard judgment. The fact should make us quite humble. Faith is certainly a gift that must be accepted and cultivated, but in any event it is a gift, and no one can claim it as his exclusive possession.

The prayer of a foreigner in the Temple (1 Kings 8:41-43)

Solomon built the Temple, but to the Israelite mind his action, however praiseworthy, was not unproblematic, because it is impossible to enclose the Lord within a temple; we can neither force him to answer our prayers nor prevent him from answering the prayers of others.

Earlier in this chapter of the First Book of Kings, Solomon had explained to the people his reasons for building a temple (1 Kings 8:14-21). Then, after praying that there might always be a successor to the throne of David, Solomon prays for the entire people that God would hear them in every circumstance. Finally (in today's pericope), he prays for foreigners as well, that is, for those not of the race of Israel. It is not surprising that foreigners should in fact come to the Temple, since they too would have heard of the great things God had done and was doing for his chosen people. The Scriptures predicted, after all, that all the peoples of the earth would acknowledge the power of the Lord.

Solomon's prayer thus anticipates the situation we find described in the Gospel: the foreigner, too, that is, the man who does not belong to our religion, may have authentic faith. The fact should not vex us but rather make us praise God, who wishes to save all men. At the same time, it should make us reflect on ourselves. For us, faith has been made easy in so many ways; it has been fed by so many gifts of grace (the word of God, the sacraments). Do not this very ease and these very gifts condemn us for our lack of faith?

Either serve Christ or please men (Gal. 1:1-2, 6-10)

The Galatians are in trouble. Some individuals seem to be preaching to them a doctrine that is not in conformity with the gospel. Paul complains of the rapidity with which they have abandoned the gospel of Jesus that he had preached to them. The real problem lies in the Jewish-Christian milieu and its opposition to Paul's teaching that neither circumcision nor the observance of the Mosaic law were necessary for salvation. Paul therefore feels obliged to remind his readers that he has been sent by Jesus himself whom the Father had raised from the dead. His words to them are stern: There is only one gospel, and no one, not even an angel, has the right to come preaching another. The Galatians must remain faithful to the gospel of Christ that he, Paul, has preached to them.

It is difficult for Paul to write in this vein. However, he is not seeking to satisfy men but to preach the truth as it is. His real interest is in serving Christ, and "if I were still pleasing men, I should not be a servant of Christ."

Except for the contingent circumstances that caused Paul to write this Letter, we today face the same problem Paul faced; in fact, it is a problem that the Church, and each authority in the Church, and, in the last analysis, each Christian has always had to face. There are moments when fidelity to Christ does not allow us to evade taking firm positions and making firm decisions. The situation of our contemporary world requires that the Christian be sensitive to all the anxieties and sufferings of men, but also that he be strictly faithful to the message and teaching of Christ.

The Christian and the Church cannot hold fast to nonessential traditions that are likely to stifle the spirit, on the pretext that if they depart from these, they will displease those who frequently love what they call "tradition" because it answers to their own mind-set, their education, a type of "humanism," a specific culture. Nor can the Christian and the Church agree to moral compromises that are clearly deviations from the requirements of divine revelation; this applies not only to sexual morality but to aspects of social life and to some kinds of government.

The Church must preach the truths of the gospel; these are the true and genuine tradition! Therefore, it cannot be afraid of displeasing men by requiring, no matter what, obedience to this essential gospel. On the other hand, neither can the Church be afraid of men when it comes to adapting to the contemporary world and abandoning what is not essential in its tradition. Judgments on these matters are evidently not easy to make. But we must remember that Christ's Spirit is present to help the Church, today no less than in the beginning.

TENTH SUNDAY

The Gift Of Life

I say to you, arise (Luke 7:11-17)

The story of the raising of the widow's son at Naim is found only in Luke's Gospel. It is one in a series of episodes that proclaim the gift of life we are all meant to receive.

When John the Baptist sends his disciples to inquire of Jesus who he is, Jesus answers by pointing to his significant deeds; among these is the raising of the dead (Luke 7:22). The raising of the widow's son, recounted just before, is an example of this extraordinary activity (Luke 7:11-17). The prophet Isaiah had long ago predicted that this would be a sign of the Messiah: "Thy dead shall live, their bodies shall rise" (26:19).

St. Luke notes that Jesus is deeply moved with pity for the poor widow. In his emotion, however, we may see

something more than simple pity for the widow's suffering.
He is also deeply moved at the thought of the life and resurrection he will give to those who believe in him, a life
and resurrection symbolized by the raising of the widow's
son. St. Luke most certainly has this broader perspective in
mind. In addition, the raising of the widow's son will be a
sign to the Baptist that he, Jesus, is the long-awaited Messiah. In short, St. Luke reports this incident in order to
strengthen the faith of his readers in Christ the Prophet, the
God who visits his people.

St. Luke likes the phrase "God has visited his people."
The elderly Simeon uses it (Luke 1:68). Later on, Luke puts
the following words of reproach on the lips of Jesus: "You
did not know the time of your visitation" (19:44). The Old
Testament had supplied Luke with the idea and the phrase-
ology. Thus the Book of Exodus reports Joseph as having said in Egypt: "God will visit you; then you must
carry my bones with you from here" (Exod. 13:19). The
psalmist marvels at this visitation and cries: "What is man
that thou art mindful of him, and the son of man that thou
dost care for [or: visit] him?" (Ps. 8:4).

The divine visitation to which Luke refers through Simeon in the Temple (Luke 1:68) is the divine coming to
redeem and liberate, prefigured in the liberation of Israel
and the exodus of the people from Egypt. Jesus is the
Prophet who conquers death and gives life.

We should not forget that Luke is writing after the death
and resurrection of Jesus. In the account of the raising at
Naim, we have resonances of the experience of the early
Church.

See, your son lives (1 Kings 17:17-24)

The Old Testament reading is chosen so as to provide a
prefiguration of Jesus' miracle at Naim. The incident chosen is the raising of another widow's son by the prophet
Elias. (The Second Book of Kings has a parallel case: the
raising of the Shunammite's son in 4:32-37.)

What is the relevance of this miracle, and of the miracle at Naim, to our lives today?

Scientific progress and a resurgence of paganism have made us forget that life and death are in God's hand. This applies not only to physical life, but also to the resurrection and the life in God that will come at the end of time and are prefigured in the miracles of Scripture. It is the Lord who bestows this definitive life on us and thus brings us to our fulfillment. Baptism as new life, and the other sacraments that sustain this life and cause it to intensify until the coming of Christ — these are the realities ultimately meant by the miracles we have been considering, as well as by the resurrection of Lazarus, which prefigures the resurrection of Christ and our own resurrection.

When we think of this gift of life and of the complete fulfillment, in the world to come, of all that we are meant to be, we must not narrow our vision and focus solely on a life given to each of us as individuals. We must think rather of a life that is given to the people of God in its entirety. The Church, which has been commissioned by Christ to raise the spiritually dead, must look to the Lord for her being and life. She is meant to be a sign of resurrection for each individual, and though the reality of the resurrection exists only in promise, she nonetheless gives us real pledges and anticipations of that unending life.

When all is said and done, the whole preaching of the Church rests on a single foundation: on the resurrection that is given to men even now (in pledge and promise) and on the sacraments that free men from sin and give life to the Church and her members as they journey toward the life that will never cease. The miracles of resurrection that the Church works are not spectacular like those of Elias or those of Christ at Naim and Bethany, but they are utterly real, and the Church is constantly working them in anticipation of the last day.

Our Christianity is a religion of life. It supposes indeed a kind of death through asceticism and renunciation, but this death is only a means of liberation. Christian existence in fact develops in an atmosphere of profound and intense life. How often we find in someone who is an invalid or ill or dying the signs of a life far more intense than what we find in the healthy! It is this deeper life that is signified by baptism and the Eucharist (sacraments of the "living") as well as by the sacrament of the sick, which looks to the life of both body and spirit. We Christians are being perpetually raised up to new life, and we don't seem to realize it! And yet the world should be able to see in us witnesses to a life constantly being poured into us by Christ, the Son of the living and life-giving God.

To preach your Son among the Gentiles (Gal. 1:11-19)

This is not the first time, of course, that the Sunday readings have urged us to reflect on the missionary activity of the apostles. In today's passage Paul tells us that as an apostle the message he passes on is that of Jesus himself, the Good News that Jesus came to preach.

We are confronted here once more with the mystery of God's choice. Paul had done nothing that he should be chosen and sent to preach the mysteries of Christ. Quite the contrary! Yet in fact he was chosen from his mother's womb, and later the Lord revealed his Son to him so that he might preach that Son to the Gentiles.

Paul received a call, as had all the prophets before him. This is something on which he lays great stress, as he does on the fact that he was fully an apostle, having been chosen directly by Christ himself. He saw the risen Christ, who entrusted him with the preaching of the gospel. He visited Peter indeed, but it was not from Peter that he received his appointment to the work of evangelization.

Meditation on this passage should be combined with meditation on the other texts in the lectionary. It is a very relevant passage. Paul is unexpectedly called, God choosing him without him having been in any way prepared; he responds to the call. His mission is to preach the gospel of Jesus Christ; he carries out his mission, always remaining in contact with the other apostles.

The task of the missionary of today is exactly the same as Paul's. It is for the sake of the gospel alone that all, each according to his own vocation, are sent out to the nations of the world. Our vocation is to be witnesses to the gospel of Jesus Christ, and we must answer the call faithfully and to the best of our ability.

ELEVENTH SUNDAY

Sin Forgiven

Forgiveness and love (Luke 7:36–8:3)

The story of the sinful woman who bathed Jesus' feet with her tears, dried them with her hair, covered them with kisses, and anointed them is one of the best known in the whole of Scripture. In our day, interpreters have endeavored to apply it, without qualification, as a proof of the primacy of "love" (an ambiguous word that needs to be used with more care).

The important thing for us here is the parable that Jesus speaks to his host when the latter doubts the prophetic powers of a man who does not seem to realize what kind of woman has approached him. It is a simple parable, and we shall not go over its details. The concluding application to the woman, however, may leave us a bit puzzled, but this depends on how the verse is translated. The point is that the woman is forgiven much because she has shown great love; one who shows little love is not thus forgiven. The woman's love has been shown in the way she approached Jesus. It is for that reason that he tells her, "Your sins are forgiven."

As usual when Jesus uses these words, those present ask: Who is this who even has power to forgive sins? The real problem is: How are they to see God in this man? Jesus gives them the answer when he says to the woman: "Your faith has saved you." She has come to realize that salvation is from God alone. She has the faith that every Christian must have.

Christ then continues on his way, preaching the kingdom of God. The fact that he forgives sins has brought home to many the presence of the kingdom.

The Lord has put away your sin (2 Sam. 12:7-10, 13)

The story of David, in the first reading, prepares us for understanding the Gospel of the day. What we should focus on in the reading from the Second Book of Samuel is not so much God's stern rebuke as David's immediate repentance. The story then has God's forgiveness follow just as immediately; no sooner has David admitted his sin than he is forgiven. The liturgy has shortened the passage somewhat by cutting out part of the divine reproaches; this is quite legitimate, since the emphasis today is on God's mercy.

The two accounts in today's liturgy — from the Second Book of Samuel and from St. Luke's Gospel — are fully relevant today, since the Lord continues to act as he is shown acting in these stories. That is to say, where he finds repentance, he immediately forgives. The two readings provide two examples of this pattern.

Catholics who have difficulties today with the sacrament of penance may well find them resolved if they meditate on these two stories. The fact is that an act of faith in the Lord who is present to us through the Church, which is his instrument and "sacrament," forgives sin, and the past is blotted out. The thing that has probably created the obstacle that some cannot overcome is too much human casuistry and a presentation of God as a difficult and irascible being. The sacrament of penance has come to be seen in too negative a light; it does not sufficiently radiate the paschal joy of reconciliation, and there is not enough sense of the life the Lord wants to give again to those who repent.

Reconciliation with God requires an act of faith and therefore an act of adoring, joyous worship. Communal penance celebrations may help to gradually restore the true meaning of the sacrament, provided they present the sacrament chiefly in a positive way, as the renewal of sinful man and the restoration of his union with the Lord.

Christ lives in me (Gal. 2:16, 19-21)

We find Paul expatiating here once again on the theme of justification by faith. Four times in a row he uses the verb "to justify" (in vv. 16-17). Let us recall briefly what the term means for him. To the Jews, the justified person was the one whom God will accept on the day of judgment; in language more familiar to us, the "justified" man is the man who is "saved."

The Galatians must realize, says Paul, that they are not justified because of their practice of the (Jewish) law, but because of their faith in Jesus Christ. No one becomes just by fulfilling the Mosaic law. Paul's thought is well expressed in a short sentence that we ought to keep in mind: "I through the law [which put Christ to death] died to the law, that I might live to God" (v. 19). In other words, Christ accomplished the final purposes of the Mosaic law (salvation from sin) when under that law the Jews put him to death. With that death the Mosaic law ceased to exist. That death, accordingly, liberated Paul from the Mosaic law and justified him; he has therefore ceased to live under that law and lives instead for God. That which justifies is faith in the

Christ who died and rose from the dead. If the practice of
the law could justify, Christ's death would have been without purpose.

What are we to do, then? How should a Christian live
who wishes to be saved? Even in his human condition he
must live by faith in the Son of God who gave himself for
him. In his present life he is to live as one nailed to Christ's
Cross; it is no longer he who lives, for Christ lives in him.

That kind of life is not reserved for the mystics but is to
be the life consequent upon baptism. If our spiritual life is
not of that kind, it is really non-existent, an appearance
without reality.

TWELFTH SUNDAY

The Suffering Messiah and Savior

Take your cross and follow Christ (Luke 9:18-24)

Once again, Jesus makes known his messianic dignity.
The crowds have not yet gotten a clear idea of Christ's person, but he wants the disciples to be really and fully convinced of his true identity. Jesus first asks the disciples who
the crowds think he is. The apostles are aware of what the
crowd thinks, and they tell Jesus. Then Jesus goes a step
further: "But who do you say that I am?" Peter speaks immediately for the others, and his answer is clear and straightforward: "The Christ of God." At this point Jesus once
again forbids the disciples to say anything of this to others.

We shall not repeat what we said earlier about the significance of the "messianic secret," especially since the
point of the Gospel pericope, as read in the light of the first
reading, is that the Messiah must suffer in order to redeem
mankind. It is on this prediction of the Passion that we

should dwell, and on the consequences of the Passion for every disciple of Christ. For all who will believe in the suffering Messiah and in the efficacy of his sufferings will have to share them with him. That is why Jesus here sets forth the basic program of every Christian life: Take up your cross daily; lose your life in order to save it.

St. Luke does not emphasize the messianic secret the way Mark does, but in this passage he does link it to the prediction of the Passion. The crowd is not capable, despite Isaiah's prophecies, of accepting a suffering Messiah.

The evangelist emphasizes the Messiah's sufferings and the part they play in God's plan of salvation that was conceived before the world began: "The Son of man *must* suffer many things." Everything in Christ's life is part of the carrying out of God's plan. Luke is here closely attuned to John, whose whole Gospel echoes the theme of the Father's will and its accomplishment by the Son.

But if the Messiah is to suffer a great deal, he is also to rise from the dead. Thus it is the whole paschal mystery that Jesus predicts here. From this point on, the apostles know the journey that Jesus must take. Do they fully understand it at this first mention? It would be difficult to say with certainty; at least we can say that their reactions at the time of the Passion, which presumably they believed would come, show them to have been inadequately prepared for the reality.

Peter's act of faith, spoken in the name of the other disciples, and Jesus' detailed prediction of the paschal mystery of his death and resurrection lead to the statement of the principles that must guide the Christian's life. Follow Christ, take up your cross daily; save your life and you will lose it, lose it and you will save it. Here we already have the foolishness of the Cross of which Paul would later write.

They shall look on him whom they have pierced (Zech. 12:10-11)

St. John (19:37), in a passage used on the feast of the Sacred Heart (Cycle B), applies this passage from Zechariah to Christ. The words of the prophet are not crystal clear and apparently underwent several revisions. Whom did he have in mind when he spoke of the man who is pierced and who attracts men's eyes to himself? An earlier passage had spoken of the messianic king as riding on an ass (9:9-10). In the present passage, this messianic king has been misunderstood and killed. But his sufferings and the sufferings of Jerusalem that put him to death will purify the city. We are reminded here of Isaiah's fourth song of the Suffering Servant (Is. 53).

This first reading is an invitation to emphasize, in the Gospel, the sufferings of the Messiah and the efficacy of his purifying Passion. But we must go a step beyond contemplative meditation and learn to share in the Cross of him who was pierced for our sake.

Clothed in Christ (Gal. 3:26-29)

The Gospel sets down the basic plan for Christian life. In this second reading Paul reminds us of our baptism and of the fact that we share deeply in the life of Christ, so much so that we can be said to be clothed in Christ. So fully are we transformed into Christ that there is no longer slave and freeman, male and female among us, for we are now all one in Christ Jesus. This is the main point of this passage from the Letter to the Galatians.

The fact that we have been united to Christ through baptism allows us to connect this reading with the other two of today's liturgy. Baptism is an act of faith in the suffering and rising Messiah. It is an act of faith that clothes us in Christ to the point where we are closely associated with all he did. His paschal mystery of death and resurrection becomes ours. Since we are clothed in Christ, we must accept our own daily cross in order to rise up with him.

Baptism thus presents us with a whole program of life. Each Christian is baptized into the suffering Messiah. No wonder, then, that his sufferings take on their full meaning only when seen as a dying with Christ in order also to rise with him. If we truly believe in the Messiah or Christ, then that is what we believe. Take this faith seriously and you have the answer to so many otherwise unintelligible things that happen.

THIRTEENTH SUNDAY

Follow Without Delay

Do not look back (Luke 9:51-62)

This passage has evidently been chosen in order to teach us what it means to "follow Jesus" and what demands the decision to follow him makes upon us. Even the first part of the reading, in which we see Jesus courageously going up to Jerusalem, is part of the lesson, since Jesus is going to Jerusalem for his Passion; we are being told indirectly what "following him" ultimately entails.

The will to follow Jesus requires a blind self-surrender, without any security for the future. The Son of Man, we are told, had no place to lay his head. Following Jesus also means that everything takes second place to the preaching of the kingdom. Jesus is unyielding on this point: "Leave the dead to bury their own dead; but as for you, go and proclaim the kingdom of God" (Luke 9:60). Following in Jesus' steps also means not looking back. Once we have abandoned everything, we must not think of the past but simply move on ahead; we must not try to evaluate what we have done or ask whether some other way might be better.

Leave everything (1 Kings 19:16b, 19-21)

The story of Eliseus' call will help us to a better understanding of the Gospel. Eliseus is called while he is out plowing; the call comes in the midst of his daily work. The circumstances are significant, but we often find God calling men in this way in both the Old and the New Testaments. Moses (Exod. 3:1), David (1 Sam. 16:11), and many others were called while tending their flocks, Simon and Andrew while at their fishing (Mark 1:16), and Matthew while sitting in his tax office (Matthew 9:9). The call is unyielding in its insistency. True enough, Eliseus, though he immediately leaves his possessions, asks that he may say goodbye to his father and mother before following Elias. But then he slaughters the oxen that were the means of his livelihood.

It would be a mistake to apply these texts solely to a religious vocation or a call to the priestly ministry. Doubtless there is need of frequently recalling the requirements of these particular vocations and the manner in which men should answer them. But it is also true that every Christian receives a call and must respond to it. For simple examples, we might think of the requests people make to be allowed to meet a given pastoral need. There can be no doubt, of course, that obligations to family come first; it would be neither just nor prudent to neglect them and perhaps destroy a necessary cell (the family) in the Church's life for the sake of what might seem more heroic but in this case would be illusory.

On the other hand, many Christians feel able to meet a need of the community with generosity and without having to be asked. Sometimes they will set their work aside for a time and deprive themselves in order to respond in the Lord's name to what is asked of them without looking back and with the intention solely of answering what they rightly think of as a call from God. Holiness is not the prerogative of religious and priests.

Today's texts should make us review our attitudes. Perhaps we are closing our ears to divine inspirations and accustoming ourselves to waiting until we are good and ready.

Called to freedom (Gal. 5:1, 13-18)

St. Paul returns here once more to the problem of the law. Christ has set us free. We might better say: Christ has freed us for freedom; such a way of putting it, modeled on Hebrew idiom, reinforces the image and helps us grasp the reality more fully.

The law imposed on God's people represented a first step toward their salvation. Its purpose was to educate, but it was also meant to be observed, and we know that it was not. What the law in fact did, therefore, was to make men realize their sinful state, to enslave them rather than to free them from the guilt of sin. Fulfillment of the external obligations of the law could not lead man to total freedom; on the contrary, he found himself more fettered than ever.

Christ came to free man completely. The promise of liberation had been given long ago to Abraham, whose faith in God justified him. We too find freedom through faith in the liberation that was promised and given in Jesus Christ. Christ frees us from sin and from all the external constraints of the law.

Such teaching would evidently offend converts from Judaism who thought that while they must follow Christ, they must also still obey the law of Moses. In their eyes, justification or salvation depended on both of these obediences. Paul, however, tells them that justification is a gift freely given to all whom God wishes to save, even if they are not members of the Jewish people. The only necessary condition for salvation is faith.

The passage read here reflects the doctrinal and practical situation that was causing a crisis among the Galatians. Paul bids them realize that they have been freed; they should not put on themselves once again the chains of their ancient bondage. The gospel is a revelation of freedom; we should not assign to the gospel the characteristic traits of the law and assimilate it to the law!

FOURTEENTH SUNDAY

Joy and Peace

Joy springing from mission (Luke 10:1-12, 17, 20)

Today's reading is parallel to the passage from Matthew
for the eleventh Sunday in Cycle A (Matthew 9:36–10:8).
There are, however, some special details in Luke's account
that merit our attention. In addition, the first reading of the
day constitutes an invitation to read the Gospel with a particular theme in mind: that of the peace and joy which is
the lot of those who have carried out their mission of
preaching the kingdom.

Jesus first chooses those he will send. The emphasis here
is not so much on the individuals he chooses (for this, see
the eleventh Sunday, Cycle A) as on their missionary activity and especially on the joy it will bring them. (This is not
to say, of course, that being chosen as a messenger who will
proclaim the coming of Jesus is something inconsequen-
tial!) We see Jesus sending his newly chosen disciples ahead
of him to the places he himself intends to visit. Their
mission will be chiefly to announce his coming, to present
him to the crowds, to open their hearts to faith, and to
arouse in them a desire for his coming. The whole passage
thus carried a special meaning for those who would be
reading Luke's Gospel, since in the early Church, the
Church described for us in the Acts of the Apostles, disciples would still be chosen and sent (see Acts 1:24; 6:3-6;
13:2-3; etc.), and their mission would consist in announcing
the Christ who would come at the end of time.

Jesus urges prayer to the Father that he would send
laborers into the harvest, as we have already heard him urging his disciples in St. Matthew's Gospel (13:39). Then he
goes into detail concerning the missionary activity of those
he is sending. The part the missionaries must play is not an

easy one, for it is that of the sheep who is sent among wolves. Despite this opposition, which at times will lead men to reject them, they are to wish peace upon every house they seek to enter. How could it be otherwise, since they are coming in order to proclaim God's kingdom?

The peace of which Christ speaks is almost like a concrete, material entity: "If a son of peace is there, your peace shall rest upon him; but if not, it shall return to you." This peace, which is a fruit of the Holy Spirit (according to Gal. 5:22), is linked to the coming of God's kingdom. This peace is the only thing the missionaries are to bring with them. They are to expect food in exchange for the incomparable service they perform in bringing peace with them into men's homes. St. Paul tells us the very same thing (1 Cor. 9:14; 1 Tim. 5:18). The missionaries are then to stay awhile in the village and confirm their proclamation of the kingdom by curing the sick and saying (which amounts to the same thing): "The kingdom of God has come near to you."

The missionaries who bring peace and the message of the kingdom are not always received. If they are refused, they are to give the prophetic sign of judgment in God's behalf. The Acts of the Apostles tells us that Paul and Barnabas used the same gesture at Antioch when they were rejected there: they shook the dust from their feet (Acts 13:51). God's judgment will be more severe on the towns that hear the message of the kingdom and reject it than it was on Sodom.

Today's pericope omits some verses of Luke and passes immediately to the return of the missionaries. They come back rejoicing and filled with youthful wonder that even the demons obeyed when expelled in the name of Jesus.

Jesus' response to their enthusiasm encourages the disciples and gives them further theological instruction concerning the efficacy of the mission they have carried out in Jesus' name. Their apostolic work in his name means that the end of the reign of Satan is at hand; Jesus even sees him fall like lightning from heaven, an apocalyptic vision of the end of time. Jesus has given them his own power to crush serpents and destroy the powers of evil. He now encour-

ages them and gives them a new cause for joy by telling
them that their names are written in heaven.

The joy and peace of the messianic age (Is. 66:10-14c)

The sorrowing are here urged to rejoice. For her infidelities, Jerusalem has been punished by exile, but the exile
is now over and the exiles are gradually coming home; the
city is coming to life again. The prophet expresses his joyous amazement at this in the verses just preceding today's
pericope (v. 8). Peace is now returning to Jerusalem, like a
river that the Lord is making flow in her direction. The
prophet describes the joys this peace brings with it.

The joy that Isaiah speaks of is also described for us in
psalms with which we are quite familiar; for example:
"When the Lord restored the fortunes of Zion, we were like
those who dream. Then our mouth was filled with laughter,
and our tongue with shouts of joy. . . . The Lord has done
great things for us; we are glad" (Ps. 126:1-3).

This Sunday conveys to us something of the vibrant emotions of the early Church as she saw the slowly ripening
fruits of her missionary activity in the name of the Lord
Jesus. We can feel a touch of her joy, of her awareness of
the presence of the God whose kingdom was spreading. Do
we still feel any of that joy today? Has not our enthusiasm
diminished somewhat? The centuries have passed, it is
true, and yet history, despite its sometimes unedifying
pages, surely provides in the past and at the present time a
magnificent vision that should stir us to joy and fill us with
peace!

Each of us should ask himself the same questions we put
to the Church as such. Is our missionary zeal sufficiently
focused on the proclamation of Christ's kingdom? Do we
spread peace and joy to others? Do those who come in
touch with us sense that we are filled with peace and joy
because we are convinced that the kingdom is among us
and that we are experiencing it? These are important ques-

tions, and the answers are more important than any considerations of missionary technique, for technique is of value only if we are spreading peace and joy because the kingdom is at hand. They are questions each of us must answer individually.

_____

Bear in your body the marks of Jesus (Gal. 6:14-18)

The two verses preceding today's pericope recall the trouble caused by the Jewish Christians. The latter wanted to make salvation dependent on belonging to the Jewish people and on circumcision. These Jewish Christians wanted to "glory in your flesh" (Gal. 6:13), that is, they were still proud of belonging to a people they regarded as privileged and of observing the Mosaic law. In fact, however, they "would compel you to be circumcised, and only in order that they may not be persecuted for the cross of Christ." In other words, the Jewish Christians regarded their membership in the Jewish people chiefly as a means of protecting their lives and their peaceful existence.

Paul, on the other hand, wants his readers to be faithful to what Christ has done. We now live a new life in a new world. It was the sufferings of the crucified Christ that saved us; they are the mark of our salvation and of our belonging to a new people. We should bear them in our own bodies and make them our source of pride.

It is clear that Paul fears a return to the law. May we not fear the same for ourselves? In what sense is such a return possible for us? It is possible for us paradoxically to feel proud and secure because we are faithful to certain observances and because we receive the sacraments — as though the sacraments were chiefly meant for security instead of being a way of sharing in Christ's sufferings so that we may also reach the resurrection with him. The tendency to seek refuge in the letter of the law or in practice will be a trap for human beings until the end of time. We must be conscious of the danger and on guard against yielding to the tendency, lest we easily slip into a life based chiefly on practices and develop a kind of Christian pride of caste.

FIFTEENTH SUNDAY

The Law Of Love

Who is my neighbor? (Luke 10:25-37)

St. Luke was a disciple of St. Paul. It is not surprising, therefore, that he has relatively little use for the letter of the law and is much more concerned about compassion and the spirit of the law. This is his frame of mind when he tells us the parable of the Good Samaritan.

The lawyer's question, "What shall I do to inherit eternal life?" is typical in that it is wholly concerned with obligation and fulfillment of a law. But the lawyer does know the law, and his answer to Jesus' own question is perfect. Then, moved by a desire to justify himself, he asks a second question, and it shows that he has not gotten to the bottom of the problem of love and that his grasp of the law he has quoted is superficial. This is not a negligiable point, since Christ has just told him, "Do this, and you will live" — that is, observe the law of love for God and neighbor, and you will have life therefrom. If the lawyer does not really understand the law he has quoted, he cannot fully observe it.

It is clear that Christ does not reject the Jewish tradition that the lawyer has just quoted to him from the Book of Deuteronomy (6:5) and the Book of Leviticus (19:18). On the contrary, Christ tells us that the attainment of eternal life is bound up with the concrete fulfillment of the twofold commandment of love for God and neighbor.

The purpose of the parable is to shed light on what "neighbor" means. The priest and the Levite who pass by have no understanding of who their neighbor is. Jesus deliberately chooses a Samaritan, a person the Jews regard as a heretic, to illustrate the true concept of "neighbor."

Live by the word of God (Deut. 30:10-14)

Moses is concerned to show that the law is not something outside of man, remote, majestic, and as inaccessible as if it were stored up in heaven. On the contrary, the law is very near; it is even in man's mouth and heart as a dynamic principle of life. It should never even be thought of as distinct from practice; that is, "law" by its nature is something to be put into concrete practice. The law is not beyond man's power or out of his reach, for it is within him. We should read here the earlier passage in which the commandment of love is enunciated (Deut. 6:4-9); in this latter passage the law is presented to us as a source of life that slowly fills the man who puts the law into practice.

These passages from the Book of Deuteronomy lead us over to the gospel and its demands. Our age, like the Book of Deuteronomy and the Gospels, is hardly legalist-minded, but this does not mean that we have nothing to learn from these passages.

Christianity is characterized precisely by the dynamic practice of love for God and neighbor; indeed, such practice is the most direct proof we can give the world that our faith is living and powerful. Love must be in our mouths and in our hearts, and we must put it into practice.

Our age thinks it has discovered the reality of the "other," yet it is a time when ever more numerous rifts are dividing men. In the very groups that should be marked by the practice of genuine love, we find men devouring one another in the name of openness. Evidently, then, the lessons of this Sunday still have their point! The commandment of love is directly related to life, and true life is impossible if the commandment is not put into concrete practice in relation to each and every person. Many an ascetical effort, many an hour of prayer and contemplation are rendered ineffective for the Church's life because these words of God on love are not found in the mouth and the heart, or if they are, are dead words that do not influence men's lives. "By this all men will know that you are my disciples, if you have love for one another" (John 13:35). Do men know us as his disciples by this sign?

All things were created through Christ and for him (Col. 1:15-20)

Verses 12-14 of this first chapter of the Letter to the Colossians were a prayer of thanksgiving for our translation into the kingdom of Christ, in whom we have redemption and the forgiveness of sins.

The pericope read today is a great hymn to the glory of Christ, who is the image of the invisible God, and the Creator and Redeemer. It is divided into three parts: the first gives praise to Christ as Creator of all things; the second gives thanks for the Redeemer, the Head of the Body which is the Church; the third honors him who has reconciled everything in himself.

Christ is the Creator. This action, however, is not to be isolated from another action of his: redemption. It is he who creates, and it is he who remakes creation so that it is better than it originally was. Christ is the image of the invisible God and the sacrament of our encounter with God. He is the first-born of all creation; he has primacy in the created order because he is the man-God. Everything has been created through Christ, in Christ, and for Christ. If he is the first-born of all creation, it is because he is above all other creatures and because he exists before them. Creation through Christ means that included in the creative plan is the incarnation that is to restore the created order.

Christ is also the Redeemer. Creation already contains within itself the second creation, because through his paschal mystery Christ creates a Body, the Church, of which he is the Head. The fact that the creative and redemptive roles of Christ are so closely united gives us a rounded idea of God's plan and helps us look at redemption, not as though it were an event apart, but as an internal force that shatters the old world in order to create it anew. It is one and the same Person who, as image of the Father and as Word made flesh, creates, re-creates, and forms a Body of which he is the Head. In fact, he re-creates the world as a single reality (John 17) which he organizes and of which he is the Head.

Christ has reconciled everything in himself, and he is the fullness of all. By the blood he shed on the Cross he has reconciled everything on earth and in heaven. He humbled himself, "emptied" himself, and accepted poverty and self-stripping, especially in his Passion (Phil. 2:7), but now he is filled and is the source of life in the fullest possible sense of this last term. Because he dedicated himself to the Father's will and lowered himself beneath the angels, he has been exalted and has received the name that is above every name (Phil. 2:9).

We are called to share the fullness that is in Christ; in fact, we are already in contact with that fullness because we are members of the Body whose head Christ is. We also have access to this fullness every time we receive a sacrament (for example, the sacrament of penance, which we do not think of often enough from this point of view), and especially when we celebrate the Eucharist, as on Sundays. The Christ who created all things continually re-creates us.

This is evidently a very active outlook on the life of Christ and the life of his members. It is an outlook that will spur us to action and to constant renewal. We must be willing to be re-created by Christ, in his Body the Church, as he wishes and in the way he wishes.

SIXTEENTH SUNDAY

God Visits Him

Receive Jesus in your house (Luke 10:38-42)

Today's Gospel contains several points of teaching. In particular, we could well find help here in solving the ever current problem of activity and "contemplation." We should not let ourselves go overboard in this direction, however, since, as the first reading shows, the Gospel passage was chosen chiefly for the idea of God's visit to us. The fact of that visit should be the focus of our attention. It is also important to see how and under what conditions we should receive God's visit.

The Lord's visit presupposes an attitude on the part of those he visits, and from this point of view today's passage is especially valuable. The evangelist does not tell us the name of the place Jesus visits, but he does tell us the names of the two women who are thus favored. This naming of names is unusual, for Luke does not normally give the names of the people who enter into dialogue with Jesus. Perhaps Luke had an intuition that this passage would be of permanent importance in the life of the Church, since it tells us how to receive Jesus. For that reason, too, the evangelist goes somewhat into detail.

There are two possible ways of receiving Jesus. One is symbolized by the attitude of Mary as she sits at the feet of Jesus. Is her attitude one of mere contemplative idleness? No, she listens actively to the Lord, and her sitting is the sitting of the disciple at the teacher's feet. Thus, the crowd sits down around Jesus and waits to be taught (Matthew 12:47; Luke 8:19-20); thus, too, a man freed from demons sits at Jesus' feet (Luke 8:35). The other attitude is one of activity that is inspired by respectful love of the Lord. So respectful indeed is Martha that Luke lets us feel a certain anxiety in her behavior, as well as a zeal so sure of itself that she can call on the Lord to be witness to all she does, while her sister abandons her to do the work alone.

In his answer to Martha's complaint, Jesus gives his judgment on the two attitudes. It is less one-sided than people sometimes seem to think. For example, his answer in no way condemns the zeal of Martha, and it would be very subjective, to say the least, to see in his words a condemnation of zeal and apostolic activity in the Church! If we are to interpret the words properly, we must attend to the context in which Luke places them. It is easy to see that the evangelist wants to emphasize the hearing of the word and the attitude of a disciple. Receiving Christ requires, first and foremost, hearing him and having the soul of a disciple. But Jesus' response does not make a choice of one attitude against another; that is, the Christian is not forced to choose between acting and contemplating. The point is rather that he must first of all listen and receive Christ with interior peace and simplicity. Any reproach of Martha is for her anxiety, not for her zealous activity in receiving Jesus.

Unfortunately, the text of Jesus' answer raises problems of literary criticism that have not been resolved. In the Jerusalem Bible translation, Jesus says: "Martha, Martha, you worry and fret about so many things, and yet few are needed, indeed only one." This translation is possible because the original text is found in three different forms: "few things are needed"; "only one thing is needed"; and "few things are needed, even only one." This third text joins the first two into one; the reading is attested by important manuscripts, and many editions have adopted it.

The first reading (and translation) would seem to mean that Martha should not worry because only a few things are needed. Such a reading would render Jesus' remark completely trivial, and as a matter of fact there are few manuscript witnesses to this reading. The second and third readings really mean the same thing, namely, one thing is necessary. What is that one thing? In the context of the proclamation of the Gospel, and given the attitude of Mary

who listens to the Lord, the one thing needed is evidently
God's word. Everything else is secondary when compared
to this listening to God's word.

"The good portion" (or "the better part") that will not be
taken from Mary does not mean her not being at the service
of others; it means only her listening to the word of God.
This is doubtless why the reading used to be used on the
feast of the Assumption of the Blessed Virgin, who, beyond
all others, listened to the word and kept it in her heart. We
must repeat once again — for the point is important — that
Jesus was not reproaching Martha for her service to others,
but only because she tended to overemphasize and give
priority to what should be secondary in relation to listening
to God's word.

God comes and fulfills his promise (Gen. 18:1-10a)

The story from Genesis is like a fairy tale that transports
us into a world of Oriental warmth and hospitality. We
could well be carried away by the story and be led to imagine that it is intended to encourage the virtue of hospitality. The author of the narrative goes beyond any such intention, however. What he is concerned with is the Lord's visit
to Abraham as the patriarch sits at the door of his tent.

The story has its strange side. The Lord appears — but in
fact three men are suddenly standing in front of Abraham.
He greets them, but he addresses only one of them, and he
uses both singular and plural pronouns in his invitation to
them. Some Fathers of the Church, such as Augustine and
Ambrose, see in these three men the Trinity; others think
one of the three is the Word, and they concentrate on him.
Exegetically, of course, neither of these interpretations is
justifiable, but the passage remains a literary conundrum.

In any case, the story depicts divine messengers or perhaps even God himself, manifesting himself in this triple
form. The three ask Abraham: "Where is Sarah your wife?"
and they promise him a son. Here God is fulfilling the promise he had made to Abraham if the latter would leave his

homeland. Abraham had first received the Lord in the latter's word and promise ("I will make of you a great nation"; Gen. 12:2), and had done so with faith. Such faith now brings the fulfillment of the promise.

The Gospel, as we have seen, follows the same line of thought, since listening to the word is a way of receiving the Lord. This does not mean that the warm welcome Abraham gives his guests is useless. The point is rather that receiving God by accepting his word and promise is more basic and more important.

The responsorial psalm reverses the perspective and sings of God's hospitality as he receives us into his house. It also tells us the qualities required if a man is to be God's guest. Between this Psalm 15, which praises God's hospitality, and the reading, which tells us of Abraham's hospitality, there is a close connection. The two together describe the exchange thus set up between God and men, and amount to a new way of expressing the covenant that exists between them.

It seems to me inappropriate to compare the two readings (Genesis and Luke) in detail. The reader might point out contradictions; for example, Sarah, who bustles about to serve the guests, is rewarded, while Martha does the same and is reprimanded. But such criticisms would show that the reader has not understood the two passages. The real point in both is the priority that must be given to the reception of the word and its heralds, and the fact that this reception is not primarily a matter of outward actions but of an attitude of listening.

The commentaries have too often seen in these texts an opposition between action and contemplation. Only an excessively anecdotal reading of the text could have created such a simplistic, moralizing opposition.

We must look more deeply than that and see a point that is important for us today. The point is that listening to the Lord is the primordial Christian activity. The welcome we give to him consists first and foremost in our receptive attitude of attentive faith. The first thing we have to do is to

understand what the Lord wants of us and, therefore, to be
alert to hear him. This first step is the basis for the whole of
concrete Christian life. We can call this listening "contemplation" if we want. Certainly, if we want to hear Jesus, we
must find a quiet place apart from the noise of the crowd;
we must find the time to read the Scriptures; we must have
the courage to avoid the discussions, the endless round tables, sharings and workshops that are now fashionable so
that we have the opportunity to listen to Jesus in silence.
We can also hear him, however, in the midst of our work,
on the train, amid physical or moral suffering. The interior
attitude of love is the decisive thing when it comes to
hearing God.

The mystery hidden and revealed (Col. 1:24-28)

St. Paul requires us to accustom ourselves to an unfamiliar terminology. As we use the word today, a "mystery" is
something hidden that we can neither see nor understand.
We like to call religious realities "mysterious," but we tend
to mean by speaking of, for example, the "mysteries of
Christ," that there are aspects of Christ that we have trouble understanding, for example, the Eucharistic presence.
In the language of St. Paul and of later theology, however,
"mystery" is just the opposite of the hidden and incomprehensible. It is a word applied to God's plan, which was
indeed hidden through the ages but which has now been
revealed in order that we might share in it. This "mystery"
is Christ himself, present among us, our hope of glory.

St. Paul is a prisoner when he writes this letter, but his
sufferings do not disturb his joy, since he puts up with
these sufferings for the sake of the Church. His attitude is a
"moral" one, but also a good deal more. Christ's sufferings
were undoubtedly efficacious and do not inherently need to
be completed. But the Body of Christ is unfinished and is

constantly being built. It is therefore the sufferings of Christ as experienced by his Body that Paul shares through his own sufferings. The Church is always in the process of carrying out God's plan more fully. As a minister whom God has chosen, Paul is intimately involved in this constructive work that completes what was lacking in Christ's sufferings, that is, his unfinished Church. Paul's ministry in behalf of this construction is twofold: a ministry of suffering and a ministry of evangelization.

The mystery hidden through the ages and revealed in the person of Christ is now at work in the world and leading the world to its fullness and completion. The purpose of every apostolate is precisely to lead man to his full being in Christ — to lead him, that is, to an interior balance that will enable him to bear suffering in Christ so that the Church may grow.

SEVENTEENTH SUNDAY

Ask and You Shall Receive

Learn to pray (Luke 11:1-13)

St. Luke wishes to show us how Jesus prayed. He is not the only one, of course, to record Jesus' teaching on prayer. St. Matthew, too, tells us how Jesus saw the act of praying: "When you pray, go into your room and shut the door and pray to your Father who is in secret; and your Father who sees in secret will reward you" (Matthew 6:6). Prayer in secret is effective. But Matthew also emphasizes the presence of Christ when men gather to pray together: "If two of you on earth agree about anything they ask, it will be done for them by my Father in heaven. For where two or three

are gathered in my name, there am I in the midst of them"
(Matthew 18:19-20).

St. John lays special emphasis on the efficacy of prayer
"in the name of Jesus." "In my name" means "united to
me": "If you abide in me, and my words abide in you, ask
whatever you will, and it shall be done for you" (15:7). If we
ask in Jesus' name, our prayer will be answered: "Whatever
you ask in my name, I will do it" (14:13); ". . . so that whatever you ask the Father in my name, he may give it to you"
(15:16); "ask, and you will receive" (16:24) provided we ask
in the name of Jesus (16:23, 26).

Both Matthew and Luke show us Jesus teaching his disciples the Our Father. In St. Luke's account, Jesus' teaching is elicited by a request from the disciples themselves:
"Lord, teach us to pray, as John taught his disciples." The
disciples who followed a prophet wanted to learn of the
prophet's own experience in prayer.

Luke, like Matthew, has preserved the prayer that Jesus
offers as a model. We may be surprised, however, to realize
that the two texts of the Our Father are not identical. This
means that the evangelists did not think it necessary to
transcribe verbatim the model prayer offered by Jesus but
only to capture its essential content.

Many of the Fathers, of course, wrote commentaries on
the Lord's Prayer. In addition, the ancient ritual for the
catechumenate contained a "handing over" (*traditio*) of the
Our Father to the catechumens; on this occasion a short
commentary on the prayer that was preached so that the catechumen might use the prayer intelligently.[33] In the Roman
liturgy the Lord's Prayer was originally sung immediately
before Communion. Pope St. Gregory the Great, however,
shifted it to its present position immediately after the Eucharistic Prayer; he was astonished that we should use prayers
composed by men during the main part of the celebration,
while postponing the Lord's own prayer to a much later
point.[34]

The liturgy uses the version of the Lord's Prayer that St.

Matthew supplies. Here are the texts of Matthew and Luke set side by side for comparison.

Matthew 6:9-13	Luke 11:2-4
Our Father who art in heaven,	Father,
hallowed be thy name.	hallowed be thy name.
Thy kingdom come,	Thy kingdom come.
Thy will be done, on earth as it is in heaven.	
Give us this day our daily bread;	Give us each day our daily bread;
and forgive us our debts, as we also have forgiven our debtors;	and forgive us our sins, for we ourselves forgive every one who is indebted to us;
and lead us not into temptation, but deliver us from evil.	and lead us not into temptation.

In St. Matthew, the Our Father is followed by a commentary on the second last petition: "For if you forgive men their trespasses, your heavenly Father also will forgive you; but if you do not forgive men their trespasses, neither will your Father forgive your trespasses" (6:14).

The structure of the Our Father is evidently similar to that of traditional Jewish prayers, with their exclamation of praise and their petitions, which are another form of praise. We have already analyzed this structure on several occasions.

Prayer to the "Father"

It would become customary in the Latin Church to address prayer to the Father, though Jesus Christ, in the Holy Spirit. Psalm 89 had long before expressed God's own wish that men should address him as "Father": "He shall cry to

me, 'Thou art my Father'" (v. 26). Nonetheless, even
though the Old Testament had a very true and loving idea
of the fatherhood of God, both as Father of the nation he
had brought into being and as Father of the individuals
who made up the people, the Lord's Prayer is typically
Christian. According to St. Paul, only the Spirit makes it
possible for us, after our baptism, to address God as *Abba*,
"dear Father" (Gal. 4:6; Rom. 8:15); this is because in baptism the Spirit of Jesus, the Son, becomes our Spirit and
enables us to address God as Jesus did.

St. Matthew's version of the prayer amplifies the address
"Father" into "Our Father, who art in heaven," whereas St.
Luke is content with the simple name. That is how Jesus
often addresses the Father in the Gospels. Commenting on
the Lord's Prayer, St. Ambrose writes: "You have changed
from evil servant to good son. . . . Therefore, lift your eyes
to the Father who begot you through the bath, the Father
who redeemed you through the Son." [35] The commentary
on the Our Father that accompanied the rite of the presentation of the prayer to the catechumen follows the same
line of thought: 'These are the words of a free man, and full
of confidence. You are to live in such a way that you may indeed be children of God and brothers and sisters of Christ." [36]

St. Luke seems to reflect better the original prayer as
spoken by Jesus, inasmuch as, like Jesus, he addresses God
simply as "Father," without the "our" and the "who art in
heaven." The prayer is thus rendered more intimate. At the
same time, however, it is surely less apt for a communal
celebration.

Hallowed be thy name

"Name" in the Bible is a way of designating the person
himself. But what can it mean to say: "May you be hallowed (sanctified)"? St. Ambrose raises the question and
gives an answer: "What does 'sanctified' mean? . . . It
means 'May he be hallowed in us,' so that his holiness may
reach us." The commentary on the presentation of the Our

Father says: "We ask that his name be made holy in us, so that after being sanctified in his baptism, we may continue as we have begun."

How did St. Luke himself understand this holiness of the Father's name? In the *Magnificat*, the holiness of God is associated with his mercy and power: "He who is mighty has done great things for me, and holy is his name. And his mercy is on those who fear him from generation to generation. He has shown strength with his arm" (Luke 1:49-51). God is holy because he carries out the work of salvation in behalf of his people and because in so doing he manifests both mercy and power.

In the prophet Ezekiel, the Lord proclaims that despite the infidelities and profanations of which his people are guilty, "I will vindicate the holiness of my great name, which has been profaned among the nations . . . and the nations will know that I am the Lord, says the Lord God, when through you I vindicate my holiness before their eyes" (36:23). This mighty and merciful action of God will be manifested when he puts a new heart and a new spirit into his people (Ezek. 36:26).

Thy kingdom come

The Lord's name is sanctified when he continues his mighty and merciful action in us and we respond to it. Such a response must be continued until the fullness of time when the kingdom of God comes. St. Ambrose writes: "The kingdom of God comes when you have obtained his grace. For he himself says: 'The kingdom of God is within you.'" Closely following Ambrose, the commentary at the presentation of the Lord's Prayer says: "But when does our God not reign, since his reign is unending? Therefore, when we say, 'Thy kingdom come,' we are asking that our kingdom may come, the kingdom promised us by God and won for us by the blood and suffering of Christ."

According to these commentaries, then, the petition looks to the end of time. At the same time, however, the petition

is also an exhortation to Christians who were contemporaries of Matthew and Luke, and to all of us as well, to
manifest and promote God's rule in our lives.

Thy will be done . . .

St. Luke omits this petition, which is, in fact, an explicita-
tion of the preceding, inasmuch as the sanctification of
God's name and the desire that his kingdom should come
necessarily imply the doing of God's will. However, St.
Ambrose sees in the accomplishment of God's will the successful carrying out of the plan of salvation: "'Peace is bestowed on all things in heaven and on earth by the blood of
Christ' (Col. 1:20). Heaven has been sanctified, and the
devil has been expelled. He is now on earth, along with
man whom he deceived. 'Thy will be done,' that is, let
there be peace on earth as there is in heaven." The commentary in the ritual of presentation understands the doing
of God's will as referring especially to us earthlings: "Thy
will be done in the sense that what you will in heaven, we
who dwell on earth may accomplish in an irreproachable
way."

Give us our daily bread

St. Matthew adds "this day" and thus puts the emphasis
on the present day; we ask for today's bread without being
anxious for tomorrow's. St. Luke adds "each day," thus
stressing rather the fact that the Father cares for his children day after day.

The petition is thus in a line with Jewish prayer, in
which there was frequent petition for earthly food.[37] The
prayer is, moreover, the prayer of one who is poor, and the
thought of the poor must inevitably come to mind as we ask
for "our daily bread." In addition, the Fathers thought at
this point of the Eucharist. St. Ambrose writes:

> He spoke of bread but called it *epiousios*, that is,
> "substantial." This bread is not the bread that enters

the body but the bread of eternal life that strengthens the substance of our souls. That is why it is called, in Greek, *epiousios*. The Latin text calls it a "daily" bread, because the Greeks call "tomorrow" *ten epiousan hemeran*. Thus, the Latin and Greek texts are both useful. The Greek, however, captures the two meanings in a single word, while the Latin expresses only the "daily" aspect. . . . Receive each day what is of profit to you for each day.

The commentary on the presentation says: "The 'bread' here is to be understood as spiritual bread. Our real bread is Christ, who said: 'I am the living bread who have come down from heaven.' We speak of it as 'daily' because we must always be asking to be preserved from sin so that we may be worthy of the heavenly food." It is clear that the spiritual and liturgical interpretation can differ from that reached by a straight exegesis of the text. The use of the Lord's Prayer in the Eucharistic celebration has given it an undeniable Eucharistic meaning.

Forgive us

St. Luke has us pray for the forgiveness of our sins, while St. Matthew speaks of the forgiveness or cancellation of debts. We may find it odd that Luke did not keep the image of a debt, since he is the one who has preserved for us the little parable about the creditor who forgave two debtors (Luke 7:41-42). In any case, we must note that in the Lord's Prayer, Luke immediately goes on to say that we must forgive those indebted to us if we would ourselves be forgiven by God.

The measure of our forgiveness by God will be determined by the measure of our forgiveness of others. After explaining that Christ has cancelled our debts by shedding his blood, St. Ambrose continues: "Pay attention to what you are saying: 'As I forgive, so do you forgive me'! If you forgive, you make an agreement that you in turn will be forgiven. If you do not forgive, how can you expect God to

forgive you?" The commentary on the presentation clarifies
the petition by reference to other words of Jesus: "The
sense of this petition is that we cannot win forgiveness of
our sins unless we first forgive those who have offended us.
As the Lord says in the Gospel: 'If you do not forgive men
their sins, your Father will not forgive you your sins.'"

And lead us not into temptation

In St. Luke's version of the Lord's Prayer, these words
are the final ones, while in St. Matthew's version this negative appeal is followed by a more positive one: "but deliver
us from evil." St. Ambrose seems to have correctly grasped
the meaning of this petition, and many modern commen-
tators agree with him:

> He does not say: "Do not lead us into temptation,"
> but, like an athlete, he wants a testing such as human
> nature can sustain; he wants each person to be deliv-
> ered from evil, that is, from the enemy, from sin. But
> the Lord who has taken away your sins and forgiven
> your offenses has power also to guard and protect you
> against the snares of your adversary the devil. . . . He
> who entrusts himself to God has no fear of the devil.
> For if God is for us, who is against us?

The liturgical commentary at the presentation of the Lord's
Prayer says simply: "'And lead us not into temptation.' That
is, do not let us be led into temptation by the Tempter, who
is the source of all corruption."

After recording the Lord's model prayer for his readers,
St. Luke continues his teaching on prayer by recording a
parable that Jesus spoke to his disciples. It is the familiar
parable of the importunate friend, and its main point is the
unwearying constancy with which we must pray. The parable is easily applied to the man who prays, but especially to
God who hears our prayer: "Ask, and it will be given you;
seek, and you will find; knock, and it will be opened to you.
For every one who asks receives." The parable is an exhor-

tation to both confidence and perseverance in prayer. For if among us men, who are evil, a father cannot refuse his child anything, how much more will God be willing to answer our prayers!

This teaching on prayer would doubtless be somewhat dangerous if it did not follow upon the model prayer just given. A simplistic mind — and this kind of simplism does exist, even among highly educated people when they deal with things religious — might think that we need only have this shameless persistence and unshakable faith, and we will obtain anything we want from God. The Lord's Prayer corrects such an impossible theology of prayer. It tells us that what we can obtain with certainty is the sanctification of God's name, the coming of his kingdom, and the doing of his will. We obtain forgiveness, but only on certain conditions, whose fulfillment depends on us. If God, being a Father, gives us what we ask, he is not, however, forced to answer any and every petition whatsoever; prayer is not something that works mechanically. God hears our petitions only if they are in keeping with his will and if we do our best to carry out what he wants of us for our salvation.

Pray tirelessly against all hope (Gen. 18:20-32)

Nothing could better show that prayer is a bold dialogue with God than this passage form the Book of Genesis, in which we see Abraham speaking with the Lord and almost straining the limits of respect in an effort to catch God, as it were, in the snare of his own goodness and his own sense of justice. The whole dialogue should be read in its entirety, for in it we see the Lord being pushed to the extreme of mercy.

The style and manner of proceeding are truly Semitic. The appeal to God's honor and reputation for justice might seem to us highly disrespectful; as a matter of fact, however, it shows great confidence in God and demonstrates the "friendly" intimacy of God with Old Testament man. Abraham makes it clear that along with Moses, Samuel, and

Jeremias, he is one of the great spiritual men of all time, one of those whose spirit of trusting prayer is an example for every generation. In the psalms, too, we find God taken to task and "forced" to save his honor by hearing the prayers of his people: "Not for our sakes, Lord, but for your name's sake you must give us what we ask"!

The responsorial psalm, Psalm 138, praises God for being always attentive to our prayer: "On the day I called, thou didst answer me." He stretches out his hand to save us and exerts his power for us, "Thy steadfast love, O Lord, endures for ever. Do not forsake the work of thy hands."

Buried and risen with Christ (Col. 2:12-14)

It is a known fact that Christians used to think of the baptismal font as a tomb in which we are buried with Christ, but also as a maternal womb that brings us to new birth. These symbolisms were connected with the very expressive rite of immersion. But the ritual that symbolized and effected this death and new life has power to do so only if the recipient has faith in the God who raised Jesus from the dead.

Sin and death, death and resurrection with Christ, faith and baptism — these are correlative terms of which Paul reminds us in his brief but pregnant statement. Because of the perspective he is adopting, he adds that forgiveness of sin means liberation from the law and its observances — law, sin, and death being connected, as he teaches in his Letter to the Romans (7:7-9). Here Paul uses an extremely expressive image: the law has been nailed to the Cross.

EIGHTEENTH SUNDAY

The Passing and the Abiding

Rich in God's sight (Luke 12:13-21)

Today's Gospel speaks to our instinctive tendencies and concerns, in order to put us on guard against them: "Take heed, and beware of all covetousness; for a man's life does not consist in the abundance of his possessions."

Following his usual catechetical approach, Jesus is not content with this abstract warning but brings it home to his hearers with the help of the parable of the rich man who piles up possessions against the future, driven by a concern that is familiar to every generation: "Soul, you have ample goods laid up for many years; take your ease, eat, drink, be merry."

If, in Jesus' eyes, riches are suspect, the same is already true of the Old Testament. The latter undoubtedly does regard wealth as a sign of God's blessing. Thus the patriarchs were wealthy (Gen. 13:2; 26:12; 30:43). Deuteronomy shows us God concerned for the prosperity of his people (Deut. 8:7-10; 28:1-12). Abundance goes with uprightness of life (Ps. 37:19).

At the same time, however, the Old Testament is also conscious of the dangers that accompany wealth; evidence of this attitude is especially to be found in the Wisdom literature. "Blessed is the rich man who is found blameless, and who does not go after gold" (Sir. 31:8); "Let not the rich man glory in his riches" (Jer. 10:23); "The rich answer roughly" (Prov. 18:23); "Your [the city's] rich men are full of violence" (Micheas 6:12). Riches are unprofitable: "Truly no man can ransom himself, or give to God the price of his life" (Ps. 49:7); "The surfeit of the rich will not let him sleep" (Eccles. 5:12). When life draws to an end, riches prove useless: "He [the rich man] swallows down riches and vomits them up again" (Job 20:15); the rich man "is like the beasts that perish" (Ps. 49:12); "Riches do not profit in the day of wrath" (Prov. 11:4); "The ransom of a man's life is his wealth" (Prov. 13:8); "Riches do not last for ever" (Prov. 27:24).

Wealth is, then, a gift of God, but it must be handled carefully, and it never becomes an unqualified good nor the most important of blessings. Wisdom must be preferred to it (1 Kings 3:11; Job 28:15-19; Wis. 7:8-11; Prov. 2:4; 3:15; 8:11). Moreover, it is difficult to remain faithful in time of prosperity, for an easy life tends to blunt the heart's sensitivity (Deut. 31:20; Ps. 73:4-9). In the Book of Isaiah we even find riches being cursed: "Woe to those who join house to house, who add field to field" (5:8). The prophet here anticipates the "Woe to you that are rich" of the Gospel (Luke 6:24).

Jesus adopts the same perspective in the parable of today's Gospel: wealth may not be intrinsically evil, but it does make it difficult to lead a life centered on the reign of God.

Leaving one's possessions to an unknown (Eccles. 1:2; 2:21-23)

The text might lead us to think that we are to be uninterested in work or progress: "All is vanity!" But that would be to mistake the author's thought. He is really preaching a balance: work should not become the main concern of our life; our attention should be focused primarily on God. The real need, therefore, is to give work its proper meaning. This meaning does not clearly emerge, however, from this highly realistic book of the Old Testament.

The Sermon on the Mount gives us Christ's thinking on wealth. The Sermon must be completed, however, by the Lord's teaching on the precious pearl (Matthew 13:45), on the obligation of serving only one master (Matthew 6:24), on the difficulty of following Jesus along the way of perfection (Matthew 19:21), and on the necessity of renouncing all one's possessions in order to be a disciple of Jesus (Luke 14:33).[38]

There is a danger that riches may cause us to close our hearts. The responsorial psalm (Ps. 95) puts us on guard against this danger: "O that today you would hearken to his voice! Harden not your hearts."

Seek the things that are above (Col. 3:1-5, 9-11)

The balanced moral outlook on life should result from what one has become in virtue of baptism. As one raised up with Christ, he must seek the things that are above. This quest is the very meaning of his life. The Christian is a new man and is constantly being remade anew by the Creator in the latter's own image so that he may attain to true knowledge.

The Christian must put to death in himself the vices Paul lists in verses 5-8 (verses 6-8 are omitted from today's reading), where the emphasis is on the appetite for pleasure and the worship of idols. But he does so for the sake of the true knowledge that leads him to a share of God's glory, his goal being to appear someday with Christ in glory. That we should seek the things above is not only a moral precept promulgated by Paul; it is also a consequence of our new being. We belong now to the heavenly kingdom and must therefore rid ourselves of the preoccupations and ways of acting proper to the old, unreconstructed self.

NINETEENTH SUNDAY

Be Ready to Receive God's Glory

Be ready (Luke 12:32-48)

In this passage from St. Luke's Gospel, Jesus describes the attitude of expectation that should characterize his disciples in every generation. The little flock waits amid difficulty, conflict, and the sameness of every day. It knows, however, that the Father has been pleased to bestow the kingdom upon it. For that reason, an attitude of expectant waiting is quite logical, and Jesus wishes to clarify this attitude through four examples that will foster understanding.

In St. Luke's view, the four parables tell the Christians whom he is evangelizing what kind of interior outlook they should have. Each of the parables in turn brings out the nature of Christian expectation: the image of the treasure in heaven, the image of the servants who are awaiting their master's return, the image of the burglar who comes when he is not expected, and the image of the faithful and the unfaithful stewards.

These parables are still relevant to us individually and to the Church of our day. They bid us be expectant and ready. We are to set our hearts upon heavenly treasure, not because earthly things are evil, but because we rightly judge that the treasures of heaven are inexhaustible, permanent, and in every way good.

We are to be as servants awaiting their master. Those who listened to Jesus were all doubtless awaiting the reign of God; their vision of that kingdom was not always a purified one, but was frequently colored by political views. St. Luke's readers, however, like the Church of our day and like each of us, thought in terms of an encounter with God, now and at the end of time. Consequently, we are able to look beyond the meaning that Jesus' words had for many in his original audience to the meaning Jesus actually intended. This is to say that we, like Luke, look for the coming of Christ at the end of time as described by both Matthew (10:23; 24:44) and Luke himself (18:8).

These parables, which illustrate the duty of expectant waiting, doubtless lend themselves to legitimate moralizing. At the same time, however, we should not allow ourselves to forget the deeper vision they offer us of the very nature of the Christian as one who has been reborn from above. The spiritual nature of the Christian is such that he is made both to wait for and to move toward his encounter with God. If his soul is always pointed toward this encounter, he cannot be taken by surprise. His treasure is in heaven; he has received from the Lord natural and spiritual talents to be used for the advancement of the world and the good of others, and he is the faithful steward of these talents. How, then, could the Lord take him by surprise, like a burglar coming unexpectedly?

Readiness is not a kind of accessory quality, either for the Church or for the individual. It is rather something inherent in the nature of both the Church and the individual. Only forgetfulness of what he really is could allow the Christian to be surprised by the coming of Christ. If he follows his true nature, he will want that coming, look for it, await it, and regard it as a blessing.

Called to glory (Wis. 18:6-9)

This passage, with its high literary quality, shows God's people awaiting the glory of God. The night of deliverance, of which we are told in the Book of Exodus (ch. 12), had been known in advance by the patriarchs, because God had promised it to them. Abraham especially, as we know, had received the promises from Yahweh and had responded to them with faith (Gen. 15; etc.). The fulfillment of the promises necessarily implied both the destruction of the wicked and the salvation of the just; divine judgment was typified by the crossing of the Red Sea and by the Deluge before it; on these occasions God struck down his people's enemies and brought his chosen ones to glory.

It was this kind of expectation based on faith that Jewish families celebrated at the Passover. The people of God must go on celebrating the Passover in the solidarity of a people that is forming itself and striving toward completion, sharing both the good and the bad. The Passover, which commemorated God's encounter with his people in the process of forming them, ended with a song of praise (the Hallel, Psalms 113 to 118 and 136).

"Our soul waits for the Lord; he is our help and shield. . . . Let thy steadfast love, O Lord, be upon us, even as we hope in thee" (Ps. 33:20-22). These words are from the responsorial psalm and bring out the deeper meaning both of the Old Testament reading and of the entire celebration. Abraham joyfully accepted the promise, but he received it amid darkness, and faith alone enabled him to overcome that darkness.

So too, it was during the night that the people of God were liberated and formed into a new people under the covenant. That covenant was to be transformed into the final, eternal covenant by the sacrifice of Jesus, which was made present and operative both beforehand at the Supper and later on in the Eucharistic celebration of the Church. Each Catholic is invited to unite himself to this Sacrifice whereby the Lord renews and rebuilds the world. Each is called, during the night of faith, to stand ready for the final encounter unto which God calls.

This invitation and summons is most important. Everything else must take second place when it comes to having one's lamp lit and trimmed, to being a faithful steward, to being always alert and watchful by the light of faith. That is the lesson of today's celebration. The whole existence of the Church is a long, seemingly endless watch in which, century after century, she awaits her encounter with the Lord. She is ever alert and ready, confident as she is of the glory in store for her. Christ has promised that glory; more than that, he enables his Church to perceive the sign of it in the Eucharistic Sacrifice.

Look for the city of God (Heb. 11:1-2, 18-19)

By a happy chance, today's second reading fits in with the theme of the other two. It begins with a lapidary definition: "Faith is the assurance of things hoped for, the conviction of things not seen." Given the relationship between this pericope and today's Gospel, it is clear that we are being reminded chiefly of the element of expectation that is inherent in faith.

Abraham sets out without knowing his destination; faith makes him sure that something and some One lie ahead. In his eyes, the true values are those that the Lord has pointed out to him. He looks, therefore, for the city that has genuine foundations, the city of which God is architect and builder. Many of those who have been chosen by God have died without seeing the promise fulfilled, but they have glimpsed it from afar, and they insist that they have been but strangers and exiles upon the earth. They have been seeking a homeland — heaven — and yearning for a better land than the one they left. But a time of expectation is also a time of trial. Abraham had to offer Isaac in sacrifice; he stood ready even for this, because he believed that God can give life to the dead. That is why Abraham was capable of sacrificing his only son, the one from whom the promised posterity was to be spring. His son was spared, and the posterity came.

When linked with the Gospel, this passage from the Letter to the Hebrews is very relevant to each of us. We await the Lord; that is why we endeavor to bear in mind that we are indeed only pilgrims. On our journey we advance in faith toward the Lord. But belief is true knowledge, and we know therefore that we already possess the beginning of eternal life: "This is eternal life, that they know thee the only true God, and Jesus Christ whom thou hast sent" (John 17:3).

TWENTIETH SUNDAY

Signs to be Contradicted

Violence for the sake of the kingdom (Luke 12:49-53)

It frequently happens that the words of Jesus that an evangelist records without at all inventing them reflect his concerns as head of a church; in this he acts under the inspiration of the Holy Spirit. Today's Gospel pericope offers an interesting example of this kind of conjunction. On the one hand, Jesus depicts himself as having come to establish the kingdom; this requires a purification that he must undergo and that he is anxious to undergo. On the other hand, Luke expresses the concrete concern of a young community that finds itself amid a hostile world that cannot understand it.

Jesus has been sent "to cast fire upon the earth," and he tells us that he is anxious indeed for the fire to be kindled. What does he mean by describing his mission in this way? We cannot suppose that Christ's role is really to cause division. We should interpret his words, therefore, as referring to the last days and to the eschatological events that are to purify the world. In the Old Testament, fire has several symbolic references: the fire of judgment that condemns the wicked (Gen. 19:24; Amos 1:4, 7, 10, 14); the fire of the last days (Is. 66:15-16; Ezek. 38:22; etc.); and the fire that purifies (Is. 1:25; Zech. 13:9). Fire has, in our passage from Luke, its third symbolic meaning and leads over to Jesus' words about the baptism for which he longs.

"Baptism" is used here in its Semitic sense of a purification; Jesus is looking forward to his suffering. Each of those who believe in him and desire to follow him must be single-minded; they must make their choice. It is possible that in this passage Luke is thinking of concrete situations in his church. In any case, he does not hesitate to set aside an image of Christ that he himself has often presented: that of the prophet who brings peace (Luke 1:79; 2:14; 7:50; etc.), in accordance with the way the Old Testament prophets had depicted the Messiah (cf. Is. 9:5-6; 11:6-9; etc.). Here, instead, Luke portrays Jesus as one who brings fire.

One of the Alleluia chants for use before the Gospel brings out well the practical lesson this particular passage contains: "I am the way, the truth, and the life, says the Lord; no one comes to the Father, except through me." The baptism with which Jesus must be baptized and which he impatiently awaits is a baptism each of us must accept. But following Christ in his purifying Passion requires a choice that often involves opposition. The coming of Christ is thus a proclamation of peace but also of violence. That is the paradoxical position of the Church and her members. We can see it already in the story of St. Stephen the deacon. He proclaimed the peace of Christ, but in doing so he could not help suffering the violence caused by division and persecution. Christianity is not diplomatic religiosity nor the science of the religious mean.

The prophet, a man of discord (Jer. 38:4-6, 8-10)

Today's reading refers to events in such a way that we can assign them a precise date. Jerusalem is under siege by Nebuchodonosor (beginning of 588 to July 587). Jeremias is already in prison, accused of demoralizing the remaining combatants and the population at large. He seems to be seeking not the happiness but the misfortune of the people. Of what exactly is he accused? The verses preceding today's selection tell us: Jeremias has been prophesying that the city will be taken and that those who surrender to the Chaldeans will save their lives; the city will be delivered into the hands of the king of Babylon.

It is not easy for us to understand the prophet's attitude, and we may be tempted to regard him as a traitor to his country. We must, however, interpret the facts differently. The Lord is using the Chaldeans to punish his people; con-

sequently, those who had been simply pagans have now
become the Lord's servants. According to the Lord's words,
Jeremias must take the side of those who are now the
enemies of the Israelite king but God's servants, since the
city has proved unfaithful. The prophet cannot but proclaim
what the Lord bids him say. Israel, of course, cannot understand this turn of events: How can the Lord be even
imagined as having any people but Israel for his own?

Given this state of affairs, it was inevitable that Jeremias
should be destined for martyrdom. The Lord did save him
from death, and the prophet lived on. Yet his life as a whole
was a long martyrdom, for he was compelled to pronounce
God's judgments and to follow his orders faithfully. He was
always to be seemingly the cause of discord.

Psalm 40 uses language quite close to that which describes Jeremias' fate and suffering: "He drew me up from
the desolate pit, our of the miry bog, and set my feet upon a
rock, making my steps secure."

Hostility from sinners (Heb. 12:1-4)

By chance, the theme of this New Testament reading fits
in with the theme of the day. The Letter to the Hebrews
tells us the meaning of the trials and sufferings a Christian
endures, the meaning of the violence to which we must all
submit in some degree.

Jesus is both the origin and goal of our faith; it is toward
him that we advance through trials. The first opposition we
meet in our following of Christ is the sins that bind us. We
are thus faced with a choice. Jesus had to face the hostility
of sinners; he endured the humiliation of the Cross, but he
is now seated at God's side and rules with him. This fact
should encourage us. At the same time, however, the Letter
gives us a warning: we have not yet resisted to the point of
shedding our blood in the struggle against sin. A violent
course is thus set before us.

The readings of this Sunday may well be an attack on our
usual ways of thinking, for they do not present Christian

life as a life of sweet and easy peace and a facile observance of the commandment of love. Instead, they tell us that violence marks the climate proper to an authentic Christianity.

This should make us stop and think. The ideal we have to offer to today's world does not rest on a kind of resignation in the face of God's demands. Neither do we propose an earthly happiness and a human peace to be won by religious practice, no matter how exemplary. We have only one thing to offer: the Cross of Christ, which we must take up uncompromisingly. This means we must be a sign of contradiction in the eyes of men. Is that the image of Christianity we present? The point is not that we are to have closed minds and to refuse to understand others. The point is rather that while opening himself to the world and seeking to understand the varied situations of men, the Christian cannot compromise with the world's demands but must speak to the world the language of God, even though he suffer for it.

TWENTY-FIRST SUNDAY

The Whole World at the Feast in the Kingdom

The last will be first (Luke 13:22-30)

This Sunday seems to be placed under the sign of universalism, like the twentieth Sunday in Cycle A. Today's Gospel once again requires of us a liturgical interpretation that departs somewhat from a strictly exegetical interpretation. If we were to read the Gospel pericope without regard to its context in the celebration (a context determined by the first reading), we would be likely to emphasize the parable of the narrow door and to focus our reflection on the difficulties of and requirements for entry into the kingdom. Such an emphasis and focus are, of course, quite legitimate, but they do not take into account the context provided by the liturgy itself.

The liturgy does not deny that it is difficult to enter the kingdom. However, in keeping with the first reading, the fact that some have not faced up to the difficulty and are therefore unable to enter the kingdom, and that they knock at the door but find themselves refused admission, leads to an emphasis on the last two sentences of the pericope: "And men will come from east and west, and from north and south, and sit at table in the kingdom of God. And behold, some are last who will be first, and some are first who will be last." Some of the last — that is, the pagans — will be saved, while some of the first — that is, the Jews — will be rejected.

The question asked by a Jew, "Will those who are saved be few?" (a question often asked today), receives no direct answer. Instead, Jesus encourages his hearers to merit their salvation so that they will not be replaced by non-Jews. The Lord is saying that salvation belongs not to a race but to those who accept Christ.

Gather men from all nations (Is. 66:18-21)

God wants to bring together people of every nation and tongue. The author of today's first reading gives symbolic expression to this totality which God desires and to which he will show his glory. Even Moses had not been able to look fully on the Lord's glory but had been given only a glimpse of it (Exod. 33:18-23); now, however, all the nations will see it. In the midst of this immense assembly a sign will be set up, a banner telling everyone that this is the gathering of those who are given the vision of God's glory. In the verses following upon today's passage, the assembly is spoken of as utterly new: "the new heavens and the new earth" (Is. 66:22).

God will send messengers forth from Jerusalem to take charge of the distant nations that have not seen his glory.

Some from these nations will in turn act as God's servants, messengers sent out to be a light for the nations (see Is. 49:6). Their purpose will be to proclaim God's glory.

The response will be the journey of the nations to Jerusalem. Using every possible means of transportation, they will come to the holy mountain, these foreigners and these Jews from the Diaspora. All will offer a sacrifice in clean vessels. The climax of this universalist vision resides in the statement that the Lord will even draw some of his priests and Levites from among the foreigners. In the first reading of the twentieth Sunday, Cycle A, we read that all will offer sacrifice in the "house of prayer for all peoples" (Is. 56:7; cf. Matthew 15:21-28; Mark 11:17).

How can we avoid seeing in these texts an image of the Church, which Vatican Council II speaks of as "a sign lifted up among the nations" (in an allusion to Is. 11:12) and "a sign under which the scattered children of God may be gathered together" (cf. John 11:52)?[39]

The vision of the prophet is to be found again in the Apocalypse: an immense throng from every nation, race, people, and tongue, all standing before the throne and the Lamb (Apoc. 7:9). The Church of our day must live by this vision; it is this vision that explains her missionary activity. She is a sign of Christ, who, being "lifted up from the earth," draws to himself God's scattered children.

To correct is a sign of love (Heb. 12:5-7, 11-13)

This passage offers encouragement to Christians in times of trial, for it bids them stop looking at trials as a form of persecution by God and to look upon them rather as signs of God's special love for them. When the Lord loves someone, he teaches them what they should learn; he corrects all those he acknowledges as his sons and daughters.

The Christians to whom these words are directed have

already suffered a great deal and now find themselves being tested once again (Heb. 10:32-34). We ourselves, or others whom we love, may be in a similar situation. The author of the Letter to the Hebrews here offers us consolation that does not rest on empty words. The point, of course, is not that we should close our eyes and pretend the suffering is not real or that we should convince ourselves it is not as bad as we thought. On the contrary, we are to look on trials and sufferings realistically and see them for what they are, for only then will we be able to pass a correct value-judgment on them. That is why the author bids us meditate on the sufferings of Jesus — these sufferings brought Jesus to his glory!

When a man being tested reacts with bitterness, he closes in on himself and ceases to understand; he thinks life has become absurd for him. What such a man should really be doing is remembering the strengthening words here addressed to the person who suffers as a son or daughter of God. Trials are not punishments; such a view is inconsistent with God's mercy and certainly does not apply to those who have abandoned themselves body and soul to the Lord. We should rather look at trials as preparation for the glory that awaits us. There is no reason, then, to be discouraged; we should rather regard trials as means of attaining a more perfect union with God, who is proving his love for us through these very trials.

Initially, then, trials may sadden us, but if we reflect on what they really mean and if we reap the fruit that God intends from them, we experience a profound peace and joy that permeate our soul and our whole life. For when trials are accepted and offered to God, they always prove healing to the soul, a doctrine Paul confirms with citations from the prophet Isaiah (35:3) and the Book of Proverbs (4:26).

TWENTY-SECOND SUNDAY

Humble Yourself, and You Will Be Exalted

He who exalts himself shall be humbled (Luke 14:1, 7-14)

The Gospel pericope gives two pieces of advice. One is for those who are guests at a banquet, the other for the host. In today's Eucharistic celebration, we should attend more to the first piece of advice, for it fits in with the Old Testament reading from the Book of Sirach.

Let us begin, however, with the advice to the host. This will enable us better to link the advice to the guests with the Old Testament reading. The host, we are told, should be disinterested, that is, he should not invite in order to win invitations in return. Consequently, he will invite not his relatives and friends but the poor, the lame, and the blind. These were unfortunates who were excluded from the Temple. At the end of this piece of advice and of the pericope as a whole, Jesus gives an eschatological dimension to the banquet of which he is speaking: "You will be repaid at the resurrection of the just."

We may turn now to the first piece of advice, the one given to the guests and the one on which today's celebration focuses our attention. The occasion is a dinner to which Jesus has been invited in the house of a Pharisee. Such invitations to him were not infrequent. He uses them as an opportunity for dialogue, for teaching, and for the manifestation of his concern for the Pharisees, who, like others, are called to enter God's kingdom and find salvation therein. On this occasion the meal would have been a special one, since it took place on the Sabbath, when banquets were more lavish than usual. The other guests are teachers of the law and Pharisees, the host being one of the leading men. As at every worldly gathering, the guests seek to put themselves forward; conscious as they are of their rank and concerned for their reputation, they are skillful in maneuvering themselves into the places of honor.

The key to the whole pericope is at the end of the advice to the guests: "Every one who exalts himself will be humbled, and he who humbles himself will be exalted." But before we reflect on this statement of Jesus, let us look at the teaching contained in the Old Testament reading.

Humble yourself and find favor with God (Sir. 3:17-18, 20, 28-29)

The advice given in this passage shows a realistic evaluation of life in the world. At the same time, the author is not concerned solely with mundane shrewdness, for we also read as a motive: "you will find favor in the sight of the Lord." This shows that the humility recommended is not to be taken as simply a recommendation of worldly prudence, but as part of the proper conduct of a just man before God. "There is One who abases and exalts" (Sir. 7:11); "The eyes of the Lord look upon him [the man who is poor and weak] for his good; he lifts him out of his low estate" (Sir. 11:12).

The theme of humility occurs frequently in the Old Testament. Sometimes we even find it treated in a manner that reminds us of the New Testament. Thus the humble man acknowledges that he is a sinner (Is. 6:5); if a man empties himself so as to receive God's grace, God will show him favor (Prov. 3:34) and glorify him (1 Sam. 2:7). Israel learned humility through hard experience, and the psalms show a deep awareness of the fact, for they emphasize the prayer of the humble and poor. The latter, above all others, know how to praise the Lord (Pss. 22:25-27; 34:7; 69:3). The Old Testament also provides many exemplars of humility, for example the Servant whom Isaiah describes (53:4-10) and the Messiah who is expected to come as a humble king (Zech. 9:9). Pride, on the other hand, as today's text tells us, is a condition that cannot be healed, for wickedness has taken root in the proud man.

When, therefore, Jesus speaks of humbling oneself, his hearers know what he means. They had long ago heard Ben Sirach say: "The greater you are, the more you must humble yourself." The attitude of a truly wise man is to listen humbly.

The responsorial psalm (Ps. 68) bids us meditate on the prayer proper to the poor and provides an occasion for praising the God of the lowly and the poor: "Father of the fatherless and protector of widows is God in his holy habitation. God gives the desolate a home to dwell in; he leads out the prisoners to prosperity. . . . In thy goodness, O God, thou didst provide for the needy."

For us Christians, humility has acquired a new and priceless dimension ever since Jesus exemplified this virtue in his life. At the same time, however, the key sentence of today's reading — "Every one who exalts himself will be humbled, and he who humbles himself will be exalted" — does not seem to be spoken in view of Christ's own abasement in his Passion. The sentence refers rather to the humility proper to a wise man, and indeed to anyone who sees reality as it is.

Any lessons from Jesus' statement must be carefully drawn, for an extremist interpretation would make it either unacceptable or psychologically dangerous. For one thing, humility does not suppose that a man is indifferent to his situation or his work or human progress. There is a kind of "pride" that is salutary and necessary for the human advancement which God wills. Inability to accept responsibility, inferiority complexes, indecisiveness, fearfulness — these are not humility.

On the other hand, Jesus does condemn any quest of power for its own sake, any harsh domination of others, any self-satisfaction that is unconcerned about others. Between these two extremes lies humility, and it takes an ongoing effort to determine just what humility requires in the modern world. One thing that can be said is that we must search out the applications of humility, not in the light of a purely human prudence, but in respect for our own circumstances as willed by God and in respect for others as well.

The Church today is increasingly aware that authority is for service. This is one necessary form of humility. Authority in the Church is always intended for service and ministry. But while the service meant is limitless, it does not justify the intrusion of a vulgar democratism, which is not genuine humility at all. Humility requires precisely that each person keep his proper place. Concern for others will then help us to find these proper places and to readjust them, for they are always difficult to maintain and must be the object of a continual, honest examination of conscience.

You have approached Jesus, Mediator of a new covenant (Heb. 12:18-19, 22:24a)

A comparison is here being made between the manner in which the former people of God was established and the manner in which the new has now been established. At Mount Sinai, the Israelites were confronted with material realities and signs, terrifying ones in fact, since the children of Israel asked that they might not have to go on listening to this fearful voice and these fearful words.

The new covenant is established in an entirely different sort of encounter that brings with it none of those ancient manifestations. The baptized "have come to Mount Zion and to the city of the living God, the heavenly Jerusalem, and . . . to the assembly of the first-born who are enrolled in heaven." Without the ancient external, fearful manifestations of divinity, believers have approached the Lord, the community of the baptized, the Church — all those who have become one through one baptism in one and the same Spirit, and whose names are written in heaven. They are the "first-born," because they all share closely in the life of Jesus Christ, who is the first-born of all creation. Christians have drawn near to God himself, the Judge of all men, and have entered into an intimate sharing with him. He remains the Judge who knows the hearts of men, yet they have not feared to approach him. They have also been united to the spirits of the just, that is, to their dead who are now enjoying the future life and are just in God's sight.

In short, the entire Church, earthly and heavenly, was present, and to it the baptized and all Christians have come. But it is above all Jesus, Mediator of the new covenant, that they have approached. It is because he is their Mediator that they have dared cross the distance separating the human condition from the glory in which the Lord dwells. Now that they have been transformed through baptism into the Father, Son, and Spirit, they can live in intimate union with the Trinity. Such is the situation of the Christian as a member of the new people of God.

TWENTY-THIRD SUNDAY

Be Free, and Understand the Lord

Renounce your possessions and become a disciple (Luke 14:25-33)

At first reading or hearing, this passage may give an impression of disorder and incoherence. The specialists therefore attempt to distinguish between the words of Jesus himself and others that are spoken by the editor, St. Luke. Thus the two short parables are certainly in Jesus' manner, even though Luke is the only evangelist to report them.

On the other hand, verses 26-27, on the denial of one's affections and the duty of carrying the cross, are also to be read in St. Matthew (10:38; 16:24) and St. Mark (8:34);

Luke, moreover, has already recorded the words of Jesus on carrying one's cross (9:23). Even so, the words do seem to stem from Jesus himself, even if Luke is combining statements here. Luke seems to have drawn up the entire passage as an instruction for his Christians. It was extremely important that they not cherish illusions but grasp the real demands of Christian life.

The disciple is, first of all, a man who is detached from everything; such detachment is the first condition required for being a disciple. A detachment that is sought in order to be without ties and to be able to follow Jesus characterizes, or should characterize, every Christian. Since this detachment is so important, the necessity for it is expressed here in language that our psychological sensibilities find harsh and even somewhat aggressive.

We must not take the word "hate" in its narrowly literal sense. Jesus is speaking of a value judgment and a freedom from ties that have nothing in common with a refusal of fraternal love or with self-centeredness. He is demanding an unconditional love of himself that gives priority to everything that concerns him and makes everyone and everything else secondary. He is asking for a preferential love that entails the leaving behind of all else. Human affections continue to be legitimate, but they are subordinate to love of Jesus.

At the same time, however, Jesus is also asking for something that is unqualified, not for a "more or less" or a "for the most part." It is this radical and uncompromising demand that St. Luke is trying to bring out; that is why he lists the objects of our affection that must take second place if there is a conflict. He includes in the list even a man's own life, his very self. In our civilization, which is still somewhat Christian, the obligation of separating oneself even from one's family rarely arises, but it was a frequent occurrence for the Christians of Luke's day who met with opposition from their own kin when they embraced Christianity and put aside Jewish or pagan practices.

Jesus even demands that one be ready to surrender life

itself. "Carrying the cross" has come to mean for us, often exclusively, a voluntary acceptance and submission to the worries of life and to great trials when they come. In the time of Jesus, however, "carrying the cross" meant the surrender of self even to the point of accepting death. The disciples were used to seeing the torment of crucifixion imposed on criminals, who were forced to carry the instrument of their torture and death to the place of execution. For these disciples, then, the words of Jesus must have revealed a full depth of meaning after their Master's Passion.

"Following Jesus" and "carrying the cross" thus became two ways of expressing the same radical requirement of self-giving, even to the point of death. The disciple is not called to carry just any cross or to follow just any person; he is called to follow Jesus and to carry Jesus' Cross.

One may not, therefore, lightly decide to follow Jesus. In fact, Jesus himself here offers two little parables that are intended to stir the listener to adequate reflection before he decides to follow Jesus. The Christian of today, like the disciple of Jesus' time, must not be led astray by an idealistic or romantic vision of Christian life. Christianity is not a philosophy but a life to be lived. There can be no compromise; one must walk in Christ's steps unconditionally, not for a moment or a day, but for a lifetime.

Wisdom enables us to understand God's will (Wis. 93:13-18)

If in reading this passage we did not keep the Gospel pericope in mind, we might well feel fearful and discouraged. In fact, the passage reveals its deeper meaning precisely because of its liturgical context.

As we read, we may well be disconcerted at first. How, indeed, is knowledge of God's decrees to be gained, and who has power to understand them? We have trouble enough understanding what lies directly before us; how, then, are we to discover what is stored up in heaven? Only wisdom and the Spirit can reveal God's will to us. Without their intervention man must live in uncertainty and walk hopelessly in the darkness. It is of our need of wisdom that we sing in the responsorial psalm (Ps. 90): "Teach us to number our days that we may get a heart of wisdom."

In this reading, however, one sentence links the passage with the thought of the Gospel: "A perishable body weighs down the soul, and this earthly tent burdens the thoughtful mind." The words point to the need of unconditional self-denial and a radical quest for liberation. If we are to know and follow God's will, we must abandon the "earthly tent" of our body and our self-will.

The lesson of this Sunday is an important one, for it presents the charter of Christian life and shows the radical demands that Christianity makes. One may not live the Christian life unthinkingly; the life of a disciple is something that must be taken very seriously.

Onesimus is to be treated as a brother, not as a slave (Philemon 9b-10, 12-17)

Philemon is the specific addressee of this Letter, yet it is meant for others as well, in fact for the whole community. Its authors, or at least those who sent it, are Paul and Timothy. Onesimus, a slave, has run away and is therefore liable to harsh punishment. Paul becomes his advocate, and in his plea he is not afraid to appeal to sentiment: An old man, now a prisoner for Christ, asks a favor for a child to whom he, while in prison, has given the life of Christ. Paul had instructed and baptized this slave, and the two are now very close.

The modern reader may feel disappointed at the way Paul acted. Why did he not keep the slave with him instead of sending him back? But that would have been to put pressure on the owner, and Paul was unwilling to do this. He wanted the master to be free in dealing with his slave in a Christian manner. So too it was not for a very long time that the Church spoke out against slavery; in the interim she respected the social conditions of each age. It is hard for us to accept her silence, and yet our criticism of her for it would be unjust. The Church evidently attempted to better the lot of slaves, especially if they were baptized; she sought at least to improve relations between masters and slaves.

The decisive argument is kept for the last: If Philemon considers Paul his partner, that is, if he understands them to be united in the Christian community, then let him receive Onesimus as though he were receiving Paul himself.

TWENTY-FOURTH SUNDAY

The Lord's Forgiveness

Joy in heaven for a sinner's conversion (Luke 15:1-32)

The parable of the prodigal son is thoroughly familiar to us and has in fact already been proclaimed on the fourth Sunday of Lent (Cycle C).[40] Today's proclamation, however, has a different emphasis. In Lent the focus of attention was the conversion of the prodigal son and his desire to be reconciled; this emphasis was due to the fact that Lent has the paschal mystery and the renewal of baptismal conversion for its goal. In today's Gospel it is rather God's forgiveness on which we are urged to meditate.

The story gives us a glimpse of the constant concern of the father for the son who has left him. He catches sight of his son when the latter is still far off; the father had evidently been hoping for the day when the son would return, and thus hoping, had often looked into the distance and thought of his son. To this earthly father we may compare God, who does not forget the sinner but waits for him with unwearying patience.

When the father sees his son in the distance, he is seized with pity. How often God too reacts thus — with pity! He is a God of forgiveness. The Book of Exodus (a passage of which is today's first reading) speaks of the Lord as "a God merciful and gracious, slow to anger, and abounding in steadfast love and faithfulness," and to his God Moses will pray: "Go in the midst of us, although it is a stiff-necked people; and pardon our iniquity and our sin, and take us for thy inheritance" (Exod. 34:6-9).

The father does not suppress his compassion for his son; rather, it is he who takes the initiative and goes out to meet him: "his father . . . ran and embraced him and kissed him." Thus does God take the initiative at the very beginning of a conversion. We see Jesus acting in the same way whenever he finds repentance and the desire for conversion. Zacchaeus, for example, wants to see Jesus; Jesus, discovering this first movement to a new way of life, takes the initiative and invites himself into Zacchaeus's house (Luke 19:1-10); he asserts that he is following a principle: "The Son of Man came to seek and to save the lost."

The intentions of the returning son are not entirely selfless. His return home is not motivated solely by a sense of his own ingratitude and lack of love for his father. The parable shows that there is still a certain self-centeredness in the son's attitude: "How many of my father's hired servants have bread enough and to spare, but I perish here with hunger!" Here, as with Zacchaeus, we do not find in the very beginning an utterly pure intention or an authentic sorrow at having done evil. The sinner must first be drawn by the desire to escape the suffering his own actions have brought upon him. In God's eyes this beginning holds great promise, however; that is why the father runs out to meet his son.

The prodigal son expresses his regret, but the father seems so overwhelmed by joy that he hardly notices what the son says. "Bring quickly the best robe, and put it on him; and put a ring on his hand, and shoes on his feet; and bring the fatted calf and kill it, and let us eat and make merry." The father has forgotten the past. No resentment shows in his behavior; his only feeling is joy, because "this my son was dead, and is alive again; he was lost, and is found."

Not everyone understands God's forgiveness. It may be that Luke took advantage of this parable of Jesus to insist that the Christian community must accept those who have sinned but still live in the Church. Jesus himself encountered people who rejected the sinner and regarded him as rejected by God as well. The purpose of his parable is to make these people understand what God's attitude really is.

The reaction of the elder son was the reaction of some of Jesus' contemporaries and some of Luke's disciples, and it is the reaction of some Christians today. The elder son regards himself as a faithful servant, and he is indeed such. He also feels injured by his father's reception of his erring brother. He, after all, has always been faithful, yet he has never been given a banquet! But this fellow who left home and squandered his possessions is now received with honors and with a joy never shown toward the faithful servant. The elder brother is scandalized, and so are many Christians today. At least in their imagination and feelings, they find it hard to accept that a person who led a dissolute life should be welcomed by God after death no less than a person who has spent his whole life in God's service. These people have a mercenary concept of Christian life and of God's justice; it leaves little room for love.

It is this attitude that Jesus seeks to correct. He is strongly opposed to any religious attitude that is based on a kind of contractual agreement between God and men, according to which each party binds himself to give such and such. No, love must come first and be the basis for all else. The father does not value less the elder son who has always been faithful; on the contrary, he reminds him that "you are always with me, and all that is mine is yours." But the

father is not unjust toward the elder son when he chooses to
pardon and restore life to the younger son who had been
dead.

The Lord relents and does not punish his sinful people (Exod. 32:7-11, 13-14)

The people of God have gone astray and worshiped the
golden calf. How unforgivable such a sin seems when we
realize that it occurred only shortly after the promulgation
of the Decalogue!

Moses' prayer for forgiveness on behalf of the people is
the focal point of the passage. It is a bold plea based on
three solid arguments. The first is that God will be destroying his own people. This people is indeed his, for he
brought it out of Egypt by the power of his arm and hand. It
would therefore be contradictory for the Lord to destroy a
people he has saved by such spectacular means.

Secondly, since the Lord liberated his people in such a
spectacular way and since this people glorifies him far beyond other nations, it would be a dishonor for him to destroy it, the very people that is peculiarly his own. In other
words, God's own honor is at stake. If he destroys Israel,
what will be left of mankind's respect and fear of his
power? This is really blackmail, yet Moses does not hesitate to use such an argument in his prayer, for faith sets no
limits to boldness.

The third and strongest argument is the appeal to God's
own fidelity. The people may be unfaithful, but God cannot
be unfaithful. He promised the patriarchs that he would
give them a great posterity. He must be faithful to his promise.

The Lord in response decides not to punish as he had
intended. Thus, despite the enormity of a sin, it is always
possible to win God's forgiveness. Forgiveness is always
his most basic will.

Christ came to save sinners (1 Tim. 1:12-17)

St. Paul lets us know here his own personal experience: he had been a sinner, and yet God chose him as a minister; God chose to trust him. Paul's case interested the entire Church. The other apostles had been chosen by the earthly Jesus and had lived with him; now Paul, who persecuted the others, saw himself overwhelmed by grace and chosen to be Christ's servant no less than the other apostles. Paul's case might indeed be a stumbling block for some!

Paul reminds us that conversion in Christ Jesus is always possible through faith and love. More than that, he believes that his sins and his conversion are part of a providential plan: he, a sinner, was chosen "for this reason, that in me, as the foremost, Jesus Christ might display his perfect patience for an example to those who were to believe in him for eternal life."

Paul thus regards himself as the first of sinners but also as the foremost witness to the long-suffering patience of God. The main point he wants to make is that "Christ Jesus came into the world to save sinners." St. Luke shows us Christ expressing the same sentiment: "I have not come to call the righteous, but sinners to repentance" (Luke 5:32), and again: "The Son of Man came to seek and to save the lost" (Luke 19:10).

The readings of this Sunday are of great value, for they undercut all forms of rigorism. They do this, not by encouraging indulgence or an easygoing attitude toward human sin, but by exalting the forgiveness God shows to those who believe and to whom, despite their sins, he sometimes gives very special graces. We must not condemn others,[41] since God forgives and does not withhold his grace once he sees a man repenting. Thus, any pride that the "just" and observant individual might feel collapses in the face of the forgiveness God bestows so freely.

TWENTY-FIFTH SUNDAY

Mammon — Money

The service of God and money are incompatible (Luke 16:1-13)

The first part of this passage of the Gospel is so shocking to us that preachers allow themselves to pass over it and go immediately to the second part. It would be a shame, however, for the Sunday congregation never to experience this shock.

The case of the dishonest steward, whom Christ praises and offers as a model, is certainly repugnant to us at first glance. And yet every Christian is aware that Jesus cannot be praising dishonesty! We admit, therefore, that we must be missing the point of what is being said, but we would have preferred to hear from Jesus an outright condemnation of the steward. That would have been the right thing, we feel, and we would not be disturbed by the passage. Perhaps, too, we could then have felt our own superiority to this contemptible fellow!

The actual extent of the steward's fraudulent dealings does not matter. What interests us is that he is an able fellow and goes about his wrongdoing in an intelligent way: he makes his creditors his accomplices, so that they will have to take him in when the times become hard. Some interpreters think that Jesus was using a real case, not in order to condemn dishonesty (there would be no point to that, since Jesus would evidently be against dishonesty), but to turn it into a springboard for some new teaching of his own. One thing is sure: Despite efforts of interpreters to prove the contrary, Jesus is clearly defending the dishonest steward and even praising him. How are we to understand this?

Jesus seems to be anticipating and defending himself

against any accusation of complicity by his statement that "the sons of this world are wiser in their own generation than the sons of light." The sons of this world are clever and quick to make decisions when it comes to business, whereas the sons of light, whose goals is the kingdom, are often so slow and lacking in cleverness when it comes to the means of finding the kingdom. If men can show themselves so able in the pursuit of perishable blessings, why is it that we are so half-hearted in seeking the kingdom?

Thus, Jesus is not by any means praising the dishonest actions of the steward. He praises only the steward's shrewdness and regrets that such shrewdness should always be found in those who live for the present world and not in those who seek the kingdom but often seem so clumsy in their ways.

One means of entry into the kingdom is to be generous and make friends in the eternal dwellings so that they may intercede for us at our death. Jesus is here encouraging us to generosity and almsgiving. Use money in order to give generously and you will have intercessors in heaven when the time comes for you to die.

Jesus takes advantage of the parable to point out the true meaning of money. A man cannot serve two masters, namely God and mammon, or money. There are people who come close to this kind of idolatry every day. If we possess money, it is not given to us so that we should become attached to it as though it were something of unqualified value, but so that we might share it. To cling to money is to show that we have not really understood God and the absolute values he embodies. We are bidden, therefore, to use money but also to be detached from it; this we will do to the extent that we are shrewd in our seeking of the kingdom.

Greed of the merchants (Amos 8:4-7)

Amos here refers to trade that involves the falsification of weights and measures; it is another kind of fraudulent dealing. He is writing against the civilization of his day, and his protests are the same as we might make in our own day. The prophet, however, is protesting in the name of the Lord, who bids him speak. His contemporaries are observing the moons and the Sabbath, but they make use of the time to conspire and think up ways of getting greater profits. For a pair of sandals they can buy or sell a poor man who cannot pay his debts.

The connection between this text and the Gospel is rather tenuous, but both do preach the need of detachment from money.

We would misinterpret the Gospel passage if we took it to be approving dishonesty; as a matter of fact, Jesus praises only a shrewdness that he would like to see the sons of light display in their quest of the kingdom, and urges them to be detached from money for the sake of the same kingdom. Similarly, we would misinterpret the Old Testament reading if we saw in it an attack upon all trade and upon every economic system and the well-being it makes possible. What the prophet is in fact assailing is an attachment to money that makes a man closed to the needs of the poor and willing even to impoverish them further. Such an attitude is in full contradiction to the attitude of the Lord; it turns money into an idol and makes it impossible for a man to serve the Lord, who reacts by saying: "Surely I will never forget any of their deeds."

The responsorial psalm (Ps. 113) sings of the way in which God shows his concern for the poor: "He raises the poor from the dust, and lifts the needy from the ash heap, to make them sit with princes, with the princes of his people."

Pray that all men may be saved (1 Tim. 2:1-8)

We are urged here to pray for all men so that they may be saved. Such prayer is efficacious, but its efficacy derives from Christ Jesus, who gave himself as a ransom for all. The apostle's role is to bring this gift to men. The Christian community is meant to be a community of prayer, and Paul asks that in every place Christians should pray, "lifting holy hands without anger or quarrelling." This is to say that their intention must be upright; they do not pray to draw down wrath from heaven on their enemies or to further their personal ambition.

What we have here is the source of, or at least a witness to, the "general intercessions" now offered in the liturgy after the homily or Creed. These intercessions found a place in the liturgy at a very early date. In his *First Apology* (addressed to Emperor Antoninus Pius in 150 A.D.), St. Justin mentions that the intercessions come at the end of the celebration of the word (ch. 67). In today's passage from the First Letter to Timothy, we already find a simple list or litany of persons and intentions to be prayed for. It is the kind of litany we find again and again through the centuries and in our own liturgies today: "for all men, for kings and all who are in high positions, that we may lead a quiet and peaceable life, godly and respectful in every way." Even the pattern is unchanged through time: "Let us pray: for. . . , that. . . ."

Paul is here urging us to frequent prayer that is not limited to the time of liturgy. We are to be really preoccupied with the salvation of all men, for we share responsibility for them with Christ.

TWENTY-SIXTH SUNDAY

The False Security of the Rich

Final lot of the rich and the poor (Luke 16:19-31)

The parable of Lazarus and the rich man is familiar to all. Egyptian and Jewish literature of the past had contained rather similar stories, to which the commentaries on this passage call attention.

The personages of the parable represent two classic types who are contrasted in the Old Testament writings: the rich man and the poor man. The basic aim of the parable is to show a reversal of situations; in the next life the rich man is in torment and can see Lazarus at rest in the bosom of Abraham. Lazarus reclines at Abraham's side at a banquet, while the rich man is tormented by thirst. The general conditions of life in the next world are not a concern of the parable, however; the description simply brings out the new and radically changed circumstances of each of the two main personages.

What we have here is an old theme: the rich man condemned and the poor man exalted in a reversal of situations that is frequently depicted or asserted in the Old Testament. The New Testament took over this theme, as we have had occasion to note in speaking of the Beatitudes.[42]

The state of those in the next life is definitively and irrevocably determined, and a great abyss separates the blessed from the others, so much so that no communication between them is possible. The rich man who is now so unhappy can only pray that his friends on earth may be warned and give thought to changing their ways.

With this thought we come to the real point of the parable, as far as its useful lesson goes. The rich man's request misses the point: "They have Moses and the prophets; let them hear them . . . If they do not hear Moses and the prophets, neither will they be convinced if some one should rise from the dead."

Two important points are being made in this parable: the necessity of listening and hearing, and the necessity of conversion. Listening and hearing is doubtless easier for the humble and the poor, since they are not tangled up by wealth and its many consequences (pride, for example). The parable has directly in mind the leaders of the Pharisees and tells them that they must indeed listen to and heed Moses and the prophets.

But the parable also reflects the larger problem Jesus faced: The Jews did not listen or did not hear because they were hindered by their sense of security and their pride. What more can be done for them? If they did not listen to Moses and the prophets, why would they heed a dead man who came back to warn them? This is a first lesson of the parable, and it is a harsh and unsentimental one.

The other important point of the parable is the need of conversion, a need that the Gospels are constantly inculcating. Conversion is urgent, because judgment is close at hand. Many passages teach the necessity of conversion (Luke 3:3; 10:13; 11:32; 13:3, 5; 24:47), and the Acts of the Apostles shows that it was the most frequent theme of the sermons preached by the apostles (Acts 2:38; 3:19; 5:31; 11:18; 14:15; 17:30; 26:18). St. Luke evidently regarded the theme as of the utmost importance for Israel.

A corrupt civilization (Amos 6:1a, 4-7)

The prophet Amos is vigorous in his criticism of the life of his day. He is unsparing of the rich and, more generally, of the whole society of the time. It was a society bent on enjoying every luxury and indulging in every debauchery, and yet it felt not the slightest tremor of unease about itself. Amos's description could readily be applied to some societies of our own time! The life that people were living had little to do with reality; the people living it were utterly unconcerned about Israel's real situation. They were living at the expense of society generally and especially of the poor; the faith and law of Israel meant nothing. Where was the covenant in their lives?

The prophet certainly does not intend to condemn improved living conditions, but only abuses and the gulf between the lives of the rich and the poor, with the former profiting by the toil of the latter while leaving them in utter destitution. Amos addresses his criticism chiefly to those who live such a life of injustice while outwardly professing the religion of Israel.

We do not have a detailed knowledge of social conditions in Israel at this time, but the text itself makes clear the situation of those the prophet is criticizing. The prophet himself feels like an outcast, for the lives of the rich and powerful are utterly alien to the covenant. They are people who are officially the beneficiaries of the covenant, yet they are living like pagans. The situation is a scandal, and those who have caused it will be made an example of: they will be the first to go into exile; the society of revelers will cease to exist.

The reading does not relate men's excesses to their state in the next life, but it does predict chastisement in the present life. Will the prediction cause its addressees to stop and reflect? Will it be an effective sign to all?

Keep the Lord's commandments until he returns (1 Tim. 6:11-16)

Today's second reading can be linked with the other two; the fortuitous connection of themes enriches the teaching of this Sunday. As in the Gospel pericope and the reading from the prophet, we are told in this passage from the First Letter to Timothy that we must concentrate our attention and energies on faith and love; especially must we be vigilant in regard to faith and be willing to struggle in its behalf; we must keep the last day before our minds.

First of all, then, we must try to be just and devout, looking sincerely for God. In St. Paul's view, being just and devout has nothing to do with outward appearances but means that we live by faith and love, and that we are gentle and steadfast. The list of spiritual qualities here yields a picture opposite to that which Amos draws of the society of his day and that which Luke gives us of rich man during his life on earth.

Secondly, we must fight for the faith. This is indeed the chief activity of us all during the period before the last day. We have been called to eternal life, and we attain it by living the faith we have professed before many witnesses. We must also keep the commandments, for faith alone does not save but must lead to good works. We must show ourselves to be upright and irreproachable, until the time when the Lord Jesus Christ will manifest himself. The whole of our life is a preparation for the last day.

Finally, the last day is the all-important moment. On that day the Lord of lords, the King of kings, who dwells in inaccessible light and whom no one can see, will cause Christ to manifest himself.

A short doxology ends the reading and turns it into a liturgical hymn of praise that asserts the power and glory of him who gives all life its authentic meaning.

Today's readings are very pertinent to our situation. We too must keep before our minds the coming parousia; we must know how to assign all things their true value; we must be firm in the faith and live by the faith. Such is the Christian ideal. We cannot deny that too often we look for security and think we have found it in an illusory well-being that only hides approaching catastrophe. But we are made for life in the world to come. We must not think of that future life as requiring a discouraging loss of transient values! Rather, we must be persuaded that in that future state we will be forever fixed in good or evil, depending on how well and fervently we have sought God in faith during our earthly lives.

TWENTY-SEVENTH SUNDAY

The Dynamism of Faith

The power of faith (Luke 17:5-10)

Today's Gospel seems to contain two unconnected themes: an answer to a plea and a parable. If we look more closely, however, there is indeed a connection between the two.

The answer to a plea of the disciples has to do with faith and all that faith can accomplish when it is strong. The parable shows this same effectiveness as flowing from a gift of God. The apostles receive faith as a gift; the efficacity of this faith is not rooted in them and their merits, but, like faith itself, is a precious gift given to them by God.

The plea of the disciples is a touching one, but it is also limited in its scope: they know that they believe, and they ask Christ that they may believe more fully and strongly. If we are to understand what it is they are requesting, we must read the passage in its proper context. At this point Jesus is not teaching the crowd but is conversing with the disciples; this tells us immediately that the subject is serious and important.

In St. Mark's Gospel, Jesus' teaching on faith is introduced by the incident of the fig tree that he had cursed and that the disciples find dried up the next day. Christ then speaks to them of a faith that can move mountains (Mark 11:23).

In St. Matthew, Jesus' teaching on faith is given in reply to a question from the disciples, who have been unable to expel a demon (Matthew 17:19-20). Later on in the First Gospel, the same teaching on faith and its power is given again in the context of the dried-up fig tree (Matthew 21:21). In view of these contexts, we may ask whether the apostles' request for a greater faith was not prompted by a desire to perform miracles.

In St. Luke's Gospel, however, there is no hint of any such desire on the part of the apostles. To understand today's passage, therefore, we must broaden our perspective a bit and ask how Luke thinks of faith, both in the Acts of the Apostles and in his Gospel.

In the Acts of the Apostles, St. Luke connects faith with the acceptance of God's word. "Many . . . believed" or "were obedient to the faith" — this is the kind of expression we find Luke using when men hear and accept the word as preached by the apostles (Acts 4:4; 6:7; 13:12; 14:1; 17:12, 34; 21:20; etc.). In the Gospel there is not the same constant linking of faith with the hearing of the word, but it does come up in, for example, the parable of the sower (Luke 8:12-13). The Gospel also emphasizes believing in the person of Jesus, that is, abandoning everything for him and following him (Luke 9:59, 61).

All in all, then, we must not link the apostles' request for a deeper faith solely with a desire to perform miracles. They are also asking for a deeper faith so that they may better understand God's word and follow Jesus more perfectly.

The fact that the apostles do ask for a deeper faith is important for Luke's catechesis. Faith is a gift; it must be requested. It is God who "opened a door of faith to the Gentiles" (Acts 14:27). Elsewhere we see Jesus praying to the Father that Peter's faith may not fail (Luke 22:32).

In today's passage, Jesus does not answer by saying that he will give them what they ask; instead, he shows them what they could do if they did have a stronger faith.

Faith is always a gift, and so is its efficacity. The parable that Jesus uses at this point is a simple one: a slave has no right to recognition because of what he does, since he belongs to his master. Similarly, the apostles are servants, and if they accomplish great things, it is only because the Lord gives them the power to do so; he is not obliged to be grateful to them, because if they accomplish anything, it is by his power.

The just man lives because of his faith (Hab. 1:2-3; 2:2-4)

When we turn to the reading from the prophet, we find ourselves in a world of destruction, violence, strife, contention, and greed. It is a depressing world. The prophet complains that the Lord seems to be deaf to his cries; he asks how long he must endure this trial. According to the beliefs and customs of the time, to write a text on some lasting materials was in some measure to make what was written come true; the writing was a power-filled materialization of the word. God's answer is comforting to the prophet, but he still counsels patience. Finally the oracle and vision do come: "The righteous man shall live by his faith." The man who is patient and persevering will win out.

It must be admitted that the choice of this text to accompany today's Gospel was not a very good one. It is not at all clear that it adds anything to the Gospel or that it helps us understand the Gospel better. There is no point, therefore, to commenting on it during the liturgy. The prophet is counseling perseverance and a faith that can be translated as "life-giving fidelity." In the Gospel, on the other hand, we are dealing with the faith that finds expression in confidence, self-giving, and the following of the Lord. There is no reason for trying to link the two kinds of "faith."

The Gospel provides us with an opportunity to reflect on the faith that motivates and guides us and that we should be trying to rouse in others. St. Luke bids us realize that our faith is a gift and that everything we can accomplish is possible only because of God-given power in us. All that we see the Church doing in the carrying out of her mission is a gift of God; those who cooperate in that mission are servants and are simply doing their duty.

At the same time, however, we must not push such considerations to extremes. After all, Luke also speaks elsewhere of the reward the Lord will give those who have worked for him. Those who have suffered for him (Luke

6:23), those who are unselfish for his sake or abandon everything to follow him (Luke 14:14; 18:30) will all have their reward. As the responsorial psalm (Ps. 95) puts it, "He is our God, and we are the people of his pasture, and the sheep of his hand."

Bear the hardship that the gospel entails (2 Tim. 1:6-8, 13-14)

Today's reading is a very beautiful passage from a letter the Apostle Paul wrote to a disciple on whom he himself had laid ordaining hands. The gift of God that Timothy received on that occasion must constantly be revived, for it is meant to be an active gift that will serve the entire Church. Timothy must not be timid or ashamed about bearing witness to the Lord, but must accept the suffering involved in preaching the gospel.

It is a moving experience for us to read those lines and realize that the later ritual of ordination was, in its essence, already in use in Paul's day: imposition of hands, action of the Holy Spirit, the gift of God. It may even be that the kind of exhortation we find Paul delivering here to Timothy reflected a liturgical use. The person ordained received, we are told, a charism meant for the service and welfare of the Church. The charism is a spirit of courage, love, and prudence. Now that a man has received it, he must carry on his ministry and preach the gospel fearlessly. Timothy is certainly prepared for such a ministry. He has been entrusted with the truth he is to teach; he must defend that treasure and faithfully pass it on.

This passage cannot but be a stimulus to those who received the gift of the Spirit in ordination. It will also help all Christians understand better the ministry of their bishops and priests, and spur them on to aid their bishops and priests by their attitudes, service, and prayers.

Paul is here giving us a sacramental vision of the way in which the Church constantly receives its structure anew. In each generation the ministry requires self-surrender, renunciation, courage, suffering, and fidelity to the deposit of faith. That deposit must be studied, better understood, and made more explicit. It must never be betrayed, nor may personal ideas ever be substituted for it.

TWENTY-EIGHTH SUNDAY

Gratitude to God

They have not returned to thank God (Luke 17:11-19)

The cry of the lepers to Jesus is a moving expression of faith, as the two names or titles — "Jesus" and "Master" — that they apply to Jesus make clear. In the form known as the "Jesus Prayer" (Lord Jesus Christ, Son of God, have mercy on me, a sinner"), the cry of the lepers is now frequently used by Eastern monks and also by the faithful of those Churches. Its constant repetition forms a rosary of prayer. This kind of prayer is very biblical and is found frequently in the psalms (see, for example, Psalms 31 and 51).

Jesus does not immediately respond to the lepers' plea with a startling cure. Instead, he sends them to the priests, thus testing their faith still further. But as they go their way to the priest, they are cured. The evangelist does not describe the miracle directly, for that is not his purpose. His concern is with the importance of faith and of gratitude. But what he is emphasizing most is that a right faith and true gratitude can be found even in a non-Jew. The pericope ends with a sorrowful remark by Jesus: "Was no one found to return and give praise to God except this foreigner?" The others were cured, but it does not follow that they were therefore saved. It is only to this Samaritan that the Lord says: "Rise and go your way; your faith has made you well."

Naaman returns to glorify God (2 Kings 5:14-17)

In the Gospel the cure follows upon faith; in the episode concerning Naaman, the cure leads to faith. The story as read in today's liturgy begins with the moment of the miracle. We know, hwever, that Naaman was initially angered by Eliseus' order to go and bathe in the Jordan. Naaman had expected that the cure of a man like himself would be accomplished in a more ceremonious way. He does not really believe that he will be cured by bathing in the Jordan, but he yields to the pleas of his servants and obeys the prophet. Of course, he is cured. He returns to thank Eliseus and offers him a gift, which is refused. Then Naaman makes his profession of faith. His cure and his gratitude have brought him the great gift of faith.

Christians are saved by faith, which is a gift; it does not matter whether they are Jew or Gentile by descent. That is the point St. Luke wants to make, along with the value of the gratitude that Jesus received only from a foreigner. Today's liturgy shows the same faith and the same sense of gratitude at work in another foreigner, Naaman. Faith and salvation are always gifts; we cannot merit them, no matter who we are. Unfortunately, we often forget to be grateful and to show it.

We have died with Christ and shall live with him (2 Tim. 2:8-13)

Timothy has been urged to recall and revive in himself the grace given him through the imposition of hands. That grace had been a gift of courage in proclaiming the Good

News and preaching sound doctrine. Paul himself is in chains like a criminal, but the word of God cannot be chained, and Paul must carry on his mission to bring that word to others. He endures everything for that word and for the elect, those whom God has chosen as recipients of salvation and eternal glory through Jesus Christ.

This part of Paul's exhortation ends with a paschal hymn that may have been used in the liturgy of Christian initiation: "The saying is sure: If we have died with him, we shall also live with him; if we endure, we shall also reign with him; if we deny him, he will also deny us; if we are faithless, he remains faithful — for he cannot deny himself."

Exegetes have often called attention to the fact that Paul likes to make up verbs that include the preposition "with" (in Greek, the "with," or *syn*, is prefixed to the verb), as a way of bringing home our close union with Christ. This union implies that we must suffer with Christ but also that we will be glorified with him. Thus Paul speaks of us as suffering with Christ (Rom. 8:17; 1 Cor. 12:26); being crucified with him (Rom. 6:8; Gal. 2:20); being buried with him (Rom. 6:4; Col. 2:12); rising with him (Eph. 2:6; Col. 2:12; 3:1); coming alive with him (Eph. 2:5; Col. 2:13); being made like him (Phil. 3:10); being glorified with him (Rom. 817); and being seated with him in heaven (Eph. 2:6).

In the paschal hymn in today's pericope, we find the same effort to emphasize our close union with Christ: we die with him (see also 2 Cor. 7:13); we live with him (Rom. 6:8); we reign with him (1 Cor. 4:8). This union is why Paul sees Christian suffering as such a splendid thing.

TWENTY-NINTH SUNDAY

The Prayer of Faith

Pray unwearyingly and with faith (Luke 18:1-8)

Today's parable hardly needs explanation, but though simple, it contains important lessons. If a judge, however lazy and neglectful of his duty, finally does justice to a poor woman simply so that she will leave him in peace, how much more surely will the heavenly Father hear the patient and persevering prayer of his chosen ones? If we read this parable with the attitudes of Jesus in mind, we may think that Jesus' attention is focused on the judge in the story. St. Luke, however, who is concerned for the needs of his flock, seems more interested in the widow and her perseverance in prayer, since she is a model for Christians.

The final verse of the passage turns our attention to the second coming. Will Jesus still find faith when he comes again? The point is that faith is connected with perseverance in prayer. Perhaps St. Luke is alluding to the difficulties and persecutions amid which the first Christians were living. Prayer was necessary if they were to remain faithful and await the coming of the Lord as men confident that their petitions were being heard.

The power of Moses' intercession (Exod. 17:8-13)

The Amalekites and the Israelites were locked in battle. As long as Moses kept his hands raised, his prayer for the Israelites was heard. His hands grew weary and fell, but his perseverance was such that he had others support his arms, and he remained in this intercessory posture until sunset, and the Israelites were finally triumphant.

Moses' example of perseverance is important and encouraging. Care must be taken, however, not to interpret it in too mechanical a manner, that is, as though the physical raising of Moses' arms were the decisive thing.

To the Old Testament passage we might join the words of Jesus at the end of the Gospel pericope, where he says that faith can move mountains.

Continuous prayer inspired by faith and accompanied by submission to God's will has always been the ideal of the Church. Christians have always attempted, though in different ways, to "pray without ceasing." The liturgy today urges us to reflect on the fervor with which we pray and the methods we use.

Be inspired by the wisdom of Scripture and proclaim the word (2 Tim. 3:14–4:2)

St. Paul continues to give wise and valuable advice to the disciple he had ordained. Timothy must respect the oral tradition he has received from his teachers, for Scripture alone is not the guide of the Christian, but Scripture as read in the Church and by the Church. He must also, however, continue to make himself familiar with the inspired writings themselves, for the teaching of an apostle must be based first and foremost on Scripture.

With this as his background, Timothy must devote himself to preaching the word. The task is an urgent one. Paul is insistent, and we can see how utterly serious he is. He charges Timothy, by the Christ who is to come again, to preach the word and to do so in season and out of season. He must rebuke evildoers and encourage all, but always with patience and always trying to instruct men.

THIRTIETH SUNDAY

The Prayer of the Humble

The tax collector is justified by his humble prayer (Luke 18:9-14)

It is considered good form to condemn the Pharisee and to be gracious to the tax collector for his attitude. But this facile approach may well be pharisaical itself. It is easy to acknowledge oneself a sinner without really believing what one says; there is a humility that is in fact a form of pride and that remains an idea in the mind without ever becoming a conviction of the heart.

It is our impression that Luke has deliberately reported this parable in order to provoke reactions from his Christians, especially from those among them who were tempted to live secure in their own sense of uprightness. Those to whom St. Luke is addressing this parable of Jesus might best be compared to those practicing parishioners who are quite sure of themselves and convinced of their fine observance. It is to such people as these that Jesus' words are addressed elsewhere in the Third Gospel: "You are those who justify themselves before men, but God knows your hearts; for what is exalted among men is an abomination in the sight of God" (16:15). At the same time, we must not be too hard on all of the Pharisees, for among them there must have truly just men who really obeyed the law. The real problem with the Pharisees generally was their self-sufficiency and pride.

There is no point in giving a description here of the divergent attitudes of the two extremes, the Pharisee and the tax collector. The conclusion alone is of interest to us: the tax collector went home "justified." The word is important. The just man is one whom God makes just; he receives God's favor, not because he is already just, but because in his humility he believes that God can be merciful to him and forgive him his sins. The deeds of men, even if these deeds be not all evil, could never be such as to merit forgiveness; only the sacrifice of the incarnate Son has that power. Because of that sacrifice, the Spirit bestows forgiveness on those who believe, and they return home justified.

The prayer of the humble man pierces the clouds (Sir. 35:12c-14, 16-18b)

The most important part of this passage is the verse that describe the conditions of prayer. "He whose service is pleasing to the Lord will be accepted, and his prayer will reach to the clouds." God thus makes no distinctions among them; that is, he does not hear only the rich or those who have an official ministry of prayer and belong to a priestly caste. Men may offer him the finest gifts, but what brings from him a benevolent answer to prayer is the absence of formalism and an attitude of generous service. The person praying may be a widow or an orphan, the kind of people so often subjected to injustice. No matter — the Lord hears them, as he hears anyone whose prayer shows a readiness to serve him wholeheartedly.

All this amounts to saying that prayer must be prayer in Spirit and truth. If we take the time to read the whole of this chapter 35 in the Book of Sirach, this impression is strengthened. The writers speaking of the kind of sacrifice that God finds pleasing. There must be operative in a man's life profound attitudes toward God that express his interior sacrifice and without which the sacrifice is unauthentic and ineffective. The writer becomes more concrete and explains, through the use of images, that the substance of our sacrifices must be our very selves, our inner dispositions, the uprightness of our life.

We may note once again that the liturgy does not hesitate to modify the strictly exegetical sense of a text by introducing and emphasizing a spiritual sense. On this Sunday the spiritual emphasis is on the idea that God alone is the true

Judge and that he alone justifies men, that is, makes them just, if they present themselves before him with a selfless faith.

Anyone with even an elementary understanding of the Scriptures will know that the situations of the widow and orphan in Sirach are real, concrete situations, whereas the humility of the tax collector is a spiritual and moral attitude. In themselves, therefore, the two texts deal with two different types of situations. Nonetheless, the liturgy, while aware that the two situations cannot be really paralleled, uses the passage from Sirach to reinforce the central idea of the Gospel pericope and the lessons we are intended to draw from it.

"Pharisaism" is not dead, and doubtless never will be until the second coming of Christ. Moreover, we must be humble enough to recognize that none of us is wholly free of its taint. It is difficult, even in prayer, not to feel secure; the reception of the sacraments may even serve to confirm us unconsciously in a way of life that is not in conformity with God's will. People are not always fully conscious that they pay lip-service to an ideal but live rather differently.

One lesson we must take with us is that our prayer is ineffective at times because it is not integrated into our lives or because we lack (for example) a real sympathy for others, or because other factors are at work that it would behoove us to search out. We are weak human beings, and God knows it, but while recognizing the fact, we must also try to change our ways.

Receive the reward of a winner (2 Tim. 4:6-8, 16-18)

St. Paul has come to the end of his earthly life. He is a prisoner, condemned to death, and he may be called to execution at any moment. He therefore looks back over his life and sums it up for us, for he is ready to leave it. He has fought the good fight; he has been faithful. Now he looks forward to his reward from him whose coming he has always longed for.

During the trials and interrogations he underwent, Paul was always supported by the Lord, even though all others had abandoned him. How can this same Lord fail to strengthen him when he departs for the kingdom? He has a pledge of this: his own fidelity and the Lord's. If the Lord was with him in all he has suffered, the Lord will certainly be with him as he enters the kingdom.

Paul's confidence is encouraging to all who want to be faithful and to live their faith as members of the Church. Their fidelity is a pledge that Christ will be at their side to help them into his kingdom.

THIRTY-FIRST SUNDAY

The Compassion of a Loving God

The Son of Man has come to seek out and save what was lost (Luke 19:1-10)

Today's story from the Gospel is one of the most moving in the entire New Testament. It has many facets and conveys many lessons, but its proclamation in the context of the first reading turns our attention in a specific direction. The central point today is not the coming of Jesus into the house of Zacchaeus, as it is when this passage is read at the dedication of a church. Our attention should be focused rather on the salvation Jesus brings, and especially on the divine search for the sinner and God's unwearied patience as he waits to transform the sinner as soon as the latter shows a willingness to be converted.

Zacchaeus is a short man and finds it difficult to see Jesus as he passes by. Zacchaeus' conscious motive is probably simple curiosity, yet hidden within that is a secret desire to meet Jesus and enter upon a new kind of life. He feels, and is, cut off from his fellow citizens, since he works for the Romans and has grown rich in the process. He seems to feel a certain disgust with himself, and this surely plays a part in his desire to see this Jesus of whom he has heard so much.

Zacchaeus' motives, such as they are, are enough for Jesus, and the latter now takes control of the situation. God has patiently waited for Zacchaeus; Zacchaeus has taken a first step; the Lord now reaches out to him — to the scandal of the bystanders: "He has gone in to be the guest of a man who is a sinner"!

Zacchaeus' conversion is somewhat spectacular. He gives half of his goods to the poor, and if he has defrauded anyone, he makes fourfold restitution. Jesus makes the situation clear: despite what Zacchaeus has done in the past, he too is a son of Abraham. Jesus has brought him to salvation because "the Son of Man came to seek and to save the lost" (an idea that is a favorite of St. Luke's; see 15:6, 9, 24, 32).

There is no point to dwelling here on other facets of this story, since the liturgical context points us in a very particular and limited direction.

The lengthy patience of God, who urges men to conversion (Wis. 11:22–12:2)

The Lord can do all things. Therefore he takes pity on men and overlooks their sins so that they may repent and be converted.

God has created everything that exists. How, then, could he possibly hate the sinner? Nothing could perdure in being, after all, if God did not will it to exist; he is Creator and Master of life, and loves all living things.

The passage contains a fine theology of God's "anxiety" for the creature, his creature, who has rejected him. This anxiety is the source of all God's efforts through history to create anew what sin has destroyed.

Above all, the text emphasizes the lengthy and unweary-

ing patience of God, who does not abandon the fallen sinner but little by little corrects him and brings him back.
The Lord does not act in a brutal manner; he respects his
creature, even when it is faithless. This divine respect for
the creature is something that modern man finds very attractive. God respects even the man who has been unfaithful to him; he does not punish brutally. In fact, God's first
reaction is not to punish at all but to convert. He warns men
and reminds them of their sinful state. He wants them to
turn away from evil and believe in him. Does not a conversion originate in a great faith in a God who has created all
things and who can and will do everything to bring them
back to him?

In today's readings the Church is telling her children of
God's marvelous pedagogy and the ideal she herself seeks
to follow. We may think that in the passage from his Gospel, St. Luke, mindful of the fact that his Christians are not
yet free from all sin, wishes to teach them that sin should
be seen in the perspective of God's mercy rather than exclusively of his justice. The New Testament sees sin as an
offense against Christ, but its primary reaction, when the
thought of sin occurs, is to think immediately of Jesus'
mercy and forgiveness.

The responsorial psalm (Ps. 145) reminds us that "the
Lord is gracious and merciful, slow to anger and abounding
in steadfast love. . . . The Lord upholds all who are falling, and raises up all who are bowed down."

In these passages, the Scriptures are not encouraging
either the Church or us individually to be indulgent toward
sin. They are simply telling us the attitude we should have:
Our first reaction to the sinner and to sin should not be
either despair or a determination to punish, but a desire for
conversion. We are to wait patiently for the sinner, take the
occasion to reproach him gently, speak to him of God's
mercy, teach him faith in the power of God, who through
his Holy Spirit can lead all back to the right path.

The formula of absolution in the new rite of penance emphasizes this mercy of God: "God, the Father of mercies,

through the death and resurrection of his Son has reconciled the world to himself. . . ."

_____

The Lord Jesus, glorified in us (2 Thess. 1:11–2:2)

The hopes and wishes that fill the Apostle's heart will be fulfilled at the coming of Christ. Will the Thessalonians be judged worthy of the call God gave them? Paul prays that they will. They have been called to faith, and this faith must be an active faith; that is, they must do all the good in their power. But none of that can be accomplished without the help of God. It will indeed be accomplished, and Christ will be glorified in them.

This is a theme to which, despite the Second Vatican Council, we are not yet accustomed: that the Church, as a living community, is a sign of the glory of God, a sign of Christ present in the world. It is the responsibility of the Church and of each of her members to see that she is indeed such a sign.

If their fidelity hastens the coming of Christ, the Thessalonians should not on that account grow fearful or listen to false prophecies. St. Paul denies writing any letter to the effect that the Day of the Lord has come. Some people in their religion will always be looking for the extraordinary or the frightening or for new revelations. St. Paul is against this approach to Christianity. The mark of the Christian is not extraordinary deeds of any kind but a life that bears witness to Christ's presence in the world.

THIRTY-SECOND SUNDAY

The God of Life

All receive life from God in the world to come (Luke 20:27-38)

All peoples in every age have been keenly aware of the problem of life's meaning and of what happens after death. Our contemporaries may not make their own the naïve (and insidious) questions of the Sadducees, but they are nonetheless often quite preoccupied with the next life. Now, as in Jesus' time, these are questions men have at heart. In the apostolic period, after Jesus' departure, the evangelists must have met with similar kinds of questions; St. Paul's Letters reflect them at times, and the Acts of the Apostles reminds us that the Sadducees did not accept the idea of a resurrection from the dead, although this had become regular teaching in Judaism (Acts 23:8; Dan. 7:13, 27; 12:2).

In today's Gospel pericope the Sadducees think they have gotten Jesus into a corner and will be able to make fun of him. They ask what they regard as a tricky question to which he can give no satisfactory answer: If a woman successively married seven brothers, whose wife will she be after the resurrection?

Jesus does not attempt to describe the kind of life lived by those who will rise from the dead. All that can be said is that while remaining themselves, they will also be different, and that sexual life as we know it on earth will have no place in the next life, because our bodies will be transformed.

What Jesus chooses to emphasize is the fact of the resurrection. His answer may strike us as weak, but this is very likely because we do not have the same kind of biblical sensibility that the contemporaries of Jesus or of the evangelists had. In any case, it seems Jesus might have chosen more persuasive proofs from Scripture.

All three evangelists report this incident, probably because all three had been asked questions about the next life and felt obliged to pass on to their communities the replies of Jesus and his teaching on the subject. St. Matthew and St. Mark emphasize that the answer is to be found in the Scriptures: "You are wrong, because you know neither the scriptures nor the power of God" (Matthew 22–29; Mark 12:24). If God is not a God who gives life, and if Abraham, Isaac, and Jacob are forever dead, then what can it mean to say we have entered into a covenant with the God of the living?

All three evangelists quote Jesus as saying: "He is not God of the dead, but of the living." Luke, however, adds a further explanation: "for all live to him." Others translate "to him" as "through him" or "because of him" or "thanks to him." This second set of alternative translations makes better sense of what immediately precedes: God is a God of the living and therefore gives life. Yet this interpretation is far from being evident, and not all scholars accept it.

The overall argument is nonetheless cogent: If the patriarchs lived for God but are now forever dead, then their life was a great mistake and the covenant is meaningless.

Raised up for eternal life (2 Mac. 7:1-2, 9-14)

Jesus might well have used this text from the Book of Maccabees as a proof of the resurrection and a justification of Jewish belief in it. As the fourth of the seven brothers was about to die, he gave clear expression to his belief: "One cannot but choose to die at the hands of men and to cherish the hope that God gives of being raised again by him. But for you there will be no resurrection to life." Several of the other brothers likewise express their belief: "The King of the universe will raise us up to an everlasting renewal of life"; "I got these [limbs] from Heaven, and because of his laws I disdain them, and from him I hope to get them back again."

The responsorial psalm (Ps. 17) expresses the same confidence: "As for me, I shall behold thy face in right-

eousness; when I awake, I shall be satisfied with beholding
thy form."

The Church knows that the risen Christ is only the first of
those to be raised from the dead. She knows, too, that the
Holy Spirit transforms men and women into new creatures
and adopted sons and daughters, and therefore she is sure
of the resurrection. Christ died to give us life — not a passing life but a life that lasts forever. The Letters of St. Paul
makes it clear that the Church held to these beliefs from the
very beginning. God's love for men and the love of the redeemed for him in return make the resurrection sure, even
though we cannot now penetrate the mystery and know
anything of the life to be lived by those who rise to eternal
happiness.

The Lord is faithful; he strengthens us and protects us from evil (2 Thess. 2:16–3:5)

St. Paul is again offering the Thessalonians a message of
hope. A Christian's life may be one of struggles and difficulties, but God loves him and gives him consolation and joyous hope as well as strength to do good and proclaim the
gospel.

The Christian must pray that the gospel may be spread
and God's word heard everywhere. The spread of the Gospel will bring persecution from non-believers, but God is
faithful; he protects his messengers from evil and gives
them courage and strength. We must therefore persevere on
our journey.

This passage is short but bracing, and can be of great help
in our everyday routine and when we are tempted to get
bogged down and grow discouraged. The certainty of God's
love for us and of the help he gives us will raise us up and
keep us from dwelling too long on the big and little afflic-
tions of life.

THIRTY-THIRD SUNDAY

The Day of the Lord

Persevere through suffering so as to obtain life on the Day of the Lord (Luke 21:5-19)

The thirteenth chapter of St. Mark's Gospel reports the same discourse but gives it a somewhat different context. Jesus is emerging from the Temple, and one of his disciples calls his attention to the splendid building Herod had constructed. Jesus then predicts that of this building which was to defy time, not a stone will be left upon a stone. A group of four disciples then accompanies Jesus to Mount Olivet, where he speaks to them alone.

In St. Luke's account, Jesus is in the Temple, and the whole crowd is listening to him.

In the other two evangelists, the destruction of the Temple has relationships with the end of the world. The question of the date and the preliminary signs has to do only with the destruction of the Temple. However, in both Luke and Mark, the discourse of Jesus is not limited to the destruction of the Temple but also covers the catastrophe at the end of the world and the glorious coming of the Son of Man. St. Luke seems to be clearly dissociating the destruction of the Temple, in 70 A.D., from the events at the end of time and from the glorious coming of the Son of Man; the destruction of the Temple is not one of the signs that the end is at hand.

In this discourse Jesus first tells of the events to come; then he gives instructions on how Christians are to react. He tells them they must be wary on two counts. They must not let themselves be led astray: "Many will come in my name, saying, 'I am he!' and, 'The time is at hand!' Do not go after them." Secondly, they must remember that wars and tumults are not the sign of the end and have no connec-

tion with the final events. St. Mark regards such wars and
tumults as the beginning of the sufferings that will come
(13:8).

Jesus then describes the various catastrophes: struggles
of nation against nation, earthquakes, great and terrifying
signs in the heavens. The precise description of these
events is irrelevant. The important thing is that when they
occur, the Christian will know that his salvation is at hand.

Prior to these events, Christians will be subjected to persecution. St. Luke is here bent on instructing his community, which must live in the time between their liberation
through baptism and the return of Christ. During this
period the gospel must be preached, but it is precisely this
that will lead to persecution. The disciples must not be
afraid. Jesus himself will give them a wisdom and words
that their enemies cannot withstand. Yet the situation will
be an extremely difficult one, for even the members of a
disciple's own family will betray him, and Christians will
be universally hated because of Jesus' name. Even the hairs
of their head are numbered, however, and no evil can touch
them. He who perseveres will be saved.

Jesus here exhorts his disciples, and all who hear him, to
perseverance. In St. Luke's view, persecutions are not a
sign that the end is near. They are part of the normal Christian condition, for the Christian is constantly bearing witness amid a perverse world. Each Christian must therefore
cultivate patience and perseverance. A firm faith, the acceptance of God's word, fidelity to God's word despite persecution — these make up the Christian attitude.

The Day of the Lord, a blazing oven for the wicked, a sun of justice for the good (Mal. 4:1-2a)

This text refers to a time of great discouragement for Israel. The exiles have been back home for fifty years, and
the Temple has been rebuilt, yet there is great disillusionment. The returning exiles had not been very well received: their possessions had been taken by others; they

were isolated and poor; there was little concern for them. The city was insufficiently fortified and often subject to raids. All this had serious repercussions on the religious life of the people. They were disillusioned, and their faith was weak; fidelity to the covenant was endangered. The disillusionment is summed up in words that Malachi quotes a little before today's pericope: "It is vain to serve God" (3:14).

Malachi now endeavors to revive the people's spirit by telling them that the Day of the Lord is coming. First, the wrath of God will be unleashed against the wicked and the arrogant. They will burn up like straw, and there will be neither root nor branch left of them. Straw, brush, trees — these are comparisons other prophets had already used (for example Nahum 1:10; Amos 2:9; Is. 5:24).

Fire symbolizes the chastising wrath of God. Thus in the Book of Deuteronomy, the Lord says that the fire of his anger has been lit (32:22), and in the Book of Job we read that on the wicked "God looses all his burning wrath" (20:23 JB). In Jeremias, fire as a symbol of divine vengeance occurs a number of times: ". . . lest my wrath go forth like fire" (4:4; 21:12); "in my anger a fire is kindled which shall burn for ever" (15:14; 17:4). Ezekiel makes use of the same image: "I will blow upon you with the fire of my wrath" (21:31); "I have consumed them with the fire of my wrath" (22:31).

The image of the tree is also used by other authors. In the Book of Job, "wickedness is broken like a tree" (24:20). In the Book of Jeremias, God's wrath is poured out on the trees (7:20). In the Gospel of St. Matthew, John the Baptist says that "the axe is laid to the root of the trees" (3:10).

The second phase of the Lord's coming will be the appearance of "the sun of righteousness," the rays of which bring healing. The Israelites, especially during their exile, were familiar with cults of the sun, but that is not a comparison Malachi is using here. In this passage the sun symbolizes the powerful intervention of the Lord in defense of the poor and the oppressed.

Are today's readings meaningless for today's Christian?

Will he regard them as poetry from another time? Yet it is the Lord himself who speaks in these passages. Has he nothing to say? Does he not wish to be heard? Does he intend the passages to be simply museum pieces? That is impossible. We must therefore attempt briefly to see how the teaching in these passages certainly applies to us today.

Some Christians are habitually disillusioned and therefore close to abandoning all zeal and discipline. In what way are they disillusioned? Often they expect of their faith and religious practice what it is not meant to give: earthly happiness. Christianity makes no promise of earthly happiness.

Faith and fidelity do not guarantee happiness in this world. On the contrary, faith and fidelity often lead to persecution and misunderstanding, even between members of the same family. Some forms of disillusionment are thus due to an incorrect understanding of Christianity. For these people, the vision of the Day of the Lord can be salutary, reminding them that the Christian religion exists only for the sake of that last day and makes no sense except in its light.

Disillusionment may have other causes. For some, it is the lack of spiritual depth in many areas of the Church. They see laxity, infidelity, weak faith, moral weakness, and, everywhere uncertainty. Even in religious Orders hitherto fervently dedicated to the expectation of the Lord's coming, they find a betrayal of purpose. In all this, however, disillusionment is nonetheless an insidious temptation. Its causes may be objectively there, but the clear vision of our destiny in God makes illegitimate any kind of morose disillusionment; on the contrary, it should, as in Malachi, rouse our courage and make us vigilant.

More serious still is the danger in which many live who make no efforts to come to grips with the problems of their own life or the life of the parish to which they belong. Without realizing it, these people live lives of carefree conformity; the world will never persecute them, because their religious lives attract no attention of any kind and have no impact on their environment. To these Catholics, who do not feel in any way at odds with their world, today's readings should be a summons to profitable reflection.

Nothing worthwhile is acquired without suffering. If a parish community and its members experience no suffering in their effort to lead a religious life, they may well be simply tepid. They have lost the sense of their mission in the world; they have become closed in on themselves or are content to work solely for the advancement of human values, but have no interest in spiritual values. These communities and individuals are living off their capital and gradually using it up; when the time comes for mobilizing every resource in order to proclaim the primacy of God's kingdom, such people may have nothing left.

These readings, then, urge upon us a valuable confrontation with our final destiny. They urge upon the Church and upon all her members a confrontation with the ultimate meaning of life itself.

Earn your own bread (2 Thess. 3:7-12)

This passage suggests that some of the Thessalonians had developed a distorted attitude. A somewhat perverse "contemplation" of the Day of the Lord had led them to abandon all work and to spend their time talking about the parousia, imagining its conditions, and calculating the time of its occurrence.

St. Paul is critical of this state of affairs. He reminds his readers that he has worked for his livelihood, even at a time when his ministry gave him a right to support from others. He takes the occasion to emphasize that a Christian is one who works. Anyone who can work and will not is not to be fed by others. This is not simply a piece of advice — it is an order.

It is always possible, even today, to get an unbalanced

view of what a life lived for God means. There have been
periods when the practice of the "contemplative life" was
thought to be a claim to support from others when it came
to material needs. Such an attitude is impossible in our day
(other deformations remain possible!), and we should
doubtless regard it as a divine favor that in our day everyone must work for his living while he tries to achieve a
correct balance between prayer and work in his life.

THIRTY-FOURTH SUNDAY

A Crucified King

Jesus crucified, remember me when you come as King (Luke 23:35-43)

"Gospel" means "good news," the news of salvation. Today's Gospel makes this point for us when it says: "Jesus,
remember me when you come in your kingly power," and
when Jesus replies: "Truly, I say to you, this day you will
be with me in Paradise." Here is the proclamation of salvation through the Cross, and a promise made by a crucified
King.

This King is conqueror of death; of this, Jesus' answer
leaves no doubt. His words are not a vague promise, but the
statement of one who is truly in command. The Good Thief
drew from Christ an answer that will give hope to all generations until the end of time: the hope that death is the
door to Paradise and that "to be with Christ" is indeed the
goal to which all Christian life is leading and the reality
that lies beyond death.

David, anointed as shepherd and king of Israel (2 Sam. 5:1-3)

There were numerous symbols and prefigurations of this crucified King. David, for example, is such a prefiguration and type, for he receives royal anointing as shepherd-king.

We must dwell for a moment on the special character of a king in Israel. He was not a king such as the pagans had. The people of Israel were God's people and belonged to him alone, so that the king's role could only be to direct and lead the people for the time they were entrusted to him. The king was thus meant to be a manifestation on earth of God's presence and power. If the king wins a victory, it is God who really wins it (2 Sam. 5:17-25; 8:1-14; 19:10).

At the same time, his function is a sacred one, for he is the anointed of the Lord. God manifests his presence to his people through the person of the king; through him, too, God manifests his sovereignty, power, and glory (Pss. 72:8; 110:1). He is thus a sign of God, but since he remains also a weak human being, he often experiences opposition, although this never goes to the extreme of denying any and every royal power. The person of the individual king is open to criticism, but the kingship itself is an indispensable condition of Israel's life and a guarantee that God is always present to his people.

In these circumstances, it is quite to be expected that Israelite literature, and especially the psalms, should paint an idealized picture of the king. He becomes a symbol of hope, and at times the hope is precisely for a truly just king who will lead Israel. It is along these lines that we are to understand Jeremias when he sees rising out of the family of David a virtuous branch who will reign as true king and save his people (Jer. 23:5-6). Ezekiel, too, has a vision of a future king who will be a true shepherd and gather together the scattered nations (Ezek. 34:23; 37:22).

The hour of salvation is gradually drawing near, and when Jesus comes on the scene, a few people will realize that the hour is now at hand. The prophets, especially

Isaiah, will depict the coming king as a servant who humbles himself and gives his life in order to establish his kingdom (Is. 53).

In the kingdom of the beloved Son (Col. 1:12-20)

In this passage St. Paul describes the unfolding of Christian life in relation to the history of salvation. In God's plan, first came the Son, the image of the invisible God and the first-born of all creation. By the shedding of his blood he re-established the primacy that had been his at the beginning of creation. Now all things find their total fulfillment in him.

The Christian takes his place in this plan of reconstruction, and his life unfolds in accordance with that same plan. We shall enter into the kingdom the Son has founded by restoring creation to its rightful state and by reconciling all things in himself and through himself, making peace through the blood of his Cross.

This part of Paul's Letter to the Colossians is a hymn to the glory of God. By our baptism we have been incorporated into Christ the King, who is Head of his Church; we have thereby become a holy nation and a royal people.

Today's first reading directed our attention to the awaited messianic king; the Gospel shows us how the crucified Jesus by his Cross brings the history of salvation to its goal. The second reading is a hymn of praise to all that Christ, King of the universe, has done to establish the kingdom of which we are now a part. We are all thus being urged to live a life under a King, as part of a kingly people, but under a King whose kingdom is not of this world.[43]

June 29

SS. PETER AND PAUL

The two pillars of the Church, each of whom has his own basilica at Rome, have always been celebrated together by the Church of Rome. The Philocalian Calendar and the Hieronymian Martyrology (June 29) show that a feast was being celebrated at Rome as early as the middle of the fourth century. These two documents announce the feast and tell us that it was celebrated successively at St. Peter's on the Via Aurelia (a liturgy in honor of St. Peter), at the catacombs on the Via Appia (a liturgy in honor of both Apostles), and at St. Paul's on the Via Ostiensis (a liturgy in honor of St. Paul). A fifth-century hymn confirms the fact of this triple liturgical celebration on the one day.

We cannot go into the archeological and historical studies that have been done on the history of the feast and on the place where the two Apostles were martyred and buried. The reader will have ready access to material on these questions.

Readings

Matthew 16:13-19	You are Peter, and on this rock I will build my Church (see p. 123)
Acts 12:1-11	The Lord has rescued me from the hand of Herod
2 Tim. 4:6-8, 17-18	Receive the reward of a winner (see p. 385)

August 15

THE ASSUMPTION OF THE BLESSED VIRGIN MARY

The Greeks gave the name *Koimesis* (Falling Asleep) to this feast that celebrated not only the Blessed Virgin's Assumption but also her death. Some of the Latin names for it were: *Dormitio* (Falling Asleep), *Depositio* (Burial), *Natale* (Birthday), *Transitus* (Passage). As a matter of fact, however, we know nothing of how the Virgin's earthly life ended.

In the middle of the fifth century, the feast appears in the liturgical books. The liturgy of Rome had a feast of the Virgin on January 1, which has been restored in the new calendar; there was no other feast of Mary in the Roman calendar until the seventh century. But we must realize that the official establishment of a feast usually follows upon the existence of a long-established devotion; in the case of the Assumption, such a devotion can be traced back very far. The dogmatic definition of the Assumption in 1950 thus simply confirmed the faith of the entire Christian people. It can be said that the liturgical feast of the Assumption was first celebrated at Jerusalem toward the middle of the fifth century; in the seventh century it spread throughout the whole Latin world as an official feast.

Readings

Luke 1:39-56	The Lord has exalted those of low degree.
Apoc. 11:19a; 12:1-6a, 10ab	A woman clothed with the sun, with the moon under her feet
1 Cor. 15:20-27	In Christ shall all be made alive (see p. 180)

The presidential prayers of the Mass give clear expression to the faith of the Church and the spirituality of the feast. The assertion that the Blessed Virgin ascended body and soul into heaven is forcefully made in the opening prayer, in the prayer over the gifts, and in the preface.

The preface says that God preserved from decay in the tomb the body that had carried his Son within it and brought the Author of life into our world. The preface also speaks of the Blessed Virgin as the perfect model of the Church as it will be in eternity.

The Church places herself under the protection of God's Mother, who is now in heaven, for Mary sustains the hope of God's people on their journey (preface). She lifts our hearts to the things that are above (opening prayer); she intensifies our longing for the resurrection and our own entry into heavenly glory (opening prayer; prayer after Communion).

November 1

ALL SAINTS

It was in the East that Christians first had the idea of celebrating all the martyrs together on one day; we find such a feast celebrated at the end of the fourth century on the first Sunday after Pentecost. A similar feast was celebrated on May 13 at Edessa, and another in eastern Syria at the beginning of the fifth century, during the Easter octave. A lectionary of the sixth-seventh centuries indicates such a celebration in the West on the first Sunday after Pentecost. Finally, in 835, Pope Gregory IV decreed a feast of all the saints for November 1, in the territory of Louis the Pious.

Readings

Matthew 5:1-12	The reward of the just.
Apoc. 7:2-4, 9-12	A great multitude, from every nation, from all tribes and peoples and tongues.
1 John 3:1-3	We shall see God as he is.

The feast focuses on the intercession of the saints in heaven for us who are still on earth; the opening prayer and the prayer over the gifts allude to this intercession. In general, the celebration has a strongly eschatological tone. The preface describes the saints as singing eternally the praises of the Father. Yet even this eschatological vision should be a source of encouragement for the entire Church as she walks by faith, helped by the example of the saints (see the preface). The prayer after Communion, which has its usually eschatological orientation, asks that we may pass from the table at which we are still pilgrims, to the heavenly banquet.

NOTES

[1] "Anaphora" means "offering" and is the word used in the Oriental Churches for the Eucharistic Prayer in which Christ and the Church make offering to the Father in prayers of thanksgiving.

[2] *Sermo* 27, 2 (*SC* 22bis:152–54).

[3] See Volume three, pages 37–47.

[4] St. Ambrose, *De sacramentis* IV, 14–21 (*SC* 25bis:108–14).

[5] The text of Hippolytus, *Apostolic Tradition*, ch. 4, is in B. Botte, *La Tradition Apostolique de saint Hippolyte: Essai de reconstitution* (Liturgiegeschichtliche Quellen und Forschungen 39; Münster, 1963), pp. 12–16; and in A. Hänggi and I. Pahl (eds.), *Prex Eucharistica: Textus e variis liturgiis antiquioribus selecti* (Specilegium Friburgense 12; Fribourg, 1968), pp. 80–81. [I have followed Botte in his interpretation of obscurities. — Tr.]

[6] *De sacramentis* IV, 15 (*SC* 25bis:108).

[7] *Ibid.*, IV, 14–17 (*SC* 25bis:108–10).

[8] *De mysteriis* 52 (*SC* 25bis:186).

[9] *De sacramentis* IV, 14 (*SC* 25bis:108–10). Italics added.

[10] *Ibid.*, IV, 21 (*SC* 25bis:114).

[11] Text in M. Férotin (ed.), *Le Liber ordinum en usage dans l'Eglise Wisogothique et Mozarabe d'Espagne du cinquième au onzième siècle* (Monumenta Ecclesiae Liturgica 5; Paris, 1904), col. 322; *idem* (ed.), *Le Liber mozarabicus sacramentorum et les manuscrits arabes* (Monumenta Ecclesiae Liturgica 6; Paris, 1912), no. 1440.

[12] *De sacramentis* IV, 27 (*SC* 25bis:116).

[13] *Liber mozarabicus sacramentorum*, no. 627; *Liber ordinum*, col. 625.

[14] Text in Hänggi-Pahl, *op. cit.*, p. 131.

[15] See *Notitiae* 7 (1971) 35–42, 74–77, 94–95, 134–36, 276–80, 409–10.

[16] See above, pages 9–19.

[17] See Volume 3, pages 198–205, for the theme of the Good Shepherd on the Fourth Sunday of Easter.

[18] See e.g., J. Daniélou, *The Bible and the Liturgy* (Notre Dame, Ind., 1956), pp. 177–90.

[19] *Catecheses mystagogicae* IV, 7 (*PG* 33:1101, 1104; *SC* 126:140–42).

[20] *De sacramentis* V, 12–13 (*SC* 25bis:124–26).

[21] *In Christi Ascensionem* (*PG* 46:692).

[22] *Explanatio in Psalmum* 22 (*PG* 69:840).

[23] St. Cyprian, *Epist.* 63, 5 (*CSEL* 3:703).

[24] Origen, *In Canticum Canticorum* III, on ch. 2, v. 4, of the Canticle (*PG* 13:154–55).

[25] St. Ambrose, *De Cain et Abel* I, 5, 19 (*CSEL* 32/1:356).

[26] Council of Trent, Sess. 24 (Nov. 11, 1563), in H. Denzinger and A. Schönmetzer (eds.), *Enchiridion symbolorum* 32nd ed.; Freiburg, 1963), no. 1799.

[27] See Vol. 1, p. 111, "Characteristics of our messianic age."

[28] See Vol. 3, pp. 66–95.

[29] See Vol. 3, p. 85f.

[30] *Ibid.*

[31] In the Christian reading of Scripture during the liturgy, there are three reasons for not using the name "Yahweh": (1) the word was never pronounced by the Jews; "Lord" is therefore preferable in English; (2) we read the Old Testament as Christians; on this score, too, "Yahweh" is unsuitable; (3) the avoidance of "Yahweh" is especially to be urged in the psalms. In these, we should at times see Christ and the Church praying to the Father, at times the Church praying to Christ. Particularly in this second situation is the name "Yahweh" unsuitable.

[32] Ch. 21; text in B. Botte, *La Tradition Apostolique de saint Hippolyte: Essai de reconstitution* (Liturgiewissenschaftliche Quellen und Forschungen 39; Münster, 1963), pp. 56–57.

[33] See J.-P. Audet, *La Didachè: Instructions des apôtres* (Paris, 1958).

[34] The text of this commentary is translated in Volume 2.

[35] *Epistula ad Joannem Syracusensem*, in *Registrum Epistularum* 9, 26 (eds. Ewald and Hartmann, 2:59–60).

[36] *De sacramentis* V, 19 (*SC* 25bis:128–30). The following quotations from St. Ambrose on the Our Father are from *De sacramentis* V, 20–30 (*SC* 25bis:130–36).

[37] See Volume 3, p. 37ff.

[38] See the commentary on these passages in the various Cycles.

[39] *Constitution on the Sacred Liturgy*, no. 2 (Flannery, p. 3).

[40] See Vol. 2, p. 169ff.

[41] See this Sunday, Cycle A, p. 138–140.

[42] See sixth Sunday, Cycle C, in Vol. 1, p. 421ff.

[43] On this point, see the conclusions drawn from the readings for the thirty-fourth Sunday, Cycle A, p. 180 above.